TRANSITIONAL SAFEGUARDING

Christine Cocker, Dez Holmes, and Adi Cooper

First published in Great Britain in 2024 by

Policy Press, an imprint of
Bristol University Press
University of Bristol
1-9 Old Park Hill
Bristol
BS2 8BB
UK
t: +44 (0)117 374 6645
e: bup-info@bristol.ac.uk

Details of international sales and distribution partners are available at
policy.bristoluniversitypress.co.uk

British Library Cataloguing in Publication Data
A catalogue record for this book is available from the British Library

ISBN 978-1-4473-6556-3 paperback
ISBN 978-1-4473-6557-0 ePub
ISBN 978-1-4473-6558-7 ePdf

Cover design: Liam Roberts Design
Front cover image: iStock/Delpixart
Bristol University Press and Policy Press use environmentally responsible print partners.
Printed and bound in Great Britain by CPI Group (UK) Ltd, Croydon, CR0 4YY

FSC
www.fsc.org
MIX
Paper | Supporting responsible forestry
FSC® C013604

Contents

List of figures and tables

Figures

Table

Acknowledgements

Writing this book has involved many people. We would like to offer our grateful thanks to those who shared their experiences with us who are working to achieve change within their organisations and in partnership with others across their local areas; the members of the Transitional Safeguarding Reference Group, supported by Partners in Care and Health; Professor Michael Preston-Shoot; Sarah Williams and Fiona Bateman from Safeguarding Circle, colleagues in the School of Social Work at the University of East Anglia; colleagues at Research in Practice; the National House Project; and the National Leaving Care Benchmarking Forum. Finally, a big thank you to Jean Luc, who has yet again supported Dez's nerdy hobby.

Foreword

Rebekah Pierre
Care-experienced author, activist, and social worker

When asked to write a foreword for a book on Transitional Safeguarding, I was initially cautious. I expressed as much to two of the co-authors, Dez Holmes and Professor Christine Cocker. The three of us were sitting on a picnic bench outside the EuSARF Conference 2023, where much discussion had taken place on this very theme.

'To be honest I'm not really a fan of the term *Transitional Safeguarding*,' I said.

Much to my surprise, Dez apologised.

'What for?' I asked. 'It's not as if you invented it, is it?'

'Actually, yes,' she said, and I felt the ground beneath me open up. 'But I welcome any challenge!'

At this point, I realised I could not back-peddle my way out. So I outlined my concerns directly.

'Children in contact with social care experience enough instability as it is,' I said. 'I mean, how would you feel if your environment, family life, and the services you rely on were described as transient? Wouldn't it make you feel anxious?'

Both agreed.

'You should put that in the foreword!' they said in unison.

Within the first few pages of reading this book, it was clear my assumptions were false. Transitional Safeguarding (excellently outlined in Chapters 2 and 7) is entirely at odds with placing children on the proverbial conveyor belt towards the cliff edge of care. In fact, it advocates for *more*, not *less* support during the critical crossover years between childhood and adulthood. If you are reading this with a view to streamlining services, you may as well stop here.

Practice and policy are culpable for shoe-horning young people's voices as an afterthought. But what makes this book so refreshing – so needed – is that co-production is the golden thread running from cover to cover. Young people are the researchers at the heart, not just the periphery.

Transitional Safeguarding is at once ambitious – advocating for entire system change underscored by relational, evidence-informed, and rights-based support – while being grounded in the realities of austerity, the cost-of-living crisis, and a post-pandemic landscape. This balance is seen in Chapter 9, where good practice is referenced to demonstrate what innovation and dedication can achieve, even against a backdrop of socio-political and financial challenges.

Its wisdom lies in understanding that young people exist outside westernised concepts of time; that their needs and strengths evolve in ways which rarely conform to age norms. The unique biological, socio-emotional, and developmental needs of adolescents are discussed at a depth not seen elsewhere in modern social work discourse. Or indeed within government, who frame children as children where it benefits them (for example, to prevent minors voting), but as adults when it does not (as seen in the introduction of care-less accommodation for 16- and 17-year-olds).

Rather than adding to the chorus of those who frame 'independence' as the ultimate goal – something to be achieved at the arbitrary milestone of an eighteenth birthday – this book highlights that young people, like all of us, thrive best in community.

Introduction

Becoming an adult is a process, not a single event. Having the 'official' date of this marked as turning 18 is a social and legal construct. There are many other points at which young people can legally take part in activities that are seen as adult. A child is legally accountable for a crime at age 10 in England. The age of consent for both heterosexual and same-sex relationships is 16 years. Joining the armed forces is possible at age 16. A young person can have a driving licence from age 17. A young person is presumed by law to have the capacity to make decisions about any area of their life from age 16, unless they do not have mental capacity (as defined under the Mental Capacity Act 2005). However, in safeguarding and protection, someone's eighteenth birthday is the key date when the safeguarding approach that they experience, should they meet eligibility criteria, changes from being underpinned by the Children Act 1989 (affecting children under 18) to the Care Act 2014 (affecting anyone over the age of 18). This means young people often fall off a 'cliff edge' at 18 as the available services do not meet their developmental needs or circumstances and the majority of young people turning 18 will not be deemed eligible for those services. For young people who have safeguarding needs as 17-year-olds, it is increasingly apparent, the more we know about extra-familial harms, that these needs do not disappear on their eighteenth birthday. It is the agencies who are tasked with supporting and protecting these young people that often disappear.

Harm does not stop at 18, nor do the traumatic effects of harm; young people continue to develop until their mid-twenties and many other areas of policy and legislation recognise the fluidity of adolescence and early adulthood. It makes little sense for the professional safeguarding response to be so rigidly age bound. Yet that is the current situation, with two wholly distinct safeguarding systems for those over and under 18 years old – and neither is designed with teenagers and young adults' needs in mind.

Transitional Safeguarding is a concept developed to specifically challenge the inadequacies of this binary approach and enable us to think differently about how to support young people as they navigate their early adult lives. This book defines and explores what Transitional Safeguarding is and is not. This is the first book that has been written about Transitional Safeguarding and, in this regard, it marks a point in time where we are all on a journey of discovery, growth, and innovation. The book has been written for anyone working to help young people be and feel as safe as possible, to help them understand the context and systems which support young people in dealing with the risks and harms in their lives. This includes those who are not working directly with young people themselves, but who manage or lead services and organisations responsible for supporting them. It will also be of interest to academics, teachers, trainers, and people working in many relevant areas, but it is not a practical 'how-to' book for practitioners. One of our key objectives in writing this book is to inspire readers to think differently about the systems they work in and maintain and consider how they might change them so young people are more effectively safeguarded. Wherever you are in the system, as a practitioner or leader, you can influence change.

Exploring Transitional Safeguarding definitions, language, and key cohorts

Transitional Safeguarding is 'an approach to safeguarding adolescents and young adults fluidly across developmental stages which builds on the best available evidence, learns from both children's and adult safeguarding practice and which prepares young people for their adult lives' (Holmes and Smale 2018, p 3).

The specific use of the term 'safeguarding' is significant. We deliberately use this term because safeguarding encompasses preventative activity, as is set out clearly in statutory guidance (HM Government 2020; Department of Health and Social Care 2023), it is not only the protective response to harm. Importantly, we use safeguarding as a verb, not a noun. We do not use the term to mean statutory services, a specific team, or a threshold to be reached.

Indeed, we would argue that using safeguarding in this way has contributed to the cliff edge facing young people. Safeguarding is – and must be – a verb; it is the collective action we undertake when people's sense of safety is undermined (Holmes 2022a). Lastly, Transitional Safeguarding is not a catch-all term for the types of harms that young people can face, it is the response to those harms.

In this book, we define young people using the United Nations description of 'youth' as those aged between 15 and 24 (United Nations 2020). We are aware that, in-so-doing, we straddle both safeguarding systems in this country. The key tenets of these systems are outlined and considered in relation to their current abilities to meet the safeguarding needs of young people. Both systems have strengths and both have areas for development; these are highlighted and discussed. The use of a boundary-spanning definition of 'young people' is a conscious effort to challenge and interrogate current system binaries.

In some instances in the book we refer to 'complex needs' and it is important for us to define what it is we mean by this term. 'Complex needs' is a term used in health to describe the interface and interaction between physical health needs, mental health needs, and learning disabilities and autism. However, social aspects may provide further complexity, such as the experience of abuse and neglect as a child. Van den Steene et al (2019, p 63) define it as:

> Children and adolescents with profound and interacting needs in the context of issues on several life domains (family context, functioning and integration in society) as well as psychiatric problems. The extent of their needs exceeds the capacity (expertise and resources) of existing services and sequential interventions lead to discontinuous care delivery. As such, existing services do not adequately meet the needs of these youths and their families. Cross-sector, integrated and assertive care delivery is necessary for safeguarding the well-being, development and societal integration of these young people.

When considering the safeguarding risks young people face, we use the term 'complex needs' to include a range of different factors such as experience of trauma and inequalities. We do not use terms such as 'complex cases' or 'complex lives' because young people are not cases and (as explored in Chapter 10) all human beings are complex so we are keen to avoid negative connotations.

Another important linguistic distinction to address is the difference between Transitional Safeguarding and transitions planning. As explored in Chapter 7, these terms are linked but they are not the same. Many young people receive specific support from organisations outside their families in their teenage years to help with their journey to adulthood. Various policies and guidance support transitions planning, for example, the special educational needs and disability code of practice (Department for Education and Department of Health 2015) and the National Institute for Health and Care Excellence guidance on transition from children's to adults' services (National Institute for Health and Care Excellence 2016a, 2016b). It is important to note that poor transitions planning or transfer between services can create or worsen risks and harms for a young person, which is why understanding this intersection is important.

In terms of defining which groups of young people are 'in scope' for Transitional Safeguarding, this will vary according to local context and individuals' needs. Young people's safeguarding needs may already be identified by the services they are known to, and while under 18 years of age their safeguarding needs would be addressed through child protection systems and services (HM Government 2020). However, many would be ineligible for safeguarding adult services as they are unlikely to be assessed as having 'care and support needs' that affect their ability to protect themselves from abuse or neglect (Department of Health and Social Care 2023). For the general public 'safeguarding adults' is a relatively new concept, compared with 'safeguarding children'; interpretation is often broad, including a range of safety issues and risks that any adult may face, particularly adults who may be seen as vulnerable to risks due to their particular circumstances. 'Safeguarding adults' through the statutory enquiry duty applies to a narrower group of adults and this is where confusion and misunderstanding can often take place.

It is important to emphasise that Transitional Safeguarding is not only focused on care-experienced young people, those with complex needs, or those facing exploitation. We pay particular attention to these groups as there is compelling evidence to show that they are poorly served by the current binary approach to safeguarding. With this caveat in mind, we have identified three broad cohorts of young people very likely to be known to children's services and who are often not eligible for statutory adult services, which is where the cliff edge presents. Many of these children and young people's needs will not have changed overnight. How they are viewed by systems and services is what has changed.

The three, often overlapping, groups are:

- Young people with health, mental health, and special educational needs. A commonality is that these children are already known to health, education, or mental health services. The process for transfer to adult services is set out in guidance documents, but eligibility for adult services needs to be determined prior to transfer and is not automatic. The guidance is clear that transitions planning for these young people should begin from age 14 but, as explored in Chapter 7, transitions planning can be highly variable.
- Care-experienced young people. Some young people who have had experience of the care system may require ongoing support to keep safe. Statutory legislation and guidance clearly outline responsibilities for supporting young people who are care-experienced. However, there are considerable gaps in provision and concerns about these young people's vulnerabilities are not new (see Stein 2004, 2006a).
- Young people facing extra-familial harm, who very often overlap with young people involved in youth justice services (YJS), including those involved in county lines, sexual exploitation, and modern slavery. However, being sexually/criminally exploited does not mean a young person will end up with a youth justice community order or sentence, or any YJS involvement. The language used to describe these young people approaching 18 often moves from 'victim' to 'perpetrator', and these discourses need challenging. Being involved in YJS does not necessarily mean a transfer to adult probation services; this depends on the type of order in place.

For both community orders and transfer for those serving a custodial sentence, transition planning has been the subject of criticism (HMI Probation 2016).

Further, there may be some young people who are not known to services, or are on the periphery, such as those facing homelessness (Neinstein 2013; Preston-Shoot 2020), those who do not have diagnosed disabilities, who may be known to universal services only, such as community health via GPs or sexual health clinics, or to voluntary, community, or faith groups (Cocker et al 2021). Other cohorts of young people, for example separated (or unaccompanied) asylum-seeking young people, may span all three of the groups listed above and are highly vulnerable, yet too often have their safeguarding needs overlooked. The other group of young people not named already are those under 18s who are – or were – the subject of safeguarding or child protection interventions and who do not have any care and support needs, so will suddenly have no support at 18. Unlike the three groups listed above, there is no transitions guidance/protocols/support entitlements. This also includes young people who are unaccompanied asylum seekers and not in care. Most young people who are the subjects of child protection activities do not enter the care system.

Where did the idea for Transitional Safeguarding come from?

What is it about an idea that enables it to gain traction and begin to influence practice? For Transitional Safeguarding, the idea was crystallised after Dez listened to a presentation by Adi about Making Safeguarding Personal (MSP) as an approach to adult safeguarding at a conference in Birmingham in 2016. Dez had been focused on supporting local innovation in relation to safeguarding adolescents for several years previously, and wondered why this approach could not also apply to young people under 18. Around the same time Dez was presenting at a conference alongside a care-experienced young person, 'Max'. Max's comment about feeling safe while in care was, 'I was in care all my life and you did keep me really safe. You wrapped me up tight in bubble wrap … but I'm 19 now and I kind of feel like I can't move my arms'

(Holmes 2022a, p 11). In one sentence Max articulated vividly why a more joined-up system is needed: the state had protected him in childhood without preparing him for adulthood; there was little focus on his self-efficacy, in stark contrast to the rhetoric of MSP and the Care Act 2014. Max had been 'kept safe' but he had not been shown how to 'keep himself safe'. Not long after, in 2018, Research in Practice published a briefing paper, 'Mind the Gap' (Holmes and Smale 2018), which critiqued the binary approach to safeguarding in current legislation and policy and coined the term Transitional Safeguarding.

Following the publication of 'Mind the Gap', Adi and Christine presented an abridged version of their many debates about the differences between child and adult safeguarding to the 2018 Leaders Forum, an event Research in Practice hosts annually. Subsequently, Christine and Adi ran a series of four national workshops for Research in Practice about Transitional Safeguarding for 88 middle and senior managers from 52 children and adult social care services. This work was later published in the British Journal of Social Work (Cocker et al 2022a). The response from professionals at all levels to the concept and their familiarity with the cliff edge facing many young people acted as a catalyst for the next five years of work.

Transitional Safeguarding builds on a range of key theoretical perspectives and these are highlighted in this book as appropriate to the themes of the different chapters. As befits a multi-agency and boundary-spanning concept, Transitional Safeguarding draws on diverse multi-disciplinary perspectives and frameworks. These include theories of human development, such as Bronfenbrenner's 1977 ecological theory of child development, and more recent theories such as life course theory (Elder 1998). The importance of strength-based (Saleeby 1996) and relationship-based practice (Ruch et al 2018) is writ large within the Transitional Safeguarding approach and a variety of psychosocial perspectives, such as attachment theory, have contributed to the way the concept has developed over time. Professional theoretical frameworks have also informed the development of Transitional Safeguarding, for example notions of containment (Bion 1962) and reflexivity are key to enabling relational and ethical practice with young people facing often emotionally distressing experiences. Aspects of leadership theory have provided useful prompts in thinking about how to move Transitional Safeguarding from the abstract to action, from concept to approach; systems leadership, boundary-spanning and adaptive leadership are particularly relevant (as discussed in Chapter 10). Complexity theory and systems thinking also both offer numerous insights relevant to the system-change endeavour of Transitional Safeguarding.

The work we have co-created since 2018 falls roughly into three areas. Firstly, there has been an emphasis on supporting policy development. We were all involved, along with other sector leaders, in the Transitional Safeguarding workgroup facilitated by the Chief Social Worker for Adults. This sponsored the development of a further briefing paper, 'Bridging the Gap', which focused on the role of adult social work and safeguarding adults. Soon after, a paper was produced for HMI Probation, exploring the interface between Transitional Safeguarding and Justice (Holmes and Smith 2022). The concept of Transitional Safeguarding has been included in cross-Government principles for responding to exploitation (HM Government 2023) and features in sector-led resources developed by and for health colleagues.[1] The work on Transitional Safeguarding has also been supported by the Care and Health Improvement Partnership programme run jointly by the Association of Directors of Adult Social Services (ADASS) and the Local Government Association (LGA), funded by the Department of Health and Social Care. Now called Partners in Care and Health, they have hosted a multi-agency reference group, which was established following the launch of 'Bridging the Gap'. Annual webinars have showcased work developed and delivered in localities in different areas taking Transitional Safeguarding forward, and some of the presentations from the 2023 webinar have been included as case studies in this book.

Secondly, we have also concentrated on developing the underpinning evidence base for Transitional Safeguarding, including publishing several articles on the subject. A paper with Fiona Bateman looked at the legal complexities in the two safeguarding systems and explored whether the law is a barrier, preventing different safeguarding responses for young people (Cocker et al 2021). Christine and Adi co-edited a Special Issue in the Practice Journal on Transitional Safeguarding,[2] which published contributions describing Transitional Safeguarding initiatives and sets out the argument for change (Holmes 2022a). Additionally, Christine has completed a study looking at Safeguarding Adult Reviews (SARs) and Serious Case Reviews/ Child Safeguarding Practice Reviews of care-experienced young people, and the findings from this are presented in Chapter 8. Along with Michael Preston-Shoot, Christine and Adi produced a paper pulling together the developing evidence base underpinning Transitional Safeguarding for use by SAR authors (Preston-Shoot et al 2022). Dez edited a book on safeguarding young people, which brought together a collection of authors that offer a critical perspective about current safeguarding practices with young people (Holmes 2022b) and includes a chapter by the three of us on Transitional Safeguarding. Beyond our own activity, academic interest in the concept continues to grow. An ESRC-funded project that explored the process of innovation in safeguarding children and young people focused one of its strands on Transitional Safeguarding.[3]

Thirdly, there has been a continuation of workshops and presentations across the country as the response to Transitional Safeguarding has been overwhelmingly positive. Despite the pressures of a pandemic and continued resource constraints, local partnerships have demonstrated a keen interest in and ambition for adopting a Transitional Safeguarding approach. Hundreds of individuals and organisations have invited us to meet with them, keen to think about and explore how Transitional Safeguarding can be taken forward in their areas. Many of these events have been and continue to be online because of COVID-19, and so between the three of us, we have had the privilege of talking to thousands of people from across all sectors. Each interaction provides further ideas, inspiration, and food for thought; it has been wonderful to see the activity across the sectors over the past five years. This book has been written to draw together what we know at this point, to promote the work that has been happening, with little or no national resource, to safeguard young people, to stimulate different ways of thinking about Transitional Safeguarding, and suggest where we might head in the future.

What does the book cover?

This book explores a number of themes relevant to Transitional Safeguarding. The impact of the current binary approach to children's and adults' safeguarding, in human and economic terms, is discussed with consideration given to how Transitional Safeguarding can span the boundary between these currently disconnected systems. The book explores the nature of harms facing young people, including structural disadvantage and discrimination. We discuss the developmental needs and characteristics of young people, including the current anomalies in policies and practice regarding work with young people. We consider the ways in which their perceived capacity and capabilities have an impact on their safeguarding experiences, and their rights and risks. Unless young people are placed at the centre of this work, then their needs will not be fully understood or addressed, and any system transformation will not achieve its goal.

The book itself is divided into three sections. The first is 'Making the case for change' and comprises Chapters 1, 2, 3, and 4.

We begin the book with the voice of young people. They are who matter. Their views on Transitional Safeguarding then set the tone and challenge for the rest of the book as they offer rich invaluable insights which reinforce the need for, and key principles of, Transitional Safeguarding. Their views are nuanced and present some complexity and ambiguity too. This complexity and nuancing are precisely why listening to young people is so vital to the development of Transitional Safeguarding and any other system-change endeavour.

The four young people who co-authored Chapter 1 with Dez are all care-experienced. The young people reflect on what it feels like for care-experienced young people to approach adulthood, wanting both more support than is available and more freedom than is permitted. In another book, Holmes (2022b) co-authored a chapter which was written with two different young people who were also supported by professionals as children and young adults. Many of the insights in both the pieces are similar. These young people – and all young people – have thoughtful and challenging messages for practitioners and leaders involved in supporting them and other young people. All have a desire to see the current systems change.

Chapter 2 sets out the argument for Transitional Safeguarding. Putting it bluntly, the current system does not work for too many young people and represents poor use of public resources. Binary adults' and children's safeguarding legislation, policy, and practice frameworks create gaps for young people to fall into; this binary fuels other binaries such as the categorisation of young people as either vulnerable or culpable. Transitional Safeguarding seeks to redress these binaries and span such boundaries. The chapter outlines the six key principles that underpin Transitional Safeguarding: evidence-informed; ecological; contextual; developmental and transitional; relational; and equalities-oriented. These address the current challenges in safeguarding young adults, exemplifying the 'both/and' ethos of putting Transitional Safeguarding into practice, leadership, and policy development.

In Chapter 3 we provide an overview of the legal and social policy frameworks that govern safeguarding practices for children and adults in England. The legal frameworks, statutory guidance, policies, and conceptual frameworks for children's and adults' safeguarding have developed differently and often in response to crises (for example, child deaths and investigations about institutional abuses). There are also differences between England, Wales, Northern Ireland, and Scotland. There are, however, similarities and synergies between children's and adults' safeguarding in terms of key principles of safeguarding practice; the 'gap' is in the paradigms for safeguarding practice rather than the legal frameworks. Risks and rights are understood differently for children and adults, protection and participation are afforded different weight. This provides a challenge for taking forward a Transitional Safeguarding approach but is not an insurmountable barrier for a more fluid and responsive system.

Chapter 4 provides an overview and commentary about 'emerging adulthood' as a developmental stage. There are key theoretical frameworks and concepts that offer useful insights to understanding young people's development, and therefore can influence how we articulate and further develop Transitional Safeguarding. However, these frameworks have some limitations and there are important critiques to be aware of, for example,

Arnett's (2000) theory of 'emerging adulthood' is situated in a particular economic, social, and historical context which is not universal, and may not stand the test of time. We suggest that it is more helpful to move beyond age-stage developmental theories and instead engage with the complexity and heterogeneity of young people's lives and identities. Life course theory seeks to do this in part, although there may also be limitations about the applicability of this theory outside of westernised environments. The need for theoretical frameworks to reflect diverse contexts chimes with Transitional Safeguarding's attention to the principle of equality, equity, diversity and inclusion, the impact of trauma on development links with the relational principle, and the developmental imperative for young people to be afforded choice and voice, which is central to the participative principle.

The second section in the book is 'Learning from current practices' and comprises Chapters 5, 6, 7, and 8. Chapters 5 and 6 present the learning from current safeguarding practices with children and adults. There is a danger that, in separating out safeguarding learning into two separate chapters, we inadvertently recreate the binaries that we are critical of. However, until we know what works well and have an opportunity to critique and evaluate these developments and learning in line with the six key principles of Transitional Safeguarding, we cannot then move on to consider what innovations and whole system changes to achieve Transitional Safeguarding outcomes might look like.

Chapter 5 sets out to explore the learning from innovation within children's safeguarding. Children's safeguarding policy and practice has, until very recently, been focused on intra-familial harm and has often been driven by responses to many crises. There are tensions between children's rights and developmental needs and the paternalism often observed within child protection. Most of these approaches to safeguarding children, such as Contextual Safeguarding, Complex Safeguarding, Family Safeguarding, and restorative practice, provide useful learning for Transitional Safeguarding. With policy attention increasingly directed towards improving responses to child exploitation and extra-familial harm, there is a potential risk of privileging specialist and bespoke services over preventative whole system support. This presents the unintended consequence of separating safeguarding young people from safeguarding the wider population. These issues are explored in this chapter.

Chapter 6 explores learning from adult safeguarding provision, which is very different from children's safeguarding. Adult safeguarding enquiry processes apply where adults have care and support needs and are unable to protect themselves because of those needs. For some young people who have had safeguarding support as children, this can mean that there is a 'cliff edge' when they become 18 because they are not considered to have care and support needs, or because these are not deemed to prevent them being able to protect themselves. Despite the enabling preventative powers of the Care Act and underpinning 'well-being' principle, lack of legal literacy, pressures on services, and limited resources and capacity can all serve to limit the support offer to young people. MSP is the key approach that underpins adult safeguarding practice. It prioritises the involvement of the person in identifying their outcomes and focuses on what they want to achieve to be safe. MSP provides a way of working with young adults that can adapt to their personal developmental needs, ensures their active participation, and provides an inclusive safeguarding response. It is aligned to the principles of Transitional Safeguarding and can be 'drawn down' to use as an approach to safeguard young people aged 16+ who are able to evaluate the risks that they face in their lives.

Chapter 7 explores the differences between Transitional Safeguarding and 'transitions' or 'transitions planning'. They are not the same thing, although there are important connections; poor transitions planning can contribute to increased safeguarding risks for young people. Transitions planning guidance and activity are largely centred on smoothing the transitions between children's services and adults' services for those young people deemed eligible for post-18 services; whereas Transitional Safeguarding is about system change, redesigning service structures including different pathways in order that all young people can feel and be safe as they grow older. Poor transitions planning, ineffective partnership working, and a lack of joined-up infrastructure have led to tragic consequences. This highlights how far we have to go before Transitional Safeguarding is viewed as a mainstream approach, but also underlines how important it is that we try.

Chapter 8 reports on research that Christine completed that investigated a number of SARs and Child Safeguarding Practice Reviews (CSPRs) of deaths of care-experienced young people. This provides significant learning through the evidence of where practice and systems need to change. We have used a whole systems model as a framework for analysis and then linked the findings to Transitional Safeguarding principles. Themes identified in this research included: poor planning for transitions and poor multi-agency/inter-professional communication; poor assessments and poor relational practice; lack of recognition of the risks and vulnerabilities that young people faced and their contexts; weak legal literacy; lack of engagement with and participation by young people, as well as evidence of their 'voices', views, and wishes; evidence of discriminatory practices, for example 'adultification'.[4] These reviews describe the multiple challenges for all practitioners and agencies in addressing practice and strategic issues to better prevent the tragedy of these deaths continuing.

Part three of the book looks at what local areas have been doing to respond to these challenges and considers how innovation in adopting a Transitional Safeguarding approach tries to address these complexities. It describes and discusses a systems-change analysis. Chapters 9 and 10 are included in this section.

Chapter 9 contains a cross section of examples to provide a picture of what is emerging locally to put the principles of Transitional Safeguarding into action. We hope that they prompt and inspire others to consider how their local area or service might be able to do things differently, to ensure that young people can be and feel as safe as possible. No one area has the complete solution, and all are on a journey with this work. The way in which change happens is a process, not a single transformative event, and this chapter explores four typologies which help situate and understand each of the examples within the system transformation that needs to be achieved.

Chapter 10 draws on theoretical frameworks from systems leadership and systems thinking literature to argue that Transitional Safeguarding should be conceptualised as a whole system change, not a discrete intervention. System transformation of this kind is not simple, of course. However, the key principles provide a path through the complexity to take small steps in the right direction – and local areas are showing that change is possible. Each key principle is then considered to explore what this might mean for anyone seeking to develop the concept and apply the approach of Transitional Safeguarding locally or nationally.

Conclusion

This book captures a moment in time; in it we summarise what we know and have learned about Transitional Safeguarding over the past six years. Make no mistake, this is complex work. It is practically and conceptually challenging and we have huge respect and admiration for all those who are trying to take this forward. We expect that, as new evidence becomes available in the future, it will inform practice and policy, and so aspects of Transitional Safeguarding will evolve over time. We are excited to see how the concept will develop. At this point, we want the contents of the book to inspire, start discussions, and bring about changes to the way we support young people to be and feel safe.

PART I

Making the case for change

1

What do care-experienced young people say?

with Desemme Jones, Jodie Kudzewicz, Sean Robertson, Louis Fearnehough, and Dez Holmes (supported by Rosie Blackett)[1]

Introduction

As explored in more detail in Chapter 2 and referenced throughout the book, there are six key principles that underpin Transitional Safeguarding. One of these argues that the design, development, and embedding of Transitional Safeguarding must be evidence-informed, which means drawing on research, practice wisdom, and expertise from lived experience. Another of the principles asserts that Transitional Safeguarding must be developed and delivered in ways that are highly participative. Young people and those who care about them are experts within their own lives and are an essential source of wisdom, critique, and challenge. For Transitional Safeguarding to be congruent with the aims it seeks in practice – that is, a rights-based, relational, and empowering approach to help young people be and feel safe – then the design process must mirror these tenets.

In keeping with this recognition that young people's expertise is a vital part of the Transitional Safeguarding knowledge base, this chapter is co-authored by four young people, each with experience of being in care and of being supported by other professional services. These young people are active members of the Care Leavers National Movement, a participation and influencing group attached to the National House Project.[2] Their ages span 17 to 22. This group explored a number of issues relating to the transition to adulthood and changes they feel would help young people make this transition well. Their insights are drawn from their own experiences; however, this chapter does not focus on their individual personal stories.

These young people make a powerful argument for holistic support services and structures which afford young people not only practical skills development, but also a sense of relational and psychological security. Their insights highlight the importance of ensuring that needs and risks do not escalate in later adulthood, and that this requires an approach which is preventative, person-centred, and non-stigmatising.

What adulthood means

As mentioned earlier, taking an evidence-informed approach is one of the six key principles that underpin Transitional Safeguarding. These sources of knowledge do not exist in separate siloes, but rather interact with each other and may co-exist within individuals. It might be assumed that young people are only drawing on their expertise through lived experience; however, the young co-authors immediately cited research evidence as a fundamental part of why Transitional Safeguarding is needed:

> I think biologically you become an adult at 25 when your brain stops developing. However, there are factors in your childhood growing up that really affect your maturity. And that can affect the age that you feel adult.
>
> I thought it was a well-known fact that your brain doesn't stop developing until 25. You're constantly learning things, neurons, I think. Like, the pathways are still connecting. So it happens gradually.

Professionals and academics note a sense of ambiguity about the age of adulthood (see Chapter 4); some of these young people expressed views about age and adulthood while others rejected this:

> I don't think an adult is anyone under 25, simple as that.
>
> I don't think there's an age to determine if you're an adult yet or not. Age isn't the factor that determines whether you're an adult or not. It's your situation, your experiences, how you feel about yourself, how you feel in the world.

Context is significant for any individual young person's experience of transitioning into becoming an adult. A person's ecosystem of relationships, environments, and experiences affects how they perceive adulthood and how ready they might be to take on the mantle of adulthood:

> Becoming an adult most definitely depends on your situation. Sometimes it [the journey or transition] can be long.
>
> I think there's a lot of things that contribute to, like, what makes you an adult or when you're ready, things like that. I think there's a lot of different aspects of it.
>
> Different experiences in your childhood will give you a different journey into adulthood.

The group discussed what being an adult meant, and what young people looked forward to about becoming adults. For these young people, adulthood was strongly associated with freedom and autonomy:

> It's freedom because then you've got more choice over your life. Like, no one can tell you 'no' except yourself.
>
> You can experience certain things as an adult as well that you couldn't as a kid, because either there were certain risks to take that you were forbidden to do then, but now as an adult, it's like, nah, those risks – I'll do it anyway. It's about the freedom and being able to drink and like going out with your friends till whenever you want and a lot of stuff like that.

> You're above the law, in a way. Not like the actual law, but, you know, your parents and that. I think people look forward to having more control over their life and what they can do.
>
> It's even just little things. Just being able to like buy whatever shopping you want and eat whatever you want and go wherever you want. Like, if you have a car, you can go off to anywhere. I think it [adulthood] it's all the freedom of that. And it's the fun and, like, the unknown. I think that's what's exciting.
>
> So [we look forward to] a sense of more freedom. Maybe a sense to be out of your, you know, the control of adults, parents, carers.
>
> You have freedom to do what you want. Yeah, see what you like. Don't have to be bossed around anymore.

Choice, control and consequences

The young people reflected that this emphasis on adulthood as freedom was likely connected to their care experience. For some of them, being in care and having a social worker was associated with having little control over their lives.

> When you turn 18, you don't always have to listen to what social services have to say. Even though they're still gonna be your corporate parent, you have your own routine to do what you want, without 'When can I do this? Can I go?'
>
> When I used to live in residential, I had to ask my social worker if I could stay at someone's house. But when you're 18, you know, you don't have to.
>
> For me the transition to move on [from residential care] was my decision. It was me telling them that I wanted to leave. They wanted to keep me up until I was 25. And I'm like, 'well, I'm independent enough. I know how to cook, I know how to clean. I know how to do pretty much everything except bills and checking gas meters.' I was ready to go. I didn't want to stay there

> any longer. I wanted to be more an independent adult rather than having the babynesss around me. Like, no, I've reached a certain age, I can do it myself. Let me go.

This in turn meant that some young people in care might want to be seen as adults before they are ready so they have control over their life.

> I'd say to escape the situation, yeah. Wanting to be free, wanting to stop that restriction and feeling of control might almost push young people towards adulthood sooner than might actually be, you know, right for them.
>
> I think the other end of this conversation is when you become too independent to the point where you're not able to accept help if it is available. So, there could be a service that helps you with that transition to adulthood, but you've learned to be too independent to trust or accept the help. It's like a fear of not being adult enough.

As such the choice to 'stay put'[3] or not can be understood less as choosing to embrace adulthood and more as choosing to reject care. This creates a paradox whereby young people who might particularly need support during this transitional phase because of their care experience are deterred from accessing support because of their care experience:

> You might still need help after 18, but you can't ask for it because you were the one that was like 'no, I'm an adult'. And that young person will suffer essentially because they would rather do anything than be in that controlling environment.
>
> Once you've decided that you want to be treated like an adult, you don't want to ask for that support because then you, it looks like you're failing as an adult, so you don't want to.
>
> You wanna keep that persona up that you're doing really well for yourself. You just don't want to seem like a failure.

> I think if a young person has left care in that way, it creates a fear of asking for help, because asking for help is admitting weakness and you know you could be put back in care. So, say a young person leaves at 16, goes into semi-independence. … Doing that and then using that to get your own flat at 17 or 18 and then turning around and being like 'actually, I'm not managing'. I feel like that's really scary.

What makes adulthood hard

Leaving care early, albeit through ostensible choice, can present longer-term risks:

> I know a young person who did something similar [declined 'staying put'] just to stop being in that environment. And it meant that when they left care, they no longer had that support and they took a lot of risks that meant they lost housing, they lost friends and family.
>
> They don't get the support that they should get until they're 25. Because they chose to get out. That's why I just stuck with it and whatever … so I know I get the support that I need.

Another key feature of adulthood was responsibility, with financial worries being particularly significant:

> The most difficult thing of becoming an adult is the more responsibilities that you take on after you've left that stage of your life behind. You had someone helping you, then when you move out to be an adult it's getting on with bills, food, budget, and everything else, it's a lot more responsibility.

For young people in care, particularly, financial concerns intersect with social and relational aspects of their lives:

> It's definitely something I worried about. I turned 18 and I was thinking about how I'm gonna pay £400

> rent for semi-independence whereas other 18-year-olds were worrying about whether they're going to go for drinks later, you know, so it causes quite a big rift.

These financial pressures play out in ways which compound the unfairness facing many young people, in a further illustration of the contradictions discussed in Chapter 2.

> One of the many difficult things is having to pay bills, having to manage your own finances. Especially as 18 to 20-year-olds only get £6.80 an hour. Minimum wage I mean – from 18 to 20 it's £6.83, and 16 to 17 is about £4.70. So you're treated like an adult and you're expected to do the exact same things that an adult is expected to do, but you're paid substantially less while expected to pay the same bills. It's hard being expected to manage the same sort of household bills [as an adult on full wage], plus your phone bills, while also maintaining a social life, you know, travel costs, trying to go to college or work.
>
> Yeah you're still treated a little bit like a child with that sort of wage because you don't have the same experience. But if it's your first job, you're not gonna have any experience.

Some young people can face even greater inequality and hardship as they approach adulthood. Refugee and asylum-seeking young people are one group identified as facing particular barriers:

> I know someone that comes to our groups from [another country]. He's been in his accommodation for like a year. They just left them there. What happens when he's 25 and they have done nothing and he don't speak proper English? How are they gonna ask for support if no one's there to help them?
>
> There's some, actually there's lot of young people in [my borough] that are not English or don't, you know, can't speak English. There's a guy in my project – we speak to him in English so he understands us, so he

> knows for the future. But then there's others that no one talks to, don't do anything. Just like to be on their own. They're never going to be able to ask for help in the future if they don't speak English.

What transitional support looks like and should look like

Current policy and practice designed to support young care-experienced people into adulthood focuses on pathway planning; this is intended to formally commence when young people turn 16, though one young person noted that it can sometimes start 'at 17 and 4 months or whatever'. The focus on practical skills, which tends to characterise much pathway planning, might seemingly influence what independence means to some young people in care:

> I guess independence is being able to do the basic day-to-day things without someone holding your hand. Without someone having to do it for you. So like washing, cleaning, hoovering, dusting. You know, all the basic things that you don't think of.

The intended benefit of ensuring young people are ready for adulthood can sometimes feel tokenistic and procedural, and can add to the pressure and challenge of transition:

> There's so much, sort of, not pressure exactly … but you turn 17; you start your pathway plan. Your placement starts talking about the expectations. So many expectations. You know, the moment you turn 17, you're starting to be built up to be able to leave. 'Right, your pathway plan.' They're going through what you can do, what you can't do. There's no sort of 'What can we help you with?' They're just ticking boxes for themselves.
>
> There's so much build-up to when you turn 18. You think that that's all been help, and you think you've received help from that, but you really haven't. It's been more [about] them ticking boxes, making

> themselves feel better. I mean, the moment you turn 18, everything changes. You go from a social worker to a young person's adviser. And suddenly that support drastically changes. So, when you ask for support, you feel almost, I don't know, I want to say a burden. It's like pressure to be this perfect adult who doesn't need any help.
>
> You do a pathway plan at 17 and four months or whatever. … And I just think 'ok it's nice writing down the things that you can do and the things that you can't do, but so what?' You need to take action.

Some examples were shared which offered promising approaches to developing young people's practical skills in terms of independent living:

> I was in residential for six years and the way that they helped kind of prepare us was [to] give us chores on a daily basis, so we knew what to do. Dishes, do the floors, clean the bathroom. And, if they felt that you were comfortable enough, they had built a downstairs for independent living. So, if they felt that you were ready, they'd move you down there and you'd have to manage that by yourself, like your own independent little flat.

Such arrangements are not commonly experienced by most care-experienced young people approaching adulthood:

> The moment you turn 18, in care anyway, most residential settings give you a period of a week to leave and then you either go into independent housing or you go into semi-independence and it's a massive sort of shock to see that. That support is withdrawn rapidly. There's no sort of … what's the word ... 'moving in period' – because the council's worried about how much it's going to cost to keep both placements running.
>
> I had to ask to move out of my independent living to stay at my nan's because it just wasn't working. I knew from my social worker that was meant to be

> teaching me like, life lessons. But like they weren't teaching me anything. I was just staying there. They didn't teach me anything.
>
> The only thing [my placement] offered was cooking lessons, but I can cook. I've got Algerian family, Turkish family, Bangladeshi people in my family. I don't need to learn to cook. My dad's mum was teaching me cooking Turkish food from like 8 years old, as soon as I could actually learn how to cook without burning my hands.
>
> Yeah it's like as soon as you're out (of care), it's right, grow up, time to build on the big man's boots, whatever you want to call it. So you've got to take on all these responsibilities before you even get the chance to understand what's happening.
>
> Yeah, and they want you to know everything overnight. They tell you something one day and they want you to learn it overnight. Like, if you have behaviour issues, they want you to change behaviour suddenly, suddenly be able to manage it.

For young people a positive transition to adulthood is not only about the practical skills of independent living that feature so largely in policy and practice. They identified a range of other gaps in support:

> There's no outside support. Like, adult mental health services is incredibly difficult to get. Because up until you're 18 you have services like CAMHS who will work with you weekly.[4] But as soon as you turn 18 there is nothing.

Further, they argue it is not sufficient to simply improve pathways from children's mental health services to adult mental health services; some young people might not need support until they enter this transitional life stage:

> There's all different types of children in care. They have all different types of situations, all different types

> of needs and stuff. But, say you've, you know, you've got a child in care who hasn't really needed a lot of mental health support. But when it comes to, like being like 17 onwards, I think it's quite hard to find yourself because that's when you first start making relationships with people and you start, you know, all that stuff.

For transitional support to be effective, it must be personalised and tailored to the individual:

> Different things will work differently for different people. You can't just do one thing and make it OK.
>
> I wish they taught me like, how to like budget *and* how to get a job *and* how to keep relationships, yes. I had to do it all on my own.

Transitional support, to be meaningful, must attend to the relational aspects of young people's development.

> It's not just the sort of skills like knowing how to pay a bill or manage a bank account or sort out your rent, those practical things. But some of that more like relational, emotional, psychological stuff.
>
> Most of the times it's like cooking classes or, you know, DIY lessons. But it also needs to think about your emotional health and your physical health as well. And professionals should be encouraging healthy relationships, you know.

The way in which transitional support is designed and delivered within leaving care services was thought by some members of the group to actually contribute to risk:

> You don't understand the changes that happen so quickly and I don't think professionals really stop to think about that. From living in foster care to a semi-independence and you're isolated from your peers. I feel like that can be quite dangerous sometimes.

These comments about relational and emotional well-being highlight the need for young people approaching adulthood to be able to access holistic and personalised support, as Transitional Safeguarding advocates for. While finance and home environment are important to a person's safety, it is not sufficient to attend to practical skills alone; a person's sense of safety is more complex than this. Transitional Safeguarding is distinct from 'transitions planning' (see Chapter 7). The Transitional Safeguarding approach seeks to ensure that *all* young people – including but not limited to care leavers – are supported to develop a sense of physical, relational, and psychological security. It aims to avoid needs emerging or escalating in adulthood, and thus sees safeguarding not through the lens of eligibility, but as a person-centred preventative approach (see Chapter 2).

Risk, safety and safeguarding

The group reflected on what the word safety means for them. While professionals might focus on being 'safe from harm', for the young people being 'safe' was broader than that. The group strongly emphasised stability and belonging as key:

> For me, safety is having that, I don't want to call it a safety net … it's more of an acceptance of your surroundings, of a community. Having those relationships with certain people. It's knowing that you can rely on them and they can rely on you.
>
> I think to me safety is stability. I think a lot of people who've grown up with um, I don't know what the word is, but when you're seen as vulnerable, yeah? It means that you can have quite a lot of big changes quite quickly. So, stability is definitely something I see as being safe as, you know, like you're in one place, you're in one situation and it's not going to suddenly change.
>
> I would say the same. Safe means stability and kind of feeling like some kind of normality. For me, I'm safe if I can just be myself and not [be] worrying that something bad's about to happen or anything like that. That's what safety is to me.

The word safeguarding has powerful, often negative, meanings for many young people – perhaps particularly those with care experience, as the group described:

> Safeguarding, to me, has always been to do with risky behaviour, stuff like that. It's always been quite a negative when in reality it's a positive because it's trying to make change. But the way that growing up vulnerable makes you see it is that the moment safeguarding is mentioned it's like 'Ohh no, someone's gonna be told that I'm not ok, that I'm not doing perfect. Someone's gonna be told that something's not right. I'm not gonna be seen as an adult because they've got an issue.'
>
> Definitely. It's got quite negative connotations and they, the professionals, don't help that very much because it is very much paperwork. All 'we've got to do this now'.
>
> In some cases, a safeguarding, like, like procedure being followed through can put someone in quite an unsafe situation growing up.
>
> Yeah, and if you're transitioning into adulthood and a safeguarding complaint is put in about you displaying risky behaviours, like you're using substances or you're hanging around with the wrong people. … It can make your life more difficult as you're not seen as an adult, you're seen still as a child. So, you sometimes don't get that respect because you're seen as risky or vulnerable.

The sense of infantilisation described here is in stark contrast to the previous discussions about being pushed into 'independent' adulthood and highlights the contradictory way in which young people are perceived and treated. The procedural, sometimes punitive, nature of safeguarding processes was considered to actually deter some young people from seeking support when they needed it:

> For instance, I was put on a DOLS order when I was 14, which benefitted me.[5] But it also made me reluctant to tell, say if anything else had happened or I was put in another situation, it would make me a

> bit more reluctant to tell them. Because it [being the subject of safeguarding intervention] can be harsh. It can feel like you're being punished sometimes, and it does make you more reluctant to come back and to say anything or to ask anyone.
>
> There's times where a situation has happened, but you feel the need to play it down because if you say how it actually is, it will be … like, what's the word, like, the process is intense and very draining to go through.

These comments illustrate the dangers that can arise when young people experience safeguarding practice as being process-driven and punitive, and they further corroborate the emphasis on person-centred and participative approach aspects of Transitional Safeguarding.

The group gave examples of the different perspectives professionals and young people have about risk. One example is cannabis use, which some young people described as being an occasional means of managing anxiety or insomnia, but many professionals would feel concerned about this. In contrast, young people felt their risks in terms of social isolation were underplayed or overlooked by professionals:

> For me and other people I know, you know, the risks associated with being on your own in isolation, were probably more than say drug use or you know, being around the wrong crowd of people.
>
> Loneliness and isolation. That's one of the things I sort of thought of when I was 18, because you're in a really strange position when you turn 18 in care cause all of your peers that aren't in care.
>
> Professionals do miss quite a lot of risks, like mental health and the people we surround ourselves with – where we don't know their background and stuff like that, it could put us in a vulnerable place.

Getting associated with 'the wrong crowd' can be a source of direct harm for young people, and can contribute indirectly to the negative consequences of labelling:

> Well, the saying where I grew up was 'if you fly with the crows, you get shot with the crows'. Uh, so if you're mixing with the wrong crowds, whatever comes your way, well if one member of that group gets in trouble, you're gonna get labelled as trouble.

Young people considered to be 'trouble' are often highly vulnerable, and the behaviours that are considered troublesome (including aggression or violence) could be their way of communicating vulnerability. This is not always understood by professionals:

> Some of them young people that do this stuff [behave badly] could be asking for help that way. That's their way of communicating for help – some young people that don't like to speak about how they feel. They just ask for help that way, and then they get into trouble and they get labelled. He's just naughty. Nothing's wrong.

Young people also explained how positive risk taking is something that is necessary for development, but that this was sometimes not understood by all professionals:

> See, for me, risks are like something that people do every day, because we're human and we want to try new things. And whether it's risky or not, we're just trying to find a place in society in a sense.
>
> You can try and keep [young people] safe, but at the same time you've got to let them try and live their life to a certain extent, but if it gets too much, then step in. Just don't overwhelm them. Let them make mistakes but be there to help them sort it out.
>
> Like some social workers don't like young people making mistakes. But you have to. If you don't make a mistake, you'll get older and you won't know how to make mistakes because you're just thinking, 'I've been told not to make mistakes. Mistakes are going to ruin me.' But you need to make the mistakes, to learn. You have to learn stuff, by making some mistakes.

Risk was felt to be something that professionals and young people thought and talked about differently. Connecting back to the earlier points about young care-experienced people feeling that they needed to seem that they were 'coping', some safeguarding issues might not be explored at all:

> Some young people can seem really, you know, independent and fine. And I feel like because of that, those conversations [about risk and safeguarding] don't occur.
>
> I think because a lot of young people do act fine. Those conversations about risk and safety ... they don't happen. I think a lot slips through the cracks if you're not a 'high-risk young person'.

A further interesting insight emerged in discussing the ways in which professionals talk with young people about risk and safeguarding. Some of the young people could not recall having a conversation about risks and harms, and their participation worker Rosie reminded them they had just hours earlier had a safety planning meeting. The centrality of relational practice shines through in their responses:

> Oh right, yeah. I think our conversation wasn't about risk, I mean, it was obviously a risk assessment but it felt more like. ... It was more a conversation about how you can help, rather than 'your risks of this, this and this and therefore we need to do this, this and this'. It was personal. And it didn't feel. ... It didn't feel like a, um, clinical sort of conversation.
>
> Like, it's not fudging it, it's not about pretending that we're not talking about risk here. It's just the language, isn't it? It's the relationships isn't it?

Good safeguarding support, like good transitional support, must be person-centred:

> What I've noticed with most services is that they have a very cookie-cutter approach, so they'll go into a

> situation or an assessment with a young person and they'll have their set of questions that's not personalised. And if you don't conform to that cookie cutter, then you're not fit for their service. I think it's important that services need to be quite personal, not intrusive.
>
> A professional shouldn't be thinking that the young person they're speaking to is going to have the exact same needs as the person before. And that seems a bit obvious, but it's not. A lot of services run like that because it's easier and there are less time constraints that way.

Self-development and identity

The need for transitions support to focus on personal development and relationships was echoed in ideas around what makes for effective safeguarding support. Supporting young people to be and feel safe was felt to be closely connected with issues of identity and self-development:

> I think that it's really important for everyone to be able to like learn, like, learn stuff about themselves. That's what I mean about self-development. Like getting to know yourself. How do we expect young people, young adults, to really know who they are if we've never explored that with them? Like, we've never helped them really think about that.
>
> I feel like, especially in residential, when you're placed with a lot of other kids, you … you lose yourself in other kids. Coming out of it when you're on your own and it's kind of like, 'ohh, like, what am I? What do I actually enjoy? Do I actually enjoy this because I like it, or do I enjoy it because someone else likes it?' Do you know what I mean?
>
> I think there's a lot of kids who have been in care since a very young age and you grow older and you don't remember anything from your childhood. You don't remember what things were like or you don't remember the things you used to do, yeah?

> I honestly think that if there were more work on that stuff, there'd be more chance of them having a better life, you know what I mean?
>
> I think there should be work done really to just help develop into themselves, you know? I mean, say that didn't happen. … You know, there was no self-development work and you was lost and you didn't really know. You go to a job. And it's like it's the same patterns – you fall in with the wrong people because that's all you know and that's how it can get worse.

The group members thought that understanding risk in the context of interpersonal relationships was especially relevant to young people in care:

> There's a lot of nasty people out there so I think what would also benefit people is kind of, like, teaching what a bad person looks like. Like, you know, someone could be very vulnerable and – not to sound horrible – naive, and they wouldn't know if someone was manipulating them. They could, you know, say if they got into the toxic relationships or say they went back to live with their parents who could be like that. And they're unaware because that behaviour is just normal to them.
>
> I think [previous young person speaking] hit the nail on the head. I don't know if anyone else has heard of DBT or dialectic behavioural therapy, but one of the key sort of lessons they teach is 'interpersonal effectiveness'. It's like how to safely manage relationships and effectively ask for what you need in relationships. I think things like that should be taught in secondary school so that while you're going through that transition into adulthood, you know you are able to spot the red flags you are able to look out for.

It is all about relationships

Relationships, as well as being a source of potential harm for young people, also represent the primary vehicle for effective support. The quality and stability of relationships between young people and professionals was a strong influencing factor on young people's experience of safety and their transition to adulthood. The importance of consistency in these relationships was a theme that came through from the group conversations.

> Some people just keep getting moved so they're there for like two months, they build relationships and then they get moved. Four social workers last year. So how are you gonna build a bond with four? How are you gonna build a bond in about three months?
>
> And if you keep getting moved then you're just not gonna build bonds with any staff are you?
>
> There's no point opening up because you know that there's gonna be a change some point down the line. I mean, I had about 20-plus social workers in six years. I think the longest social worker I had was one year.
>
> If I needed anything or if I wasn't OK, I wouldn't go to my social worker. I've had my new social worker for about six months and I still don't trust her.
>
> Well, lots of young people might have learned not to trust people. And then your social worker goes on leave and never came back. You have to wait another like three months to get a new one, so if you need something you have to call up. Talk to like three different people.
>
> You see them [your social worker] like once a month. Last time I had a phone call from my social worker was like two months ago.

Promisingly, the young people also had examples where relationships had been sustained:

> Like with my house project, I've been on it for like six months, but I knew the people for like two years before. So I built up a bond from then – If I need anything I can just go to them because actually I've known them longer than I know my social worker now.

> There are two [previous residential workers] that I still message to this day because we had that strong of a bond. And I'm very thankful for them for doing that.

Having a meaningful relationship is crucial to being able to strike the right balance between risk and rights – between protection and participation, as noted in other chapters – and for this balance to be different for each young person:

> I do think it is very difficult [to treat someone like an adult but also help them be safe] because obviously you need to think about the young person, you need to think about their safety, but then you also have to keep in mind about their needs and what they want and stuff like that. I do think it can be very difficult to get it right.
>
> There's been no one way to have a solution to every problem. Do you know what I mean? Because every situation is different, and every individual is different. It depends on the person and their circumstances. That's why you need to have that relationship.

Relationships with professionals are by no means the only important type of relationship. Building and strengthening familial relationships for young people in care was seen as key to a positive transition:

> Some children in care have – still see – their families, some don't. But it's kind of a rocky relationship. I think that there should be more, like, family time together. If it's, you know, if it's all like safe and it's what the young person wants themselves. Because it gives them a good start [for adulthood].
>
> Instead of just being fully on their own, if they've got the chance to, you know, build relationships up with family and stuff like that, I think it gives them. … It's just a lot better because when you do go into adulthood, it does get very lonely.

Young people's vision for system change

The young people argued cogently for a system of support that offers a life-course approach. They challenged the construct of Transitional Safeguarding being for up to 25 year olds, and gave examples of how the cliff edge experienced by many 18-year-olds is replicated at 25 for many care-experienced young people.

> So the other day I was speaking to the director of [a service in my borough] and they said to me something that doesn't really make sense: 'You're a young person till you're 25, and we are your corporate parent until you die.' So what about between 26 and when you die? Nothing – you're on your own.
>
> I don't know why the system shuts off at 25. I think the care system should shut off when you think. You should be the one to leave, not they get rid of you once you turn 25.
>
> There should be a safe thing. A safety net. Catch you when you fall, yeah.

In terms of the kind of support that would be helpful for young people, it might not be best delivered by social care services. Nor did young people want intensive or expensive specialist services:

> Maybe not like social care, but like someone that you can talk to, maybe like a contact. And from each borough, they should have like one person for over 25-year-olds too. Or like a few people that you can just call up and talk to, instead of just being isolated and not knowing where to go.
>
> I think young people get, well, they try to get help somewhere else. They don't want to go to social services for help. Some of the people I know, they just talk to their friends, but friends that have been in care, so they know how they feel.
>
> There needs to be support for some other people that haven't got help. Everyone needs a support bubble.
>
> I think it's more like just for someone you can rant to.

> For after you turn 25, yeah, 100 per cent. There should be, as [other young person] said, a support bubble for those young people who have nowhere else to turn because they don't want to go back to social workers especially. I've not had the best experience. I felt judged every time I turned to them.

Service improvement might be the focus for many professionals, but for these young people the goal is whole system reform, and they are clear that resourcing is part of that reform:

> Social workers are massively overworked and underfunded. So there needs to be a lot more other services that can help young people.
>
> I would just rebuild the whole social care system. … It's letting too many young people down, and it just needs to be rebuilt and have the right sort of people running it. And not those who are money orientated, people with hands-on experience, people who are passionate. We do have that already but they're massively underfunded, massively overworked and so those people slip through the net and give up on that career because it's too stressful. And I think that's a disgrace.
>
> We should be supporting those who have a passion to make a difference and to help raise the next generation of adults.

These young people are passionate about participation, and each are involved in a variety of activities and groups that aim to improve the system. Their motivations are clear:

> I do it because I think I never got listened to. I don't want other young people to not get listened to and not get the support they need.
>
> Just to make sure that the social work is … you know, we do it, so the social workers know what to do.
>
> We just want … I think we want to change things for real. We're gonna change this and maybe all the young people see it.

Their commitment to participatory system reform is exemplified by the young person who, when asked what one thing they would change if they were in charge of everything, replied:

> Well, if I was in charge, I'd just ask young people what they want to happen, what rules they want in place.

Conclusion

Expertise borne out of lived experience, just like practice wisdom and academic evidence, rarely offers simple answers. The contradictory positioning of young peoples' rights, protections, and freedoms in policy and legislation, as explored in the introduction, echoes the way that care-experienced young people face a range of contradictory experiences at the hands of professionals. On the one hand they can have their sense of freedom constrained and can feel infantilised, on the other they are propelled into independence; they can feel pushed to quickly develop practical skills while often being unable to access wider psychological or emotional support. It is unsurprising, therefore, that young people themselves express an ambiguity about adulthood. This chapter explores a number of these dual perspectives. These young people describe both craving the freedom of adulthood *and* harbouring several fears and anxieties about what is to come. These young people may be both deterred from accepting support for fear of being seen as 'not adult' *and* they firmly believe young people should be offered support. These young people want support to be and feel safe *and* they can find safeguarding processes to be an unsafe experience. These young people argue passionately for the right to be protected, *and* they reject notions of paternalism.

These seemingly contradictory ideas are not unresolvable – indeed, the core ideas underpinning Transitional Safeguarding suggest that system reform relies on a more boundary-spanning perspective being adopting within policy and practice. As the young people co-authoring this chapter have highlighted, what is needed is safeguarding support that balances rights and risks, integrates protection and participation, and is person-centred and holistic. Young people need to know that there is support available to make the journey to adulthood a positive one, and accessing such help does not undermine a person's status as an adult. By drawing on the ideas and insights in this chapter, and the expertise of local young people, local areas can develop their approach to Transitional Safeguarding and redesign their systems and structures of support. This can show young people not only that local services have an important role to play in helping them be and feel safe, but also that their voices are heard and respected. It is, after all, a partnership.

2

The challenge of safeguarding binaries

Introduction

This chapter will explore the ways in which binary notions are impeding safeguarding efforts at both a practice and policy level and will consider the human and economic cost of the current approach. The six *key principles* of Transitional Safeguarding will then be outlined, with an explanation of how each principle is deliberately intended to respond to and redress identified problems. In keeping with the theme of boundary-spanning, this chapter will then describe how each of the principles exemplify the 'both/and' ethos of Transitional Safeguarding at practice level and at the level of leadership and wider policy.

At its heart, Transitional Safeguarding is concerned with boundary-spanning, and as such is an issue of systems leadership that supports practice change. This fundamental characteristic is precisely because Transitional Safeguarding seeks to redress the binaries and inflexibilities within the current safeguarding systems, whether these are related to age, service siloes, or professional disciplines, and/or the wider way in which citizens are conceptualised. There have been significant efforts in recent years, including new statutory duties, to ensure a more fluid transitional experience for some young people – notably, those with special educational needs and disabilities, and those leaving care. However, within the safeguarding arena, a binary notion of childhood and adulthood has endured, with safeguarding responses for those over aged 18 and those aged under 18 operating to wholly different thresholds, legislation, and policy paradigms (Cocker et al 2021). This divergent approach, with little fluidity between adult's and children's safeguarding systems, means that some older adolescents and younger adults are not receiving the support they need to be safe and feel safe (Holmes and Smale 2018). As argued elsewhere (Holmes 2022a), the transition to adulthood is a process, not an event, and this process varies depending on a young person's experiences, environment, and context. While many harms facing young people under 18 continue into adulthood, and although young people's brains continue to develop until their mid-twenties (Sawyer et al 2018; Prior et al 2011), the current safeguarding approach operates to a rigid notion that adulthood suddenly occurs on a person's eighteenth birthday. This binary approach permeates practice and policy in a variety of ways, each of which undermine the ability to help young people to live safer lives. Furthermore, this binary construct reflects and reinforces an underpinning public and professional mindset. It is not simply a question of adjusting service structures and direct practice; what is required is whole system change, which in turn requires systems leadership. This is explored further in Chapter 10.

As discussed in Chapter 10, systems leadership connects to the concept of 'systems thinking' and 'whole system approaches', both of which are important when seeking to enable positive change in relation to complex or 'wicked issues' (Ghate et al 2013). Transitional Safeguarding and systems leadership are both reliant on 'boundary-spanning' (Williams 2002). In seeking to redress the unhelpful binaries of current safeguarding approaches and recognising that safeguarding is not only about practice but also about local leadership and national policy, a boundary-spanning mindset is vital.

Exploring current binaries within safeguarding policy and practice

As outlined in Chapter 3, the legislative, policy, and practice frameworks that guide safeguarding for those aged under and over 18 are distinctly different, creating a gap through which some young people can fall. This disconnected and polarised thinking manifests in several ways, which influence and drive each other. The obvious binary is in relation to age, with safeguarding services operating to the rule that a person is either a child *or* an adult, with little recognition of the liminal nature of adolescence and emerging adulthood. This binary perpetuates the challenges of safeguarding people who occupy both victim and perpetrator identities, as can be the case in many forms of exploitation (Firmin 2020), and reinforces the notion that a person is either vulnerable *or* culpable. This in turn contributes to siloed service responses, with some people receiving a criminal justice response instead of a safeguarding response; even within the same service, practice can adopt a binary position of either being protective *or* participative.

Each of these binaries interacts with the others, reinforcing and perpetuating a set of mechanisms by which many young people are disqualified from support services. These binary constructs are seemingly fuelled by the way language is used, and arguably such language has come to dictate professional responses. The term safeguarding is often interpreted through an eligibility lens, and so 'acts not as a verb – something to do with a person when their safety is undermined – but as a noun, a threshold to be reached, a place that many people cannot access despite their safety being undermined' (Holmes 2022a: 8). It follows that a teenager may not receive a safeguarding response if the harms they face are not understood to be a 'safeguarding issue' – for example, peer-on-peer abuse (Firmin 2020). Similarly, a young adult facing harm will likely not receive a safeguarding response if their needs are not deemed to meet the criteria set out in the Care Act 2014, if they are not 'vulnerable enough', to phrase it starkly. Accordingly, their clearly harmful circumstances are procedurally redefined as 'not safeguarding' despite the clear vulnerabilities it creates in the person (see Chapter 6). This creates a 'self-reinforcing loop, with terms defining actions that in turn prescribe the terms' (Holmes 2022a, p1:8). This byzantine arrangement is counter to widespread evidence, which emphasises the crucial importance of person-centred and needs-led safeguarding support and has led to calls for 'an integrated paradigm for safeguarding young people that better meets their developmental needs and better reflects the nature of harms young people face' (Cocker et al 2021).

As explored in Chapter 4, early adulthood is a distinct life stage and the current safeguarding systems do not recognise or respond to this. Some progress has been made in terms of transitions between services, and the guidance associated with this is welcome. However, it would be fair to say that the focus to date has been on promoting a smoother transition between children's and adults' *services* for those who are eligible for post-18 support, as opposed to promoting a smoother transition between childhood and adulthood itself by fundamentally reconsidering service eligibility. The difference between Transitional Safeguarding and transitions planning is considered further in Chapter 7.

One example of efforts to create a more transitional approach for young people is the extension of personal adviser support for young people leaving care up until the age of 25 (Department for Education 2018). This is rather hard to square with the government's assertion that 16–18-year-olds in care may be placed in unregulated settings, as they are being accommodated rather than receiving 'care' (Department for Education 2021), and it also overlooks the many young people who have experienced trauma and abuse in their lives but were not removed into care. This matters because care status is a poor proxy for understanding need – particularly given the argument that the granting of a Care Order under s.31 of the Children Act 1989 requires some attribution of 'significant harm' to parents, and so is not relevant to the many adolescents coming to the attention of professionals due to harm outside of the family home (Firmin and Knowles 2022). Similarly, while the special educational needs and disability (SEND) code of practice covers 0–25, there remains a disconnect between this document, which defines a young person as having a learning disability if he or she 'has significantly greater difficulty in learning than the majority of others of the same age' (Department for Education 2015), and the Care Act 2014 eligibility criteria for assessing adults' care and support needs, which specifies the person must be 'unable to achieve certain outcomes as a result of their need, which must arise from physical or mental impairment'.

Turning to other binary boundaries, the duality of 'victim/perpetrator' identities is another aspect in which current safeguarding approaches can struggle to respond effectively. This is particularly problematic in the context of extra-familial harm and exploitation, a pressing issue for many local areas (Association of Directors of Children's Services (ADCS) 2021; 2022), as young people can find themselves awkwardly positioned at the interface of justice and safeguarding systems (Holmes and Smith, 2022; Harris and Edwards 2023). Although Government guidance does acknowledge that young people *under* 18 can be both victims and perpetrators of sexual and criminal exploitation (HM Government 2020; Home Office 2018), the children's safeguarding framework and law enforcement responses are poorly equipped to manage this duality (Beckett et al 2017) and victims of child criminal exploitation continue to be criminalised (Human Trafficking Foundation 2022). There is brief acknowledgement within government guidance that those *over* 18 can be criminally exploited, but this is limited to those termed 'vulnerable adults' (Home Office 2018). This subjective terminology does not align with definitions used in the Care Act 2014 and locates vulnerability as an individualistic construct, leaving some exploited young adults facing criminal charges rather than a safeguarding response.

This binary framing reinforces the idea that a young person is either vulnerable or culpable, often depending on their age, and the professional system demonstrably struggles to hold a 'both/and' construct in mind. This echoes other binary constructs: namely that vulnerability is counter to capacity. For example, sexual exploitation in childhood and adolescence can be a driver for sexual victimisation in adulthood and evidence suggests this can lead to a number of detrimental effects on a person's health and well-being (Lalor and McElvaney 2010). Despite this, trauma is not considered a care and support need and sexual exploitation of adults is afforded only a fleeting reference within the Care Act 2014 guidance, which only acknowledges sexual exploitation as an issue for 'people who may lack the capacity to understand that they have the right to say no' (Department of Health and Social Care (DHSC) 2023). Similarly, guidance regarding 'cuckooing'[1] acknowledges that 'vulnerable adults' may become victims (Home Office 2018) but does not recognise that this form of exploitation affects not only those adults with formally defined care and support needs, but also many others who experience vulnerability and adversity beyond these narrowly defined needs

(Spicer et al 2020). In both examples, vulnerability is positioned as an individualistic construct – something which an adult possesses within themselves – rather than recognising that vulnerability is highly contextual and dynamic. It may also be the result of or be impacted by structural inequality(ies). This failure to span conceptual boundaries can lead to the 'under-recognition of young adults' situational vulnerability, and simultaneously risks pathologising young adults where vulnerability is identified (Holmes 2022a).

Manipulation and coercion can be common features of exploitation (Beckett et al 2017). This demands a safeguarding response which is highly participatory, in order to allow young people to exercise as much choice and voice as possible (Holmes 2022a). While participative 'user-led' approaches within safeguarding adults are an established concept, with benefits found for both individuals and for practice development (Droy and Lawson 2017), in safeguarding practice with young people under 18, an emphasis on rights and participation can often be lacking (Warrington 2016). Affording young people a sense of choice and agency is an important means of enabling them to exercise their rights and is particularly key in the context of coercion (Hill and Warrington 2022). A boundary-spanning practice paradigm that combines both protection *and* participation is therefore crucial. As one young survivor of sexual exploitation explains 'A lot of people have pushed us into things, have forced us to do things and made a lot of decisions for us and we don't need the people who are there to help us to do it as well' (Jago et al 2011, p 63). The tension of integrating protective and participative practice is keenly felt by children's services practitioners working to address sexual exploitation, leading to researchers urging for an approach to participation and protection which is 'both/and not either/or' (Lefevre et al 2018).

We might wonder why, in the face of clear evidence that complex issues require joined-up thinking, does this binary mindset persist? Some argue that the disconnected approach is not simply a consequence of fragmented policy and siloed services, but is also a consequence of human psychology:

> From a psychosocial perspective, the splitting involved in creating binary, 'either/or' categories (such as who

> presents 'a risk' and who is 'at risk') may be a defensive response to overwhelming anxiety and complexity, a familiar characteristic of social work and social care practice. (Huegler and Ruch 2021).

This desire for neat delineation and order is understandable, given the complexity and pressure facing professionals; however, dismantling this construct is essential to developing and embedding Transitional Safeguarding.

The human and economic costs of the current binary system

Evidence shows that many of the adversities and harms facing young people and adults are connected. For example, socio-economic inequality has a profoundly detrimental effect on physical and mental health (Marmot 2020) and poverty is a driving force for child protection and care rates for children (Bywaters and Skinner 2022). Family breakdown is a key factor in youth homelessness (Clarke et al 2015); sexual exploitation and other trauma is linked to mental ill-health and substance misuse (Widom et al 2008; Levine 2016); and experience of domestic abuse in childhood has been found to be associated with violence and gang association later in life (Children's Commissioner 2019; Molina and Levell 2020). Given these connections, it is striking that the responses to these harms (and the associated funding structures) are often highly disjointed.

This creates financial inefficiencies and, of course, bears a significant human cost. Imagine a young woman aged 17 years and 364 days and ensnared in a sexually exploitative relationship. Overnight, she will cease to be defined as a victim of child abuse and may instead be viewed as an adult with the capacity to exercise her right to make certain choices. Her circumstances, vulnerability, and needs are wholly unchanged by her birthday, but she is suddenly no longer 'everybody's business'; a somewhat ubiquitous phrase within children's safeguarding (Holland et al 2011). Her needs arising from sexual exploitation and trauma *may* escalate far enough that she is deemed eligible for safeguarding support as an adult, but she will have to experience much more harm and pain first. Should this young woman become a mother, it is very possible that children's safeguarding services might see reason to intervene, but this will necessarily be centred on the safeguarding needs of her child. This scenario highlights that, while concepts such as early intervention in child welfare services and prevention within adult social care are established within their respective spheres, there is a long way to go towards embedding a life-course approach. The practice binary noted earlier in this chapter, in which protective practices and participatory practices are perceived in opposition to each other (Lefevre et al 2018), can result in negative and even dangerous consequences for young people. Inspired by the Social Discipline Window (Wachtel 2003) that underpins restorative practice (see Chapter 5), Figure 2.1 aims to illustrate how protection and participation are inter-related and must be held in thoughtful balance according to the individual and their context. Evidently, the aim is purposeful practice with young people, which requires high levels of participation in order to promote effective protection. Conversely, if practices offer low levels of protection young people can be left in precarious situations, while a focus on protection without a focus on participation can leave young people feeling punished (see Chapter 1).

Figure 2.1: Balancing protective and participative safeguarding practice

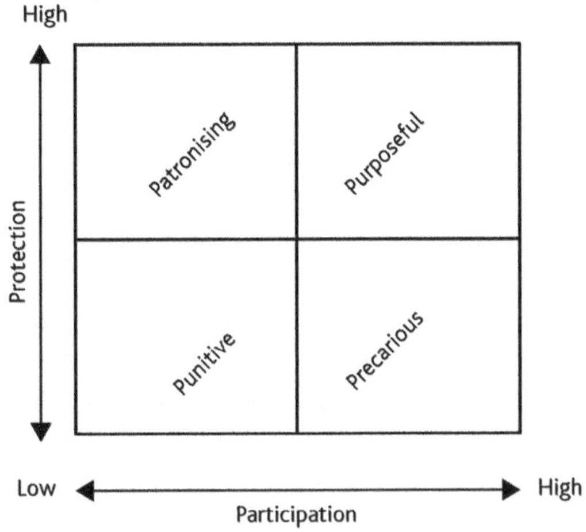

One of the most palpable detriments of the current binary approach relates to the interface between young people's safety needs and the justice system. There is clear evidence within the justice literature that young people, especially those with experience of risk factors, 'may not be fully developed until halfway through the third decade of life' (Johnson et al 2009, p 216). Notwithstanding welcome efforts within the justice sphere to better recognise the needs of young adults (Holmes and Smith 2022), there remains an urgent need to improve transitional support for young people under *and* over 18 within the justice system (Harris and Edwards 2023). The cross-party Youth Violence Commission documented evidence from professionals regarding the many young people 'around the age of 25, who badly want to leave the life of crime behind' but are trapped by a criminal justice response (Irwin-Rogers et al 2020, p 33). A vicious cycle can be seen here, with researchers noting that adults with previous criminal convictions are targeted by exploiters involved in the drugs trade (Whittaker et al 2019), and yet if they are not deemed to have care and support needs, they are likely to receive a criminal justice response for their involvement. For young people who turn 18 between offence and conviction, the binary construct of 'childhood versus adulthood' creates a number of harmful consequences such as 'loss of anonymity … only being eligible for adult sentences … and much longer rehabilitation periods which reduce employment prospects and prevent people moving on with their lives' (Helyar-Cardwell and Moran 2020, p 1). So, the professional response to a young person being exploited where they do not fit a narrowly defined construct of 'vulnerable' may be to criminalise them. This criminalisation undermines their ability to engage in the very things that reduce the risk of offending, such as employment and settled accommodation and relationships (House of Commons Justice Committee 2016), and so their vulnerability – and potentially their risk to others – is perpetuated and exacerbated.

The prospect of adopting a Transitional Safeguarding approach, or indeed any complex system innovation, is daunting given the irrefutable under-resourcing of public services. Analysis by the Health Foundation (2021) found a funding gap for adult social care of at least £2.1bn just to conduct 'business as usual' in the context of an ageing population (House of Commons Health and Social Care Committee, 2020). Another Commons Select Committee supported this analysis, adding that a lack of investment in public health services and prevention was stopping people receiving support at an earlier stage, and concluding that 'the Government urgently needs to allocate more funding to adult social care in the order of several billions each year, at least £7 billion' (House of Commons Levelling Up, Housing and Communities Committee 2022, p 24). Just as worryingly, the House of Commons Housing, Communities and Local Government Committee (2019) reported a £3.1bn funding gap for children's services by 2025, in a report published before COVID-19 or the cost-of-living crisis. A survey undertaken by the Association of Directors of Adult Social Services (ADASS) found that just 3 per cent of directors were confident that they have the resources to deliver on all of their responsibilities in 2023 (ADASS 2022). Research commissioned by children's services leaders estimated the total required to close the budget gap in-year stands at £778m, or 7.5 per cent of the national children's services budget (ADCS 2022). The current disconnected system response is not only a poor fit for the holistic human experience, but also represents poor value for money. In considering the impacts of the current disjointed approach, a tentative economic argument can be made for promoting the Transitional Safeguarding approach.

Evidence from the UK and international contexts highlights that failing to support young people's recovery from harm and trauma can lead to problems persisting and/or worsening in adulthood, creating higher costs for the public purse (Chowdry and Fitzsimons 2016; Kezelman et al 2015). Given the interconnectedness of mental health and safeguarding, the need for preventative investment across this life stage is sharply demonstrated by the finding that three quarters of mental health problems are believed to start under the age of 24 (Kessler et al 2005) and the estimated annual costs of mental health problems in England are over £105bn (Centre for Mental Health 2010). The ensuing costs of young people's unmet safeguarding needs often fall to parts of the system beyond safeguarding services – as illustrated by the over-representation of people with experience of trauma and abuse within the prison population (House of Commons Justice Committee, 2016); the bi-directional relationship between mental ill-health and homelessness (Narendorf 2017); and the stark evidence of poorer outcomes and higher costs associated with early parenthood (Public Health England 2019a).

The understanding that connected issues are best addressed through collective investment underpinned the Total Place initiative, announced by Labour in their 2009 budget, and subsequently the Whole Place Community Budgets pilot announced by the coalition government in 2011. In their guide to Whole Place Community Budgets, the Local Government Information Unit (LGIU) describe the concept as being one wherein '"joined-up", place, and community responsive services [are] based around local communities being able to achieve better results from public services for their area if the complete public expenditure in that locality can be treated as a single "budget", with institutional barriers and funding regimes relaxed, and local priorities pursued "seamlessly"' (LGIU 2013). It is unfortunate that such initiatives were not pursued. If local leaders of children's and adult's services were able to identify the collective costs associated with young people and young adults facing harm, might this not support them in leveraging investment in preventative support from those multi-agency partners to whom the costs fall? Could joining up local expenditure help to redress other binaries and siloes discussed earlier? If homelessness, mental health, substance misuse, and criminal justice services were able to influence and reduce the needs of young people before they required these services as adults, that would likely yield benefits to the public purse as well as to young people. The creation of integrated care systems offers some promise for a more flexible and joined-up response for young people, but it is not yet clear how much attention integrated care boards and partnerships will pay to safeguarding and wider well-being (Partners in Care and Health 2022).

The damaging effects of austerity and under-funding of public services over many years should not be underestimated. The intention here is not to argue that local areas must simply 'do more with less', but rather to recognise that funding constraints are both the problem *and* potential solution for those seeking to adopt a Transitional Safeguarding approach. A preoccupation with eligibility at the expense of prevention can lead to more intrusive and often more expensive intervention into people's lives. The interconnectedness of the harms, impacts, and related costs reinforces our starting premise that Transitional Safeguarding is an issue of systems leadership, reliant on the 'boundary spanning' relational behaviours that Williams highlights as essential to managing complex problems (Williams 2002).

Examining the six key principles of Transitional Safeguarding

Transitional Safeguarding is a holistic framework comprising six overarching and interdependent key principles (see Figure 2.2), designed to enable local areas to work flexibly within these principles according to context and circumstances (Cocker et al 2021). Each principle is a direct counter to the identified problems and shortcomings of the current binary safeguarding system.

Researchers arguing for a social model of child protection have highlighted the ideological resistance to recognising inequality as a driver for harm (Featherstone et al 2018), and a government-sponsored review in 2022 lamented the stigmatising approach of child protection and suggested this comes from an unhelpful mindset within practice (Independent Review of Children's Social Care 2022). To counter the risk of ideologically driven approaches, the first key principle of Transitional Safeguarding is to be **evidence informed**. This means drawing on evidence from research and data, along with professional expertise, and triangulating these sources of evidence with the expertise of those with lived experience. Evidence from professionals highlights the need for a more transitional approach (Cocker et al 2022a) and young people's stories have prompted some local safeguarding partnerships to adopt Transitional Safeguarding as a strategic priority (Office of the Chief Social Worker 2021; Walker-McAllister and Cooper 2022). It is true that the research evidence around harm outside the home, particularly criminal exploitation,

Figure 2.2: Key principles of Transitional Safeguarding

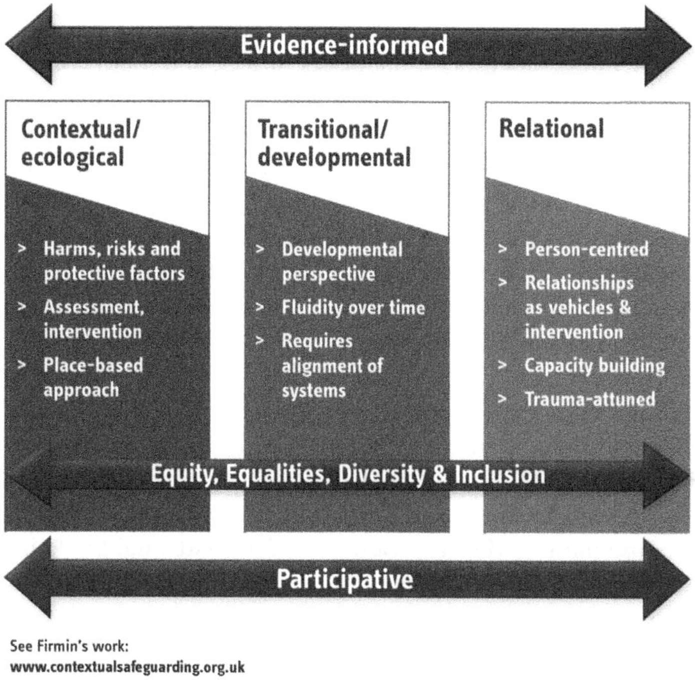

Source: This figure is derived, in part, from an article in practice on 4 Aug 2021, © British Association of Social Workers, available online: doi.org/10.1080/09503153.2021.1956449

is still evolving (Independent Review of Children's Social Care 2022) but there is compelling evidence that too many young adults are being left without support with tragic consequences (see Chapter 8). We may not know enough about what works, but we know enough to act.

Criticisms of the responses to young people facing extra-familial harm are that they are often individualistic and can locate blame with the young person and/or their parents or carers (Firmin 2020; Barlow et al 2022; Beckett and Lloyd 2022). In response, the second key principle of Transitional Safeguarding is to adopt an **ecological** standpoint (drawing on Bronfenbrenner's 1977 ecological theory of child development). This means considering the variety of 'ecosystems' that influence a young person's safety, from the individual and their family, through to their peers and community, and then wider society. In a similar vein, a **contextual** perspective – as set out within the approach of Contextual Safeguarding – focuses on the places, spaces, and social contexts in which young people are safe or unsafe and requires expansive and creative partnership working (Firmin 2020). Transitional Safeguarding is a whole-person approach, situated within a whole-place offer.

As discussed, the current approach to safeguarding young adults is predicated on the notion of eligibility and this can conflict with the clear evidence that young adults may be ensnared in harmful contexts or circumstances without necessarily having formal care and support needs. In addition, current children's safeguarding approaches are not designed with adolescents' developmental needs or risks in mind (Independent Review of Children's Social Care 2022; Hanson and Holmes 2014). To directly counter this, the third principle of Transitional Safeguarding is that the response must be **developmental and transitional** by design. Adolescence and early adulthood are distinct developmental life stages (Coleman and Hagell 2022; Arnett 2000) and a young person's developmental stage must be understood within their individual and socio-political context (see Chapter 4 for a discussion on this). As such, safeguarding systems must enable a professional response which is fluid and reflects the individual needs of the young person and their circumstances, instead of being dictated by rigid age-related boundaries. The Care Act 2014 already notes that the eligibility criteria – that is, the formal care and support needs that generally 'qualify' a person over 18 for statutory adult safeguarding enquiries and interventions – are a *minimum* threshold. This, together with the prevention principle, means that the Care Act 2014 therefore provides a framework within which local partnerships can offer more fluid safeguarding support (see Chapter 6).

The safeguarding system for children and young people has faced ongoing calls for a less process-driven approach (Munro 2011; Independent Review of Children's Social Care 2022), and the Making Safeguarding Personal (MSP) agenda which underpins safeguarding adults' practice deliberately sought to shift from a process-driven culture to person-centred practice (Lawson et al

2014). In keeping with this need to ensure personalised and strength-based approaches, the fourth principle of Transitional Safeguarding is to centre a **relational** approach. This includes recognising the impact of trauma and is particularly important where a young person believes they are choosing to be involved in contexts and/or behaviour that professionals would deem harmful (Hickle and Lefevre 2022). This kind of practice requires proactive and reflective support from management and leadership at all levels, including the recognition of vicarious trauma.

Increasing evidence of structural inequalities and marginalisation in relation to young people's safeguarding and wider outcomes is emerging. Discrimination, disproportionality, and adultification are particularly harmful to Black and other ethnically minoritised young people (Bateman 2017; Davis and Marsh 2022), and poverty, ableism, and gendered stereotypes can also exacerbate risk for many young people (Eshalomi 2020; Wroe and Pearce 2022). These intersecting issues do not stop at 18 and may worsen over time as young people bear the trauma of discrimination. In research focused on Black people's health outcomes, the cumulative effects of social or economic adversity and political marginalisation experienced over time is described as 'weathering' (Geronimus et al 2006). This recognition that discrimination and its impact can build over a person's life course is important to the development of a humane and ethical approach to safeguarding. Accordingly, the fifth principle of Transitional Safeguarding is that it must foreground an **equalities-oriented** approach in which equity, diversity, and inclusion are seen as part of effective safeguarding. This means that practice and policy must proactively seek to identify and redress inequity and injustice; it must avoid blaming young people and obscuring the structural discrimination they face; and must robustly challenge where safeguarding responses replicate discrimination and exclusion.

Research has consistently highlighted the need for young people's voices and expertise to be valued within safeguarding practice and policy (Hill and Warrington 2022). Young people with experience of exploitation repeatedly report feeling controlled by professionals trying to protect them (Hallet 2016) and many receive a punitive response. Safeguarding adults practice and policy does largely seek to empower the person at risk, and the emphasis on working in partnership with people needing support is a key tenet of MSP (see Chapter 6). However, analysis of Safeguarding Adult Reviews (SARs) for young adults who have died shows that their voices are too often missing (explored further in Chapter 8). In light of these findings, the sixth principle of Transitional Safeguarding emphasises a highly **participative** approach is needed, with young people's rights and expertise respected throughout, in order to afford them as much choice and control as possible.

Taken together, these six key principles aim to offer a coherent framework which addresses the contradictory ways in which young peoples' rights, freedoms, and protections are currently positioned within policy and legislation (Holmes 2022a) and counters key criticisms of the current binary safeguarding system.

Beware binary thinking in applying the key principles

In keeping with the boundary-spanning mindset central to Transitional Safeguarding, each principle invites a 'both/and not either/or' perspective in its application within practice and at a leadership and policy level.

The principle of being evidence-informed requires what might be called epistemological boundary-spanning, whereby different sources of knowledge are valued and triangulated to develop a multifaceted understanding of complex issues. At a practice level and at a local strategy or national policy level, this requires research evidence to be integrated with professional wisdom and expertise borne out of lived experience, rather than privileging academic evidence over other forms of knowledge (Markauskaite and Goodyear 2017; Staempfli 2020). In doing so, people's lived experience must be *both* respected as valid *and* not assumed to be representative; professional wisdom must be *both* respected and valued *and* interrogated for biases and gaps. Within research, it requires respect and attention to be paid to *both* quantitative *and* qualitative research. The former can 'provide vital information about a society or community, through surveys, examinations, records or censuses, that no individual could obtain by observation' (UKRI 2022) and the latter is essential to the understanding of relational practice (Ruch and Julkenen 2016). At both a practice and policy level, this principle reminds us that the allure of a definitive 'what works' ideology can be problematic when seeking to understand and innovate within complex systems (Bowyer 2022; explored further in Chapter 10).

The principle of ensuring an ecological and contextual perspective requires *both* attention to the context in which a young person experiences risk or harm *and* a consciously personalised approach in which the safeguarding response is tailored to individual need. Attending to the spaces and places where a young person is unsafe does not preclude the need for a deeply person-centred approach, indeed Contextual Safeguarding is intended to be highly complementary to relationship-based practice, as it 'requires practitioners to work with the contexts in which relationships form and use relationships to shift the contextual dynamics that may be undermining young people's safety. In this sense the way that relationships are used is informed by the contexts in which they exist and the relationships themselves become a source of contextual intervention' (Owens et al 2020, p 5). For practice and policy alike, it is important that a contextual or ecological framing is seen as congruent with a relational and personalised approach.

The principle of being relational should not be understood as a nebulous form of kindness. This principle requires practitioners working to safeguard young people to be *both* relational *and* methodical and defensible in their decision making. This blended 'head and heart' approach echoes Munro's assertion that social workers need to be able to use research and theory alongside skills in building relationships (Munro 2011) and chimes with research highlighting the need for child protection to be informed by professional judgement held in careful balance with procedural expertise (Samsonsen and Turney 2017). At a policy level, this requires investing in skills development across the multi-agency workforce, including those who manage and supervise practitioners; a valuing of relational practice across all disciplines; and for national actors to role-model this blending of authentic empathy with technical expertise in their interactions with the sector.

The principle of ensuring that safeguarding responses are developmental and transitional by design requires *both* an understanding of the developmental needs of young people and young adults *and* a clear recognition that each young person's journey to adulthood is unique. Care must be taken to avoid assuming that developmental milestones and experiences are universal (Chapter 4 discusses this). It is important to avoid over-estimating maturity in ways that could leave young people held responsible for their harm and/or under-estimating self-efficacy in ways that could lead to young people being patronised, punished, or treated without due regard for their rights. At a local level, this requires a nuanced approach to applying legislation that recognises fluctuating and situationally-influenced capacity; and for leaders to nurture a culture in which professionals are supported to be curious in the face of ambiguity. At national policy level, developmentally-attuned responses would be significantly improved by government departments aligning funding streams and policy priorities in order to enable local areas to design a fluid support offer that transcends age-related boundaries.

The principle of being equalities-oriented is boundary-spanning in that it requires an intersectional lens, that is a recognition of the multiple and interacting forms of discrimination that compound each other, particularly for Black women and girls (Crenshaw 1991). This multifaceted understanding of oppression must be embedded within practice, local partnerships, and in national policy. Importantly, it requires an understanding that safeguarding responses without an equalities-oriented lens can reinforce marginalisation and inequity (Davis and Marsh 2022). The disproportionate representation of Black young men within school exclusion and criminal justice populations, the over-representation of people with learning needs among the prison population, and the documented over-surveillance of marginalised and poor communities within child protection all signify that current safeguarding approaches fall woefully short in terms of an intersectional mindset. Additionally, the under-reporting of discriminatory abuse indicates an ongoing deficit in terms of recognising inequalities and identifying discrimination in adult safeguarding work (Mason et al 2022)

The final principle requires a thoughtful balance, as practice must be *both* participative *and* protective. It is vital that young people, whether over or under 18, have their vulnerabilities recognised and are not blamed for the harms they face. Equally, their vulnerabilities must not be seen as reason to disempower them, deprive them of their rights, or dilute or ignore their voices (Hill and Warrington 2022). For practice to operate in this integrative way requires thoughtful local leadership, with a whole-system response that enables choice and control while recognising that coercion and/or trauma responses may impede a young person's ability to act in their own best interests. There is much from safeguarding adults practice and policy that can inform work with under 18s (Cocker et al 2021) but such system reform requires an integrated policy framework in which young people are seen as deserving of protection without paternalism.

Conclusion

Transitional Safeguarding seeks to redress the unhelpful binaries that can create considerable human and economic costs. These can be seen between children's and adults' safeguarding, between safeguarding and justice responses, and in the positioning of young people as either vulnerable or culpable. Transitional Safeguarding is based on a set of interconnected boundary-spanning principles, intended to counter siloed working and so support whole system reform. Each principle features its own 'both/and' balancing act in application. The principles are also fractal, with implications for each level of the system, and recurring themes that reinforce each other at every intersection. This system-level perspective is considered further in Chapter 10.

3

Negotiating legal and social policy frameworks

Introduction

This chapter provides an overview of the legal and social policy frameworks that govern safeguarding practices for children and adults in England. It explores some of the drivers as well as implications of these frameworks. As we set out in the Introduction and Chapter 2, safeguarding practices use a binary notion of childhood and adulthood (Holmes and Smale 2018). This binary approach within safeguarding is in part driven by increasingly divergent social care policies and practices which operationalise the different legislative, policy, and conceptual frameworks for children and adults. Ultimately, this perpetuates the gaps through which some young people fall. These are outlined and explored later.

We also identify the key principles that underpin safeguarding practice with children and with adults. Many of the principles underpinning child and adult safeguarding are similar, but there are also some differences and these are outlined and discussed. This is further explored in Chapters 5 and 6, which examine learning from innovation and promising practice in children's and adults' safeguarding, respectively. Importantly, neither safeguarding system is specifically designed with adolescent developmental needs or behaviours in mind. Legal and social policy frameworks provide the architecture for safeguarding practice, and they can promote or inhibit ways of working.

This chapter explores the implications for developing Transitional Safeguarding.

An overview of safeguarding in children's and adult social services in England

Safeguarding practices in children's and adult social services in England have developed in accordance with different legislative, policy, and conceptual frameworks. The Local Authority Social Services Act 1970 led to the creation of social services departments and established the framework for local authority social work that is still in place today (Carr and Goosey 2017). However, the legal frameworks and statutory guidance development for safeguarding of children and adults are completely separate.

Children's safeguarding and the role of child death inquiries

The first Act of Parliament for the prevention of cruelty to children was passed in 1889 (Batty 2005). In the following 100 years, until the Children Act 1989, further legislation that specifically addressed child protection across the UK included: Children Act 1908; Children and Young Persons Act 1932; and the Children Act 1948. Additionally, the inquiries/other responses to the deaths of various children, beginning with Dennis O'Neill (aged 13) in 1945, have significantly influenced child protection practices. For example, the Children Act 1948 established a children's committee and a children's officer in each local authority after his death.

The death of Maria Colwell (aged 7) in 1973 was the first of a string of high-profile national inquiries that followed individual children's deaths from the 1970s onwards, including: Tyra Henry in 1984 (aged 21 months); Jasmine Beckford in 1984 (aged 4); Kimberley Carlisle in 1986 (aged 4); Ricky Neave (aged 6) in 1994; Victoria Climbié (aged 8) in 2000; Ainlee Labonte (aged 2) in 2002; Peter Connolly (aged 17 months) in 2007; and Daniel Pelka (aged 4) in 2012 (Batty 2003). Parton (2003, p12) argues that the death of Maria Colwell and the resulting public inquiries served to, 'establish child abuse as a social problem about which we as a society, and certain organisations and professionals in particular, had a responsibility to do something about.' These inquiries have significantly affected the development of child protection, including the introduction of children's guardians; Area Child Protection Committees, which became Local Safeguarding Partnership Boards, and then 'multi-agency safeguarding arrangements' (Children and Social Work Act 2017), known locally as Safeguarding Children Partnerships; the use of child protection conference systems; and the publication of statutory guidance, such as 'Working Together to Safeguard Children' in its various iterations from 1999, which includes child protection procedures (Parton 2004). The death of Victoria Climbié led, via the Children Act 2004, to the creation of the Children's Commissioner post in England.

There is nothing straightforward about children's safeguarding; these individual child death reviews reiterate that simple solutions to complex problems should be avoided.

> When the outcome can be as terrifying as death, society needs to appreciate the complexity of the issues raised and consequently the complexity of situations. Time and time again reviews completed after child deaths appear to point to simple solutions. However, the solutions are in reality not that simple. (Dent and Cocker 2005, p165)

Older children have also died from abuse and neglect. Of the 40 cases included in the first biennial review of Serious Case Reviews (Sinclair and Bullock 2002), six were aged between 11 and 17 years (15 per cent). In the seventh analysis of serious case reviews, Brandon et al (2020) found that 31 per cent of the reviews concerned young people aged between 11 and 17 years. The child protection system has predominantly developed in response to the experiences of young children, and it was only recently that initiatives such as Contextual Safeguarding (Firmin 2020) and approaches such as 'complex safeguarding' (Firmin et al 2019) aimed to distinguish between the experiences of younger children and older children/adolescents in determining how to approach risk and responsibilities when safeguarding young people.

Key issues relevant to safeguarding during adolescence: institutional inquiries

In addition to the individual children's inquiries, independent reviews have identified institutional shortcomings in other areas of child protection and childcare systems. These include the Cleveland Report (1988), investigating a sudden increase in child sexual abuse at Middlesbrough General Hospital in early 1987 (Butler-Sloss 1988); the Pindown Inquiry, which looked at a specific approach to behaviour management used in children's homes in the Staffordshire area (Levy and Kahan 1991); the Waterhouse Inquiry, which looked into the abuse of children in care homes in North Wales (Waterhouse 2000); and the Rotherham Inquiry, which examined child sexual exploitation in Rotherham (Jay 2014). The latter two reports examined practices that predominantly affect older children. The Jay report emphasised the importance of listening to young people and taking what they say seriously (this links back to one of the recommendations of the Cleveland inquiry report 26 years earlier), to see them as 'victims', not as having made 'lifestyle choices' – as the latter can serve to condone their own abuse. Jay was critical of the wider systems within the local area that failed to act on multiple occasions after receiving multiple referrals of child sexual exploitation going back for years. She estimated that between 1996 and 2014 over 1,400 young people (aged 11-plus) had been affected by sexual exploitation.

Three of the 17 recommendations of the Jay report related to working with minority ethnic families and the issue of race, including institutional racism, in investigating concerns. Some staff were concerned about being accused of racism (p 93), and others were instructed by managers not to refer to the ethnicity of alleged perpetrators (p 92). This is not a unique finding to Rotherham. The inquiry held into the death of Tyra Henry some 40 years earlier concluded that the white social workers were too trusting of Tyra's family and made assumptions about her extended family members because they were Black (Batty 2003). The ethnicity of the children subject to serious case review was found not to be routinely recorded (Sinclair and Bullock 2002). For example, the serious case review report into the death of Ainlee Labonte did not acknowledge or comment on Ainlee's ethnicity (Kenward 2002;

Mistry and Chauhan 2003). Again, this is not an uncommon finding. Ratna Dutt, OBE, director of the Race Equality Unit in the UK, said at the Public Inquiry into the death of Victoria Climbié:

> There is some evidence to suggest that one of the consequences of an exclusive focus on 'culture' in work with Black children and families, is [that] it leaves Black and minority ethnic children in potentially dangerous situations, because the assessment has failed to address a child's fundamental care and protection needs. (Laming 2003, p 345)

A more recent overview report on Child Safeguarding Practice Reviews (CSPRs) again highlighted issues of race, racism, ethnicity, and culture (Dickens et al 2022). Additionally, the review concerning Child Q in Hackney (Gamble and McCallum 2022) focused on adultification of Black children and racism by the London Metropolitan Police. The review of Logan Mwangi's death in Wales (Stephens and Webber 2022) emphasised that, 'Professionals did not fully explore the context of [Logan's] race and ethnicity. With the value of hindsight, we know that [Cole] and [his stepson Craig Mulligan] held and expressed racist and discriminatory views that one would expect to have made life very hard for [Logan].' (p 16)

The use of public inquiries then to spearhead developments in child protection practices has been significant. Parton (2003, p 3) states,

> In many respects public inquiries have proved to be the key vehicle through which changes in policy and practice have been brought about over the last 30 years in relation to child protection policy and practice in this country. Rather than public inquiries being ignored, they have been fundamental to the way child protection operates. In this respect, they are as much a part of the problem as they are the solution.

Systems changes

Each of these individual and institutional inquiries must be understood within its specific context, including when it took place (Parton 2004). Although influential, each individual death or review is not solely responsible for the current children's safeguarding system, but the political responses to each review's recommendations have added to the development of the social policy and legislative agenda over time, which has shaped services. For example, Parton (2004) draws out links between many of the changes in systems introduced following the death of Maria Colwell in 1973 that were then investigated in the inquiry after the death of Victoria Climbié some 30 years later.

Alongside the Victoria Climbié Inquiry report, Children's Trusts were established in England in 2003 (Bachmann et al 2009), moving local authorities children's services out of the social services departments created under the Local Authority and Social Services Act 1970. These trusts were an umbrella for relevant professions to work more closely together to improve communication and coordination of services for children and families. However, any change produces intended and unintended consequences. The Audit Commission's independent analysis of these trusts pointed to too much time and energy being spent on setting up structures and processes at the expense of improving the lives of children and young people (Audit Commission 2008). Review and scrutiny are important to mitigate any of these unexpected and unplanned effects.

Following the 2010 general election, Children's Trusts were abolished under the coalition government, which created further changes to strategic safeguarding responsibilities. Local safeguarding children's boards became multi-agency safeguarding arrangements with three statutory partners (the local authority, health and police) and an Independent Scrutineer (Department for Education). These governance arrangements could be 'old wine in new bottles' (Wood 2021, p 7). However, some partnerships report improvements:

> Safeguarding partners have introduced a wide range of new measures to ensure independent scrutiny and challenge of the new arrangements. This includes peer challenge, independent scrutineers, commissioned external reviews, engagement of children and young people, annual assurance statements by external agencies, engaging lay members, and the use of local authority scrutiny and health and well-being committees. We need

> to draw together a secure evidence base for the impact of independent challenge and scrutiny on the outcomes for children. (Wood 2021, p 8)

It is debatable whether these strategic changes were required in order for the sector to innovate.

Frameworks for Wales, Scotland, and Northern Ireland

The Welsh Government was the first country in the UK to establish an independent Children's Commissioner post in 2001. England was the last of the four countries to appoint anyone to this role in 2005 (NSPCC 2021).[1]

Much of the English legislation also applied in Wales prior to devolution in 1999. Devolution saw power and responsibility transfer from the Houses of Parliament in Westminster to national governments in Wales, Scotland, and Northern Ireland. The Social Services and Well-being (Wales) Act 2014 provided Wales with its own legislative framework for social services for children and adults, including safeguarding (NSPCC 2021).

Scotland also saw similar legislation passed to that in England and Wales, with the Social Work (Scotland) Act in 1968 and the Children (Scotland) Act 1995. The death of Kennedy McFarlane in 2000 (aged 3) was a significant turning point in the Scottish Child Protection system, akin to the effect of Victoria Climbié's death in England at around the same time. The post of Children and Young People's Commissioner was established in Scotland in 2003. The Children and Young People (Scotland) Act 2014 has provided additional support for children in care and care leavers and created early help systems to identify and respond to child welfare concerns.

The Children (Northern Ireland) Order 1995 established the legislative framework for the current child protection system in Northern Ireland. In 2003, Northern Ireland created the post of Commissioner for children and young people.

Adult protection and adult safeguarding

The history of the development of adult safeguarding is a rather different story. Adult protection in England was first addressed officially in the publication of 'No Secrets' (Department of Health and Home Office 2000), over 100 years later than child protection. Adult protection was initially directly described in national government guidance in England in a memorandum form rather than statute. This guidance underpinned safeguarding practice for more than a decade (Cooper et al 2018). It was a further 14 years before adult safeguarding duties and responsibilities became statutory, through the Care Act 2014.

'No Secrets' was developed in response to concerns predominantly about the abuse of older people (Cooper et al 2018). A key driver for producing this guidance was to achieve some consistency in safeguarding practices for adults within local authorities across the country (Brammer 2020). In subsequent years the language used in policy changed from 'protection' to 'safeguarding', with the publication of the framework for standards of good practice by the Association of Directors of Social Services (ADSS) in 2005. The change of terminology communicated that safeguarding work enables an adult 'who is or may be eligible for community care services to retain independence, well-being, and choice and to access their human right to live a life that is free from abuse and neglect' (pp 4–5); this reflected the broader emerging policy agenda in adult social services regarding personalisation (see later). The use of the term 'vulnerable' was particularly queried, 'because it seems to locate the cause of abuse with the victim, rather than placing responsibility with the actions or omissions of others' (ADSS 2005, cited in Brammer 2020, p 465).

The context for safeguarding practices with adults during the last decade of the twentieth century and the first decade of the twenty-first century was the division of social services departments and separation of children and adults' social services, following the Children Act 1989 and the NHS and Community Care Act 1990. Adult social services took a different path of care assessment and management, focused on identifying social care needs, rather than risk of harm being at the centre of assessment. Care management processes were often found to be bureaucratic and transactional; people were assessed as having 'identified needs', which were supposed to be met by whatever the market offered, provided they met eligibility criteria (Cocker and Hafford-Letchfield 2014).

The market-oriented model of care management had its limitations, with assessment and provision of care allowing service users little choice. Having successfully advocated for a social model to understand care and health needs in the 1970s and 1980s, challenging reliance on a medical model (Oliver 2013), disabled people challenged conventional practices and began lobbying for a more personalised approach to their care needs. Direct Payments became the vehicle by which service users could fund their care and support to be delivered in ways that were highly personalised, shifting the model of adult social care away from a paternalistic frame and supporting a user-led approach. Subsequently, policy directives emphasised co-production and person-centred rights-based approaches (Hall 2012). The concept of 'personalisation' became paramount in social policy in the 2000s and was legislated in the Direct Payments Act 2009 and Care Act 2014. Personalisation is about putting the person at the centre of the way in which their care is planned and delivered (Think Local Act Personal, 2018). The Care Act 2014 built into statutory guidance the fundamental principles of personalisation and empowerment through 'choice' and 'control' and personal budgets; national government policy continued to promote personalisation, despite changes in political leadership (Department of Health 2007, 2012).

The 'No Secrets' paradigm determined adult safeguarding practices: adult protection was a process led by professionals and experienced as something 'done to' rather than 'done with' people who used social services (Pritchard 2013; Williams 2013). Processes were focused on finding out whether abuse allegations could be substantiated or not (Cooper and Bruin 2017), which was compatible with a care management model in adult social care. However, in response to the personalisation agenda across adult social services, Making Safeguarding Personal (MSP) was developed (see Chapter 6). MSP started out as a programme of culture change, focusing practice on what outcomes a person might want to achieve in terms of their safety and well-being, rather than a process-driven safeguarding practice dominated by professionals (Cooper et al 2015; Lawson 2017). This provided the opportunity to develop personalised safeguarding practice; personalisation had by and large failed to impact on safeguarding practice before the development of the MSP approach (Manthorpe et al 2015). There are six principles (empowerment, prevention, proportionality, protection, partnership, accountability) specified in the statutory guidance that underpin safeguarding adults and resonate with the MSP approach. The principles reflect the fundamental double focus on well-being and safety, permeating through all safeguarding adult practice guidance (Department of Health 2017a). MSP is included in the Care Act 2014 statutory guidance (Department of Health 2017a, see Chapter 6). Further, the Care Act 2014 marked a significant change in the culture and practice of safeguarding adults. It changed the language of safeguarding adults, from labelling the person as 'vulnerable' to looking at the risks of harm or abuse that they might be experiencing and their ability (or not) to protect themselves, due to their care and support needs (Cooper and Bruin 2017). Other language changes included changing 'alerts' to 'concerns', and 'investigations' to 'enquiries', and words such as 'elder abuse' ceased to be used (Department of Health 2017a). These demonstrated a shift not only in language but also in the culture of safeguarding practice with adults.

The introduction of 'well-being' as a central principle in s. 1(1) of the Care Act 2014 marks a further shift and it is the frame through which local authorities must undertake their duties. They have a duty to promote an individual's well-being, and this includes protection from abuse and neglect, s.1(2)(c). Well-being is defined in s.1(2) of the Care Act 2014, and it is understood that there is no hierarchy in how any of the nine factors of well-being, which include safeguarding, apply to a person (see Chapter 6 for further information).

Austerity had a significant impact on how local authorities were able to deliver Care Act 2014 responsibilities and meet the care and support needs of people within their communities (see Chapter 6); adult social care budgets faced substantial cuts year on year for well over a decade (Lymbery 2014) so fewer and fewer people benefit from local authority-funded adult social care support. Only 3 per cent of directors of adult social services were confident that they had adequate resources to meet their responsibilities in 2023 (ADASS 2022). As cited in Chapter 2, there is ongoing evidence of considerable under-resourcing of adults' social care services (Health Foundation 2021; House of Commons Health and Social Care Committee 2020; House of

Commons Levelling Up, Housing and Communities Committee 2022, p 24).

Learning from institutional reviews (adults)

In England, as with child protection, though to a far lesser extent, high-profile enquiries have driven priorities in safeguarding adults' practice. Prior to the Care Act 2014 there were a range of serious case reviews of the deaths of adults. These high-profile reviews included those of the deaths of Steven Hoskins, aged 39 (Flynn 2007, cited in Brammer 2020, p 485), and Gemma Hayter, aged 27, in 2011 (Warwickshire Safeguarding Adults Board 2011). Both Steven and Gemma had learning disabilities and in both situations their abusers were 'friends' and local people. These reviews drew attention to the risks for people living in the community and indicate a theme that has subsequently developed more deliberatively in children's safeguarding work, namely Contextual Safeguarding (see Chapter 5). It was also a key theme in a SAR undertaken on 'Colin' (anonymous Safeguarding Adult Board, undated), which, after publication, was distributed nationally as the authors of the SAR and the Safeguarding Adults Board were so concerned that other areas should also learn from Colin's death.

Several reviews have also involved adults with learning disabilities, autism, and mental illness who were living in private hospitals who experienced institutional or organisational abuse. These have contributed to raising the profile of this form of abuse of adults, and in turn influenced policy and practice (see Hafford-Letchfield et al 2014, chapter 8). The review following the Panorama programme about Winterbourne View (a private hospital and assessment and treatment centre for people with learning disabilities, autism, and so-called 'challenging behaviours') triggered the Transforming Care programme. This was aimed at ensuring that people with complex mental health needs, learning disabilities, and autism would not remain living in hospitals long term unnecessarily and would be supported to live in the community (see NHSE et al 2015). Subsequently, there have been further high-profile reviews regarding deaths of people living in institutions, the most publicised being Whorlton Hall (Social Care Institute for Excellence 2022) and Cawston Park Hospital (Flynn 2021). These reviews provide evidence that safety in these settings is an ongoing challenge. In response to these and other less well-known Safeguarding Adult Reviews (SARs), the Department of Health and Social Care has supported attempts to improve the monitoring and review of the care and support for people using these services through initiatives such as conducting individual 'safe and well' reviews (NHSE 2022). These reviews have drawn attention to organisational abuse and 'closed cultures' in institutional settings, and the learning from these reviews continues to unfold.

Learning from SARs

One of the three core duties of Safeguarding Adults Boards (SABs) in the Care Act 2014 is to conduct SARs where:

- An adult with care and support needs has died and the SAB knows or suspects that the death resulted from abuse or neglect, or an adult is still alive and the SAB knows or suspects that they have experienced serious abuse or neglect, and
- There is reasonable cause for concern about how the Board, its members, or others worked together to safeguard the adult (Sections 44(1)–(3), Care Act 2014).

This duty validates the undertaking of case reviews regarding adults, which had been intermittent before the Care Act 2014. The numbers of SARs undertaken have increased year on year since these data were collected, from 60 in 2013/14 to 195 in 2021/22 (NHS Digital 2014, 2022a). The first national analysis of SARs was undertaken in 2020 and reviewed 231 over a two-year period, 2017–2019 (Preston-Shoot et al 2020). Self-neglect was found to be the most prevalent type of abuse (in 45 per cent of reviews), then neglect/omission (37 per cent), physical abuse (19 per cent) and organisational abuse (14 per cent). This pattern is quite different from the pattern of safeguarding enquiry activity, where neglect/omission is most prevalent, followed by physical abuse, financial/material abuse, and psychological abuse (Preston-Shoot et al 2020; LGA/ADASS 2019d). This indicates that working with people who self-neglect remains an important area of improvement for safeguarding adult activity, which has implications for young adults where professional perceptions regarding 'lifestyle choice' can confuse or impede responses to issues such as self-neglect (see Chapter 6).

Key learning from the national SAR analysis was that shortcomings in practice 'have an immediate and direct impact upon the individual'[2] (LGA/ADASS 2019d). The most noted practice shortcomings were: failure to attend to mental capacity; poor risk assessment/risk management; failures of safeguarding; poor recognition of carers; inadequate attention to care/support needs and healthcare needs; and absence of professional curiosity (Preston-Shoot et al 2020). Several of these shortcomings are noted in the findings from analysis of SARs regarding care-experienced young people, in particular (see Chapter 8). Additionally, factors influencing practice, that echo across the different domains utilised for analysis, included: limited resources and time pressures; lack of information sharing between practitioners; lack of case coordination; and poor guidance. Further, there were aspects of the national legal and policy context that impacted negatively on direct practice (Preston-Shoot et al 2020). Many of these factors feature in SARs regarding young people (see Chapter 8). There were areas of good practice concerning meeting individual's health needs and applying MSP principles (Preston-Shoot et al 2020).

Many of the themes identified in the national analysis of SARs have also been found in thematic and regional analysis of SARs, for example shortcomings regarding assessment and management of risk and of mental capacity (see Braye and Preston-Shoot 2017b). Thematic analyses similarly cite recurrent themes, enablers, and barriers (Preston-Shoot 2020). However, there has not been the consistent national scrutiny through triennial analysis as with children's safeguarding reviews, so it is not possible to explore what is improving over time, in terms of practice, in response to the findings of SARs.

Frameworks for Scotland, Wales, and Northern Ireland

Different legislation drives safeguarding adult practices in Scotland (the Adult Support and Protection (Scotland) Act 2007)[3] and Wales (section 127 of the Social Services and Well-being (Wales) Act 2014) (SS&WB Act 2014). In the Scottish legislation, the overarching principle underlying Part 1 of the Act is that any intervention in an individual's affairs should provide benefit to the individual and should be the least restrictive option of those that are available which will meet the purpose of the intervention. This is further supported by a set of guiding principles which, together with the overarching principle, must be taken account of when performing functions under Part 1 of the Act:

- the wishes and feelings of the adult at risk (past and present);
- the views of other significant individuals, such as the adult's nearest relative; their primary carer, guardian, or attorney; or any other person with an interest in the adult's well-being or property;
- the importance of the adult taking an active part in the performance of the function under the Act;
- providing the adult with the relevant information and support to enable them to participate as fully as possible;
- the importance of ensuring that the adult is not treated less favourably than another adult in a comparable situation; and
- the adult's abilities, background, and characteristics (including their age, sex, sexual orientation, religious persuasion, racial origin, ethnic group, and cultural and linguistic heritage).

In Wales, there are six principles that underpin the SS&WB Act 2014:

- well-being – this principle is central
- increased citizen engagement and ensuring voice and control for people who need care and support, and carers who need support
- prevention and early intervention
- the promotion of well-being
- co-production – citizens and professionals sharing power and working together as equal partners
- multi-agency working and cooperation. (Care Council for Wales 2017)

Additionally, in Wales the Social Services and Well-being (Wales) Act 2014 contains safeguarding duties for adults and children, alongside the Children Act 1989 and 2004 for children. Part III of the Children Act 1989 no longer applies in Wales and has been replaced by provisions in the SS&WB 2014 Act, particularly Parts 3 and 4 (assessing and meeting needs for care and support) and Part 6 (looked after and accommodated children).[4] This shows that it is possible for a single piece of legislation to include safeguarding duties across the lifespan. There are national safeguarding procedures for children and adults and safeguarding boards include partners set out in section 134(2), all of whom have an interest in safeguarding children and adults. One of the benefits to the Welsh legislation is the inclusion of health and social care needs for children, and arguably this should help processes for those young people with identified social care needs as they move into adulthood.

Similarities and differences in children's and adults' safeguarding in England

Brammer (2020) suggests that there is a similarity between the overarching principle of well-being underpinning the Care Act 2014 in relation to care and support, and the paramountcy principle and welfare checklist in the Children Act 1989, where the child's best interest must be at the centre of all decision making, and it is the welfare checklist s.1(3) Children Act 1989 that guides what factors should be taken into consideration by the courts. Both lists are not hierarchical. Each point should be examined separately within an assessment about that adult or child. In the Children Act 1989, the welfare of the child in its entirety takes paramountcy rather than any individual item (Cocker and Allain 2019), just as the well-being principle is primary in the Care Act 2014.

The well-being principle in the Care Act 2014 is similar to the well-being duty in the Children Act 2004, which concerns local authorities' responsibilities to promote partnership working. It also includes the need to improve the well-being of children in each local authority area regarding their social, economic, physical, mental, and emotional well-being, including protection from harm and neglect (Section 10.2). This responsibility also includes young people aged 18 or 19 (10.9a), care-experienced young people over the age of 19 (Section 10.9b), and those aged

19–25 with an Education Health and Care Plan (EHCP) or who have a learning disability or difficulty and receive services (Section 10.9c). Therefore, when safeguarding young people, both legal frameworks underpinning child and adult safeguarding prioritise balancing safety and well-being when tailoring appropriate support to protect young people.

The principles underpinning child and adult safeguarding are not mutually exclusive and are summarised in Table 3.1.

Table 3.1: Comparison of safeguarding principles for adults and children in England with the MSP 'I' statements

Safeguarding Principles for Adults (14.13 Care And Support Statutory Guidance 2020)	MSP 'I' statements (Care and Support Statutory Guidance 2020)	Safeguarding Principles for Children (Children Act 1989)
Well-being of the adult		**Welfare of the child**
Proportionality: The least intrusive response appropriate to the risk presented.	**'I am sure that the professionals will work in my interest, as I see them and they will only get involved as much as needed.'**	**Three overarching principles:** • **paramountcy** of the welfare of the child • **'no order'** principle – there is some crossover with proportionality principle in adult safeguarding • **'no delay'** principle Human Rights Act 1998 also requires a **proportional** approach when Article 8 right to private and family life is qualified. For children and adults, one must intervene only as much as is necessary to achieve a safeguarding goal.
Protection: Support and representation for those in greatest need.	**'I get help and support to report abuse and neglect. I get help so that I am able to take part in the safeguarding process to the extent to which I want.'**	**Protection:** From serious harm (s47);

(continued)

Table 3.1: Comparison of safeguarding principles for adults and children in England with the MSP 'I' statements (continued)

Safeguarding Principles for Adults (14.13 Care And Support Statutory Guidance 2020)	MSP 'I' statements (Care and Support Statutory Guidance 2020)	Safeguarding Principles for Children (Children Act 1989)
Prevention: It is better to take action before harm occurs.	**'I receive clear and simple information about what abuse is, how to recognise the signs, and what I can do to seek help.'**	**Preservation:** Every effort should be made to preserve the child's home and family links; a duty for and **provision** of services to children in need (s17).
Empowerment: People being supported and encouraged to make their own decisions and informed consent.	**'I am asked what I want as the outcomes from the safeguarding process and these directly inform what happens.'**	**Participation:** The views of children should be sought according to their age and understanding.
Accountability: Accountability and transparency in delivering safeguarding.	**'I understand the role of everyone involved in my life and so do they.'**	**Accountability:** No equivalent for children's safeguarding practice.
Partnership: Local solutions through services working with their communities. Communities have a part to play in preventing, detecting, and reporting neglect and abuse.	**'I know that staff treat any personal and sensitive information in confidence, only sharing what is helpful and necessary. I am confident that professionals will work together with me to get the best result for me.'**	**Partnership:** Services should work in partnership with parents and others with parental responsibility.

Source: Cocker et al 2021, p 148.

Of the six adult safeguarding principles underpinning adult safeguarding (DHSC 2023), there is straightforward equivalence across child and adult safeguarding for three of them: protection; prevention; and partnership. However, these terms may be applied differently in children's and adults' services. While there are some similarities in content for the other three – empowerment, proportionality, and accountability – the positioning of these principles requires exploration when considering how best to safeguard young people (see Cocker et al 2021).

Other legislation also impacts on how these principles are understood at different ages. Significant here is how mental capacity is assessed and understood. The Mental Capacity Act 2005 presumes capacity from age 16, unless proved otherwise. For anyone over 16 years of age, their mental capacity will determine the extent to which they are involved in decision making about their lives. For 16- and 17-year-olds this assumption may not fit with the protective paradigm of safeguarding children. Work with young people under 18 remains reliant on the safeguarding framework in the Children Act 1989 and child and family social workers' understanding and application of the Mental Capacity Act 2005 is variable (Preston-Shoot et al 2022). Mental capacity is often understood to mean that anyone over 16 has the autonomy to make decisions, even when these are judged to be unwise by others and that when such decisions are made, then there is nothing more that can be done by people within the professional network. As with all professionals working with adults, 'walking away' is not the appropriate response in these circumstances; rather, working with the person on their understanding of risk and using professional curiosity are still required to achieved safety, resolution, and recovery (LGA/ADASS, 2019b). Understanding the executive functioning capacity of any young person making decisions that are deemed 'unwise' is important to ascertain, particularly where alcohol, drugs, mental illness, control and coercion, criminality, and exploitation are contextual factors. This has particular importance when considering specific decision making about risk, and mental capacity must be assessed in terms of specific decisions.

The key difference between safeguarding children and adults is that in children's safeguarding, the emphasis is on 'harm' and 'significant harm' (defined in Section 31(9) of the Children Act 1989) caused by abuse or neglect that has a direct effect on a child's health, welfare, or development. Adult safeguarding involves working with adults who are at risk of or experiencing abuse or neglect, but there is a much narrower range where there is a statutory duty to intervene; someone must have care and support needs and be unable to protect themselves because of these needs to be deemed eligible for a safeguarding adult intervention (DHSC 2023, section 14.2). However, adult social care services also have duties and powers to undertake preventative work to stop care and support needs developing over time; there are opportunities for young people to be offered support, with their consent, in order to address and mitigate risks they might be experiencing, to prevent their situations deteriorating, and become eligible for safeguarding intervention (DHSC, 2023, section 14.2; see also Chapter 6).

The profile of safeguarding activities within child and adult services is also different. This is partly because of legal frameworks but also because of history, as already discussed. In adult social work, while 'adult safeguarding is everyone's business', it is more of a minority interest (Cooper et al 2018). Safeguarding is a small part of the Care Act 2014 guidance, perceived as a specialist area of adult social care responsibilities and service delivery, and involves a minority of people who use adult social care services, although all staff working in adult social care have to be vetted. In child and family social work, children's safeguarding is a core activity; further, anyone working with children in any context will be aware of child protection, vetted to work with children, and be aware of their responsibilities to report any concerns and protect them. The policy shift signposted in the care review (Independent Review of Children's Social Care 2022) advocates a return to specialist child protection roles rather than a 'safeguarding is everybody's business' approach to children's safeguarding.

Attitudes to risk in child and adult safeguarding are also different, particularly around how risks and rights are understood. Children's legal rights are different to adults. The Children Act 1989 takes into account children's wishes according to their age and understanding. For adults their well-being is key, and it is assumed that they have autonomy to make decisions about their own lives if they have mental capacity, and it is presumed people have it until proven otherwise. Even when someone is assessed as not having mental capacity, assessing mental capacity applies to each specific decision, so someone may have capacity to make some decisions but not others.

Safeguarding adults is often about risk enablement, where adults have the right to make decisions and take risks. Safeguarding children has a different emphasis. It is often 'risk averse' (Munro 2019; Gupta and Blumhardt 2016); it involves protection from harm, and this can be at the expense of children's rights – for example, right to a family life (Brammer 2020). Practice can also be risk 'blind' or risk agnostic. In children's safeguarding, the safeguarding failure, particularly regarding younger children, is catastrophic at a political and individual level, as evidenced by the political response to the death of Arthur Labinjo-Hughes (aged 6) and Star Hobson (aged 16 months) at the end of 2021. The political impact of a young person or adult's death is not as straightforward to assess and does not tend to trigger similar responses.

Although there are a number of important differences in the legislation governing child and adult safeguarding, there are a great deal of commonalities too, particularly in the principles underpinning both pieces of legislation (Care Act 2014 and Children Act 2004), that are potential enablers for Transitional Safeguarding. Preventative powers in the Care Act 2014 support Transitional Safeguarding across the 18-year threshold, and the well-being responsibilities in the Children Act 2004 extend beyond age 18. This makes it possible to explore ways in which safeguarding partners can work together to support young people affected by abuse, neglect, and extra-familial harms.

Conclusion

This chapter has given an overview of the legal and social policy frameworks that govern safeguarding practices for children and adults in England. We operate within a binary legal system where age is the key factor determining a safeguarding response. However, legal frameworks are not the only cause of gaps in safeguarding services for young people, and in fact there is much within existing legislation to support Transitional Safeguarding.

Additionally, there is learning to be gained from where local areas have successfully innovated within these legal boundaries (see Chapter 9). It is possible to do this, but it requires a willingness from practitioners, managers, and leaders within and across services to place young people at the centre of a service, and not privilege the structure of organisations over safeguarding and supporting young people.

4

Emerging adulthood as a developmental stage

Introduction

This chapter will critically review the material of Arnett (2000) and others who have spearheaded the development of 'emerging adulthood' as a new developmental stage. Arnett argues that 'emerging adults can pursue novel and intense experiences more freely than adolescents because they are less likely to be monitored by parents and can pursue them more freely than adults because they are less constrained by roles' (2000, p 475).

A key feature of adolescence is taking risks. This is about trying new things, learning new skills, having new social and emotional experiences, and finding out more about who we are as we move into adulthood. Enabling young people to take risks safely is not a contradiction in terms. However, not all young people experience risk taking in the same way. Beckett and Lloyd (2022) highlight that adolescent behaviour and harmful experiences are often wrongly viewed by practitioners as 'lifestyle choices'; this is underpinned by the idea that young people freely choose to engage in activities viewed as 'risky' and 'harmful'. Often in these circumstances, practitioners and services treat adolescents as having the same agency as adults (Beckett et al 2017), not appreciating that they may be influenced inappropriately or incurring abuse or neglect. These contradictions and tensions will be explored in this chapter and their implications in relationship to Transitional Safeguarding are addressed. This includes providing examples of two different services that address these issues.

Human development and life course theory

Since the early twentieth century, social scientists have been interested in exploring and explaining the complexities of what it is that makes us human, including identifying commonalities in experience across cultures and societies. Humans are multifaceted complex beings. We are all individuals with idiosyncrasies living within a specific historic, social, and cultural context relative to us, and yet there are some commonalities of experience that all humans share across these contexts. Most health, education, and social care practitioners will be familiar with the key psychoanalytic theories that have shaped much of the thinking about development over the last 100 years: Freud's psychosexual development theory; Piaget's theory about cognitive development; Pavlov's behavioural theory; Skinner's theory of conditioning; Erikson's theory of psychosocial development; and Bowlby's theory of attachment. There are also many critiques of these theories. For example, all the theorists listed here are white men whose experience of life was located within a Euro/Anglo/US cultural context. The voices of other social theorists whose experiences of life were and are more diverse are overlooked. This has latterly resulted in decolonising activities to expand thinking and ideas (for example, Adams et al 2015; Liebel 2021). Additionally, the previously mentioned theories are individual in focus and do not centre the cultural and political context in which people live. The work exploring this has come later.

Emerging Adulthood as a distinct life stage

Within the life course development literature, researchers have argued the developmental case for adolescence lasting from the age of 15 to 25 years (Rosenfeld and Nicodemus 2003) or even 10 to 25 years (Sawyer et al 2018). Literature from medical sciences also shows that,

> Adolescents engage in more reckless, risky, and thrill-seeking behaviours than their younger and older peers;

> they have the highest rates of sexually transmitted diseases and criminal behaviours of any age group, and even drive faster than adults. The mortality and morbidity rates of adolescents are 200 per cent greater than their younger peers, an increase that has been attributed to higher rates of what are traditionally called 'risky behaviours.' Whatever psychological features give rise to these behaviours, they do not reflect flawed reasoning capabilities or generally poor decision-making skills – those are much improved in adolescents compared with younger children. (Tymula et al 2012, p 17135)

Arnett (2000) introduced a new term, 'emerging adulthood', to address the prolonged transition from childhood to adulthood and, over the next few years, he developed a body of work (for example, Arnett 2004) that expanded this concept into a theory that explored the specificity of development issues for 18–25 year olds in industrial nations in the early twenty-first century. It has gained considerable traction. Arnett (2007) states,

> The theory of emerging adulthood was proposed as a framework for recognising that the transition to adulthood was now long enough that it constituted not merely a transition but a separate period of the life course. I proposed five features that make emerging adulthood distinct: it is the age of identity explorations, the age of instability, the self-focused age, the age of feeling in-between, and the age of possibilities. (Arnett 2004, p 69)

It is important to note that 'emerging adulthood' is also a cultural construct, along with childhood, adolescence, and adulthood. Arnett believes it is 'a new term for a new phenomenon' (2004, p 70). What he means by this is that in western nations, young people's lives have changed markedly over the past 50 years. More participate in university education than ever before, sexual relationships are much less likely to be bound by an expectation of marriage (though may still be expected among some faith groups), living arrangements might differ from previous generations (that is, young people stay living at home longer or cohabit with partners), and many adults become parents later than in previous generations. Arnett (2007) also acknowledges that there will be differences in experiences for young people, particularly in relation to socio-economic status and ethnicity, and agrees that cross-national research is limited. He also acknowledges that there are some young people for whom this stage will likely be experienced negatively – specifically young people leaving care, young people with disabilities, those with mental health problems, and those who are involved with the criminal justice system.

There are a developing number of critics of Arnett's work (for example, Bynner 2005; Hendry and Kloep 2007; Côté 2014; Schwartz et al 2015) who argue that 'emerging adulthood' is not universal. Hendry and Kloep (2007) do not think that this theory advances how we understand human development; it makes the same fundamental errors as previous psychological developmental theories in terms of repeating a falsehood about what constitutes normative behaviour, including gendered normative behaviour. This is also an issue in healthcare with the 'default male' building male bias into systems and structures within our societies (Criado Perez 2019).

> We are now in danger of having a psychology of the affluent middle classes in Western societies, with other groups being seen as deviating from that norm. This is not a problem of Arnett's theory alone. All age-bound stage theories, from Freud to Erikson, have been criticised for being ethnocentric and having social class and gender biases. (Hendry and Kloep 2007, p 76)

Hendry and Kloep (2007) think that, given the social, cultural, economic, and historic specificity of Arnett's theory, there is a danger it will become outdated, as other changes occur within our future societies, depending on technological advances and environmental challenges for example. Young people will develop different characteristics to adjust to the social contexts they find themselves in. Inevitably, some young people who have good support networks will do very well in adapting to changes while others who do not have these networks will struggle. This, coupled with the continued effect of inequality with the distribution of resources within westernised nations and indeed across the world, will affect health and other outcomes for different young people.

Hendry and Kloep (2007) encourage us to think beyond age-stage developmental theories and instead embrace the complexity of human experience, including the interplay between macro structural factors, such as our relationships with social institutions, and micro factors, for example individual agency and experience, as well as cultural imperatives. In this regard the work of Bronfenbrenner and others is important (Bronfenbrenner 2005). Systems thinking highlights the links between multiple layers of society, from the individual through to macro structures. It does not solely rely on age-stage processes, rather it acknowledges that the way individuals interact with their environment is determined by a number of different factors, including age, wealth, access to resources, culture, gender, sexuality, disability, and so on (see Chapter 10 for a discussion of systems theory and Transitional Safeguarding).

Life course theory

As a challenge to mainstream developmental theories, life course theory (LCT) (Elder 1998) aims to make sense of the multiplicity of events that occur in people's lives. It is interdisciplinary in focus, acknowledges the central nature of an individual's development, and stresses the importance of locating the individual and family within a historical, cultural, and social context (Hutchison 2014). Instead of basing a theory on age-stage developmental processes, LCT has identified five essential concepts: cohorts; transitions; trajectories; life events; and turning points. These offer a different route into examining human development over the life course. For young people, this means examining their experiences as a specific group of people born around the same time; it can be beneficial in terms of understanding the impact of historical, social, and environmental factors on them (for example, the effect of COVID-19). The transition from childhood to adulthood is also understood within a social context, not just an individual one, which provides an opportunity to consider other factors that influence young people's experiences, not just their chronological age marking the transition to adulthood.

According to LCT, transitions are 'embedded into trajectories' (Hutchison 2014, p 1588). Different trajectories intersect (for example, education, work, health, family), so people's lives are not predetermined in terms of outcomes. Life events are 'a significant occurrence involving a relatively abrupt change that may produce serious and long-lasting effects. Life events require adaptation and may produce stress' (Hutchison 2014, p 1588). They are connected to the final concept – turning points.

Rutter (1996) identified three important types of turning point life events:

- those that either close or open opportunities;
- those that make a lasting change on the person's environment;
- life events that change a person's self-concept, beliefs, or expectations.

These will be different for each person and can occur at any age.

In addition to these five concepts, LCT has six central and interconnected themes developed by Elder (1994) and colleagues that also apply across the lifespan. The three most relevant for Transitional Safeguarding are: timing of lives; human agency in making choices; and developmental risk and protection (Hutchison 2014, p 1588).

Timing of lives builds on the work of Elder (1974) and distinguishes between chronological age, biological age, and social age. In terms of definitions,

> [social age] refers to the age-graded roles and behaviours expected by society, the socially constructed meaning of various ages. Age norms indicate the behaviours expected of people of a specific age in a given society at a particular point in time. Life course scholars suggest that age norms vary not only across historical time and across societies but also by gender, race, ethnicity, and social class within a given time and society. Social age receives special emphasis in LCT. (Hutchison 2014, p 1589)

One of the key tenets of Transitional Safeguarding is consideration of moving beyond chronological age to determine eligibility or access to support for young people experiencing safeguarding issues. A developmentally-attuned approach refers to social and physiological development. The LCT focus on social age supports this approach in its flexibility regarding chronological age and move away from age norms determining responses to safeguarding a young person.

According to Hutchison (2014), human agency in making choices is one of the best contributions of LCT to understanding human development. It uses Bandura's ideas about self-efficacy (Bandura 1977) to consider how people use personal power to achieve the goals they may have in their life. However, Hutchison also acknowledges that this concept has limits. This is because of the structural and cultural influences that are specific to any historical point. In terms of Transitional Safeguarding, consulting with young people about decisions that are made about them is critical, particularly as the Mental Capacity Act 2005 says that young people aged 16 and above can and should make decisions in all aspects of their lives, unless they do not have capacity. Supporting young people's self-efficacy is important to encourage independence, but there will be ways in which other factors impact on individual young people's ability to make decisions about their future, for example, where they live.

The key feature in LCT of developmental risk and protection acknowledges the links between specific traumatic life events and the ongoing effect these might have throughout someone's life. This is not inevitable, and connects with some of the resilience literature (for example, Rutter 1996). A positive and transformational relationship with one supportive adult can be a protective or mitigating factor across the life course (Hutchison 2014, p 1593), but it will not counteract all experiences of trauma or systemic racism or inequality. An example of this protective influence is given by Werner (2001), who gives a moving account from a longitudinal study of children who survived the Nazi Holocaust. After being in concentration camps these children moved to a therapeutic placement in England. 'All the resilient survivors considered one woman to be among the most potent influences on their lives – the school teacher who provided warmth and caring and taught them to behave compassionately,' (Moskovitz, cited in Werner 2001, p 126). Howe (2005, p 278) believes that, 'if relationships are where things developmental can go wrong, then relationships are where they are most likely to be put right'. This is relevant to Transitional Safeguarding as 'relational' practice is a key principle of the approach.

Strengths and weaknesses

LCT encourages greater attention to the impact of historical and social change on human behaviour than Arnett's Emerging Adulthood theory. LCT looks at biological, psychological, and social processes, noting the interplay of these on people's lives. The life course perspective is not as deterministic as some theories in terms of acknowledging the importance of human agency. It also considers diversity in trajectories and takes into account cumulative advantage and disadvantage – so factors like class, power, and privilege are acknowledged in a stronger way than in emerging adulthood theory. In terms of weaknesses, more work should be done to understand the heterogeneity of young people at a global level. This is a challenge to all developmental theories including LCT and emerging adulthood. There is a danger that Arnett's theory only applies to affluent, late industrial societies. This is where Bronfenbrenner's Ecological Systems Theory (1974) can support better links being made between the systems within societies in terms of the impact they have on people's lives. For Transitional Safeguarding, this reinforces the importance of two other key principles: a developmentally-attuned approach; and attending to equity, equality, diversity, and inclusion. Young people are not a homogenous group (see Davis and Marsh 2022), therefore a person-centred approach relies on knowing the individual young person well (hence the importance of the key principle of relational practice). This includes understanding where they are in their journey to adulthood, as well as how structural inequalities may have impacted on this, including being aware of any protected characteristics.

Risk and risk taking

Blankenstein et al (2016) define risk as, 'choosing the option with the highest outcome variability, that is, an action that may lead to greater benefits, but may also lead to negative outcomes, at the expense of certainty' (p 77). They separate out young people's attitudes to risk and 'known' decision contexts, from attitudes to ambiguity and 'unknown' decision contexts, believing them to be separate constructs that will both influence young people's attitudes towards risk and decision making. There are neurobiological factors, for example as brain structure and function continue to develop into our mid-twenties (Sawyer et al 2018), as well as individual factors (for example, how do young people understand risk on an individual basis?) and contextual factors (for example, peer groups) that impact on young people's experiences of and engagement with risk (Firmin 2020).

Wall and Olofsson (2008) move away from biological and cognitive processing as a route to explore a young person's understanding of 'risk', to a sociologically-defined view – 'sensemaking of risk' (p 432). They are particularly interested in the everyday life context of young people and how risk is expressed in this environment.

> The individual's understanding of risk is not only an individual construct but also influenced by social relations and general beliefs about the world and life. It is in the interaction with other people that norms and understandings are created, from which the individual then makes sense of his or her surrounding world, not least risks. (Wall and Olofsson 2008, p 432)

Wall and Olofsson (2008) found that there was a difference in how young people in rural areas in Sweden made sense of risk as a collectivistic view (us–here), compared with their counterparts in urban areas, who had an individualistic view (me–there or me–where I am). This highlights the potential influence of place and space on young people's approaches to risk, particularly the interplay between individualisation and social connections (including the role of social networks) in the lives of young people. This also links back to a discussion in Chapter 2 about how risk can affect decision making, which can in turn place young people in conflict with the law. There is evidence within the justice literature that young people, especially those with experience of risk factors, 'may not be fully developed until halfway through the third decade of life' (Johnson et al 2009, p 216).

It is not a contradiction in terms to aim to enable young people to take risks safely, but risk and risk taking is not the same experience for every young person (Cocker et al 2022b). Risky behaviour can be described as activities such as drug taking, unprotected sex, driving over the speed limit, and driving while intoxicated (Arnett 2000). All are understood to be risks that young people engage in, alongside new risks and dangers that some young people experience because of their specific issues (that is, they may be care-experienced and living in a residential care home), which means that they may be more likely to be targeted and groomed (La Valle and Graham 2016). Examples of specific risks that some young people are exposed to include: child criminal exploitation; child sexual exploitation; and county lines (Glover Williams and Finlay 2019).[1] Holmes (2022a) points out that language is important here: the term 'risk taking' continues to be used by professionals in the context of exploitation and other forms of abuse and is problematic because it implies that young people are responsible for the harm, which can hide the abusive nature of it.

Again, with an eye on language, there is a danger that certain activities are conflated and viewed as 'risky' and 'harmful' by practitioners. They can also be viewed (wrongly) as 'lifestyle choices' that young people freely choose to engage in, rather than recognising that there may be constraints and influences upon young people ensnared in these circumstances or behaviours (Holmes and Smale 2018). These attitudes to risky behaviours, seeing them as 'lifestyle choices', may then affect how agencies work with young people; practitioners treat them as adults rather than viewing them as young people struggling with harmful incidents or circumstances (Beckett et al 2017). The problem is that practitioners are not necessarily taking into account the nature of adolescent development when making their decisions about risk and protection; rather they are governed by a binary understanding of child/adulthood embedded in agency structures and processes. Despite the clear evidence that risk and harms move across chronological age boundaries and adolescent development is complex, responses to safeguarding risks may be determined by age-defined childhood/adulthood. For example, young people under and over 18 are involved in moving and delivering drugs around the country via county lines. This is not a 'lifestyle choice'; these young people are being criminally exploited (see Chapter 2). Further, they will be treated differently in terms of safeguarding risks and criminal prosecution according to their age, regardless of their developmental stage. Some young adults have vulnerabilities because of drug and alcohol addictions, learning disabilities, mental health issues, prior experience of abuse, or social isolation. They might be subjected to 'cuckooing' behaviour, where gang members use their home as their base for drug dealing (Children's Society 2017; Glover Williams and Finlay 2019). This is not a 'lifestyle choice'; despite what they and others may say about the arrangements, it is abuse. Again, these young adults are being criminally exploited and the multi-agency response to anyone in these circumstances should acknowledge this (Cocker et al 2022b).

So how do these theories help us understand the experiences of young people who face considerable adversity in their move towards adulthood? Arnett (2000) suggests that accepting responsibility for one's self and making independent decisions are the two most important factors for young people that mark their move towards self-sufficiency and autonomy in some areas of life, while also recognising that there are external constraints on personal autonomy. Tyrell and Yates (2018) believe that they also apply to young people whose journey to adulthood is difficult. When developing appropriate safeguarding responses for young people over and under 18, involving young people in decisions that are made about them at every stage is critical (Cossar et al 2011), including encouraging young people to have some choice and control about what happens in their life alongside achieving the outcomes of safety and well-being (Jobe and Gorin 2013; Gorin and Jobe 2013; Warrington 2016).

The impact of trauma

For young people who are facing safeguarding issues, trauma is often something they have experienced and may continue to experience. Trauma is defined as, 'events that pose significant threat (physical, emotional, or psychological) to the safety of the victim or loved ones/friends and are overwhelming and shocking' (American Psychological Association (APA) 2016).

Many definitions rely heavily on health diagnostic criteria, such as DSM 5 (APA, 2013). Gradus and Galea (2022) offer a challenge to existing definitions of trauma, specifically, 'whether our current definition captures the full range of traumatic events that might affect populations, particularly the most vulnerable and historically marginalised.' (pp 608–609). There is evidence that, for a number of young people who have experienced trauma and adversity in their early years of life, this causes considerable toxic stress and harm, which can have a lifelong effect on their health and well-being (Mahon 2022). Trauma, like all harm, does not stop at 18, and so is relevant to Transitional Safeguarding.

Trauma-informed approaches are ways of working with young people that seek to support and enable young people to address issues and difficulties they may have faced in their lives. Hickle (2020, p 537) describes trauma-informed approaches (TIAs) as, 'a strengths-based way of working with individuals across the lifespan, rooted in a foundational understanding of trauma and the impact that experiencing trauma can have in people's lives.' Harris and Fallot (2001) initially developed TIAs and identified five key principles to underpin work with traumatised people: safety, trust, choice, collaboration, and empowerment (Hickle 2020). Viewing trauma in this way enables the impact on young people to be considered within their developmental situation, which is central to the Transitional Safeguarding approach. Also using relationships as a vehicle to help young people feel safe and move forward with their lives, as advocated by Hickle and Lefevre (2022), is included in the 'relational' principle of Transitional Safeguarding.

Over recent years, much has been written about TIAs to social work practice with young people as a way of rethinking relational practices. While this refocusing on the experiences of young people in order to understand their responses to situations they have faced is welcome, there is a danger that TIAs have become a buzzword applied to anything and everything, with the original meaning behind the concept becoming lost. This does not mean that TIAs have no value – they do – rather the danger is that a superficial understanding is applied to work undertaken with young people, instead of creating the support and services young people require that are relational, developmentally attuned, and responsive to the trauma that young people have experienced in their lives (Hickle and Lefevre, 2022). Hickle's (2020) study showed that young people valued being consulted in decisions about their futures, including having options, even if these were limited, and staff forming trusting and meaningful relationships with them in environments that were safe, calm, and respectful (Hickle and Lefevre 2022). This made a difference in their lives.

However, most services are not designed with these criteria at the forefront (Harris and Fallot 2001, cited in Hickle and Lefevre 2022). In his scoping review, Mahon (2022, p 1) comments on, 'the scarcity of empirical evidence on how trauma-informed care is implemented in systems'. Ideally, such a service should provide a secure base for young people where their strengths are acknowledged (the opposite is usually the case) and practitioners concentrate on mitigating the effects of trauma to aid young people's well-being, with the potential benefit of reducing the need for services and where the ultimate outcome is a healthy, safe, happy life in which the person has healed from trauma. Many organisations have begun to think about this at a service level, and there are a number of good resources available to help with this (for example, Treisman 2016; Wilkinson 2018; Taggart 2018). This approach includes the need to adopt trauma-informed care for staff as well as the people they work with, recognising that the climate and culture within workplaces can also exacerbate vicarious trauma for staff (Mahon 2022).

Additional issues for some young people

There are specific challenges for young people with certain experiences, such as experience of the care system or criminal justice system. Care-experienced young people face additional hurdles at age 18 when they move into independence and independent or semi-independent living. Of course, every young person's situation is unique to them; however, there are some structural factors that affect the options that care-experienced young people have at this age. By this age 'leaving care' services are responsible for supporting young people and, for most of them, this involves transferring from a system of support by a social worker to a personal adviser, whose role is to give advice and support (see Chapter 7). Concerns remain that many young people who are care experienced are 'focused on running away from their previous experiences rather than towards new opportunities', which is the opposite experience of most other young people who have not experienced care (Tyrell and Yates 2018, p 1024).

Where a young person has particular needs, such as physical or mental health issues, although the process of transition to adult services should have started a considerable period of time before turning 18, often this is not the case (see Chapter 7). Additionally, young people's experiences of trauma and abuse early in their lives can have ongoing impacts on physical and mental health. In looking at the types of behaviours young people may exhibit who have experienced childhood trauma, Downey and Crummy (2022) found that many young people had low self-esteem, experienced depression and anxiety, and engaged in alcohol and drug misuse as a coping mechanism. These problems are not new and there have been a range of policy developments geared towards improving services for young people who have experience of state care (for example, Care leaver strategy (HM Government 2013; Care leaver covenant[2]; APPG (2017) recommendations). Young people are clear about the limitations of the transition support they receive (see Chapter 1).

Experience of being in care is a poor proxy for a person's post-18 support, as it is an administratively, rather than clinically, defined population. We know that young adults with care experience are over-represented within the adult prison population (see Staines 2016 for a summary of evidence regarding this correlation), and some care-experienced young people will also have been in contact with YJS. This disproportionate experience of hardship is also mirrored within the homeless population. According to Reeve and Batty (2011), 25 per cent of those who were homeless had experienced care at some point in their lives. The concept of multiple exclusion homelessness refers to factors that contribute to safeguarding risks. These include experiences of care and childhood trauma (Preston-Shoot 2020).

As with becoming entangled in criminality, there is an emerging understanding that it is not only being in care, but wider adversity, which intersects with homelessness or unsafe living arrangements for young people. For example, research undertaken for Centrepoint by the Cambridge Centre for Housing and Planning Research explored the experiences of 16–24-year-olds experiencing homelessness. Of the 409 young people who had sofa-surfed that year (out of a survey of 2000), 90 per cent had been in care or had a social worker (Clarke et al 2015). These factors, along with social exclusion and poor mental health, provide imperatives for developing a more transitional approach to supporting all young people who have faced trauma and adversity, not only those with care experience or who have special educational needs or disabilities (see Chapter 7).

It is inappropriate for safeguarding support to young people to be contingent on having experience of care. There are other groups of young people who also face particular challenges as they progress towards adulthood, for example, young people with special educational needs and disability (SEND), young people involved with YJS, young carers, and unaccompanied asylum-seeking young people. A nuanced and flexible response is required from services supporting young people because of their particular needs and developmental stages, and this is often missing (Holmes and Smale 2018). Some parts of the wider system have already arguably created a more fluid and transitional approach towards service provision, but we are often not getting it right for young people who *do* have care and support needs and are formally eligible for services (see Chapter 7). Further, the majority of young people do not meet this threshold.

For young people facing harm who do not enter care, there are no post-18 support entitlements for those who are supported under Children Act 1989 s.47 arrangements. This includes young people who are unaccompanied asylum seekers and have not been in care. Regarding those young people involved in the youth justice system, there are many gaps in knowledge; the National Institute of Health and Care Excellence (NICE) guidance document on transitions between children and adult services (2016b) noted that, 'young offenders tend to undergo particularly poor transitions into adult services' (p 34). It also notes that research about this group of young people is lacking, despite the knowledge that they have high levels of need and, like care-experienced young people, often face poor outcomes in terms of education, work opportunities, homelessness, and mental ill-health.

There are also transition points between the justice system and the safeguarding system with an overlap between the respective populations of young people involved with both. 'Justice professionals and researchers have repeatedly highlighted the high levels of trauma, neurodiversity, learning needs, and impaired mental health among the young adult custody population,' (House of Commons Justice Committee 2016, cited in Holmes and Smith 2022, p 9). The existing Joint National Protocol for Transitions in England between youth justice and probation (HM Government 2021) has some crossover with the six principles that underpin Transitional Safeguarding (Holmes and Smith 2022). The recognition of the developmental aspects of young adulthood in the criminal justice system is evident through the use of maturity and risk assessment tools, which support practitioners to explore and assess maturity of young adults and to take these into account in the different stages of the criminal justice processes (University of Birmingham et al 2013). The work of Prior et al (2011) has explored the relationship between maturity and offending behaviour. This has influenced how the Offender Assessment System (OASys) (the core assessment process used in prisons and the community) now works with younger adults. Practitioners are encouraged to adopt a strengths-based approach – not solely viewing the behaviours of 18–24-year-olds as 'problematic' but also assessing the potential for growth and change. This approach is referenced in the case study discussed later in this chapter about the Newham Hub, and in Greater Manchester's complex safeguarding work described in Chapter 5. There are also clear requirements for transitions work with young people moving from youth justice secure settings to adult prisons (Ministry of Justice 2022).

Case study: Newham Hub

The Newham Hub is a youth justice/probation service for 18–25-year-olds. The model recognises that trusted relationships are a catalyst for change and aims to leverage strong relationships that are built between practitioners and young adults.

Newham Hub

Young adults are at high risk of reoffending, with 29 per cent of 18–24-year-olds in London reoffending between October 2019 and October 2022. Evidence also shows that 18–25-year-olds are the group most likely to desist completely from crime, demonstrating the importance of the opportunity to change the trajectory of their lives if specialist support is provided that meets their specific needs and developmental stage.

The Mayor's Office for Policing and Crime (MOPAC) and the Ministry of Justice have partnered to create the Y2A (Youth 2 Adult) Hub – a holistic, trauma-informed service for 18–25-year-olds on probation and 17-year-olds transitioning from the Youth Justice Service to probation services in Newham. Newham was chosen for the location as a complex inner-city borough with one of the highest levels of deprivation and serious youth violence in London. Between April 2017 and March 2021, Newham recorded the highest number of homicides with a victim age under 25 of all London boroughs.

The Hub mobilised in 2021 and was fully operational by April 2022. The pilot was originally funded through the Treasury's Shared Outcomes Fund for two years. MOPAC, London Probation and the Barrow Cadbury Trust funding have funded a 12-month extension (until March 2024). It includes co-location of a multi-disciplinary team, consisting of probation, commissioned services, and statutory support agencies. The team provides wrap-around support tailored to young adults' distinct needs and informed by an understanding of maturity. This co-location of probation and specialist services allows for continuous assessment of young adults' needs, information sharing between services, increased capacity to work remotely outside of the probation office (due to risk management), greater responsiveness to young adults' needs, increased engagement among young adults with services, and reduced time and travel costs.

Services were commissioned with young adults' distinct needs in mind and include mentoring and coaching, emotional well-being, speech and language therapy, accommodation support, substance misuse, restorative justice, meaningful activities, and bespoke young women's support. Young adults can also access job centre support through the hub, as well as food bank supplies and sexual health provision. All staff working in the Y2A Hub receive training in maturity, young adulthood, and typical needs experienced by young adults, as well as trauma-informed working.

Emerging impact

The pilot is subject to evaluation (process, performance, and impact). While reoffending data will not be available for some time, early evaluation findings and anecdotal evidence on the impact of the Hub have been promising, with countless stories of positive outcomes achieved and feedback from young adults that the Hub is making a real difference to their lives. Feedback from staff is also highly positive, citing the multi-agency approach as a key strength of the model.

Case study: Dorset Birth to Settled Adulthood programme

The Birth to Settled Adulthood programme takes an ecological and contextual approach to understanding the young person's circumstances and life experiences. Many differing environmental factors impact on the lives of young people, their development, and their ability to stay safe from harm as they move from childhood to adulthood. This may require the ongoing support of services past their eighteenth birthday.

Dorset adult and children's social care – Birth to Settled Adulthood programme

At a strategic level, the Dorset Safeguarding Adults Board and Bournemouth Christchurch and Poole Safeguarding Adults Board identified Transitional Safeguarding as a key focus in their strategic planning for 2021–24.

During 2019 a Local Area SEND inspection in Dorset highlighted, through feedback from young people, families, and carers, that the move to adult life was not well planned and that services needed to make the transition from children to adult's services easier. Once agreed by cabinet, a framework programme was developed and the Birth to Settled Adulthood Partnership Board was established in mid-2022, with an independent chair.

The Birth to Settled Adulthood Service has two areas of focus: redesign of the 14–25 transition service in Dorset, and the development of a 0–25 offer, comprising the four preparations for adulthood pathways identified in the Children and Families Act (2014).

The commitment between partners is to create a more joined-up response to enable young people to be supported to maintain their safety and well-being and move positively into adulthood. The programme aims to deliver a more fluid response across children's and adult services. Regular communication and meetings are taking place with partners to contextualise this work programme and understand the cohort of young people who are at risk of abuse, neglect, or exploitation but may not meet Care Act eligibility. Dorset Council, while still at a relatively early stage of this programme, has already made positive steps to achieving a more coordinated approach across the integrated care system.

The programme is specifically designed to span age bands and take a more fluid approach to service design and delivery. This will be achieved through strategic and operational partnership working with a shared commitment to and understanding of Transitional Safeguarding principles.

By working alongside young people and their parents/carers/representatives/educational establishments, and by having a better understanding of their communities, including the environmental factors or circumstances which may increase the risk of harm, the service will be able to identify structural inequalities and increase awareness of the intersectional factors which create risk, inequality, discrimination, and oppression.

Partnership work has been initiated with Dorset Youth Association and Youth Voice, recruiting young people to help facilitate conversations and capture the voice and experiences of young people.

Emerging impact

Fortnightly transitions tracking meetings, which are multi-professional meetings, monitor progress of individual young people moving towards adulthood. These explore any issues arising and agree solutions to resolve them. These meetings include safeguarding issues and identify any actions required to support or protect the young person.

Conclusion

This chapter has examined some of the literature that examines concepts and ideas linked to emerging adulthood. Although Arnett's work has enabled thinking about this as a specific stage in life development, there are some shortcomings with this approach, particularly for those young people who have experienced considerable adversity, loss, and harms as children or continue to experience them as young adults. The ongoing impacts of adversity on young people's health and well-being is important to acknowledge in terms of what this means for young people, for example when using drugs or alcohol as coping mechanisms for stress, anxiety, and depression. LCT provides a different way of thinking about the impact of key events and other factors on a person's life, as well as insight about how we conceptualise what is going on for young people, moving away from a linear way of understanding human development.

Being aware of these developmental frameworks for young people can assist those working with them to support young people in ways that acknowledge their developmental age and stage, key events in their lives, and their social, cultural, and environmental contexts. This reinforces an approach to working with young people that ensures we involve them in all decisions made about them. This is what they tell us they want. It will be specific and personal to each of them. Adopting an approach to practice and service provision that is trauma informed can create challenges for agencies. There may be existing problems with services for young people (for example, high turnover of staff) and these can exacerbate difficulties, rather than proactively address them, when relational practice and continuity of support are key. Where safeguarding issues exist, what young people tell us works in other services will also apply here; they want to be involved in decisions, to be given choice, to have the opportunity to build trusted relationships with workers, and to be able to create and be in safe environments.

PART II

Learning from current practices

5

Learning from safeguarding children and beyond

Introduction

This chapter considers what can be learned from safeguarding children in order to inform thinking about Transitional Safeguarding, aiming to complement Chapter 6, which focuses on learning from safeguarding adults. It starts by reflecting on some of the trends and ideologies apparent within child protection, exploring how policy reform has tended to respond to crises, which in turn may have fuelled a culture of blame and application of over-procedural solutions. In arguing for a different approach to system reform than has tended to be seen previously, this chapter then explores tensions and challenges observed both within 'traditional' child protection and within safeguarding of young people facing extra-familial harm. A number of innovations within safeguarding children's work are considered, along with their potential connection to Transitional Safeguarding. The chapter then discusses other parts of the wider system, beyond safeguarding, in which there are clear policy and practice efforts to consider young people's support needs beyond their eighteenth birthday. Finally, these reflections are consolidated with the intention of drawing out potential lessons for how the Transitional Safeguarding approach might be developed and embedded.

How we got here

Chapter 3 explored the legal and policy frameworks that govern how children and young people under 18 are supported and safeguarded, and noted the way that the state's response to children and young people at risk of harm has tended to be formulated in response to crises or scandals, with numerous examples of child deaths instigating high-profile national inquiries. The consequence of these public inquiries, however unintended, can be to fuel a culture in which blame is located at practice level (Munro 2004, 2011), despite these inquiries invariably identifying systemic and structural problems. A concordant feature of how reform has tended to play out can be seen in the ever-growing raft of procedural checks and balances intended, presumably, to eliminate the danger of practitioners making mistakes. Social work, in particular, has been found to be highly proceduralised (Parton 2009), with some researchers noting that the efforts to make the system safer through formalising procedures may be counter-productive (Broadhurst et al 2010). Some have argued that the notion of child-centredness within children's safeguarding practice, clearly an important tenet, has contributed to a mindset in which wider family needs or strengths are overlooked and cynicism can prevail (Featherstone et al 2014).

At the time of writing, in 2022/23, children's safeguarding policy is in a state of flux, with two major reviews shaping future policy (Independent Review of Children's Social Care 2022; Child Safeguarding Practice Review Panel 2022). The government response to these reviews suggests a move towards 'specialist child protection' services (Child Safeguarding Practice Review Panel 2022; Department for Education 2023b). This seemingly reflects a concern that the system is lacking the investigative expertise necessary to protect children from harm. This position is somewhat contradicted by evidence showing child protection investigations have soared over the past decade or so, while the number of these investigations that did not result in a child protection plan have increased by an ever-greater proportion (Independent Review of Children's Social Care 2022). Clearly there is no lack of investigative impetus within children's services. Interestingly, one of these reviews argued for a radical shift in practice and culture to avoid stigmatising parents and also advocated for specialist 'expert child protection practitioners' (Independent Review of Children's Social Care 2022). Neither the review nor the government response (Department for Education 2023b) considers how the narrow specialism model might increase the stigma of safeguarding services.

Over the years other reviews have influenced policy and practice discourse around adolescent safeguarding, which often but not exclusively manifests as extra-familial harm. High-profile inquiries regarding child sexual exploitation were instigated following media reports in 2011 about 'localised grooming and abuse' of young women and girls (House of Commons Home Affairs Committee 2013). As noted in Chapter 3, the review by Alexis Jay was one such significant inquiry, but was by no means the only review of its type. Investigations and inquiries were undertaken in a number of local areas, igniting public outrage and in some instances fuelling racialised debates (Cockbain 2013). Charities highlighted the high numbers of young people facing exploitation and the inadequacy of the safeguarding response, and those working in statutory child protection were found to be lacking confidence in dealing with harm outside the home (House of Commons Home Affairs Committee 2013). It is not that exploitation was a new phenomenon – it was the framing of it as a child protection issue that was new. Until that time, policy documentation routinely referred to sexual exploitation of young people as 'child prostitution' and victims were estimated to be two and a half times more likely than average to have a criminal record (Phoenix 2012). Many of these young people facing sexual exploitation *were* receiving a response, but it was a criminal justice response rather than a safeguarding response. As explored in Chapter 2, the same issue can be seen today in relation to young people ensnared in criminal exploitation. Perhaps child protection has not strayed too far from its early roots, in which the philanthropic drive to protect vulnerable children meshed with a sense that society also needed to be protected from the delinquency of young people (Hendrick 2003).

By this time, professional bodies were calling for a national debate on the treatment of young people facing harm and highlighting the questionable effectiveness of care for some adolescents

(Association of Directors of Children's Services (ADCS) 2013). The available evidence suggested that the current response to young people facing harm was not sufficiently developmentally informed (Hanson and Holmes 2014) and innovations regarding extra-familial harm such as Contextual Safeguarding (discussed later) were gaining traction. Government acknowledged the need for change, and in 2014 the Department for Education launched a strand of innovation funding focused on young people 'on the edge of care' (Department for Education (DfE) 2014a). New government guidance was issued in relation to children going missing (DfE 2014b) and guidance for working with children and young people affected by sexual exploitation was revised (Beckett et al 2017). By 2019, a national review was undertaken regarding child criminal exploitation (Child Safeguarding Practice Review Panel 2020) and the cross-party Youth Violence Commission was underway (Irwin-Rogers et al 2020). In less than a decade, adolescent risk and the need for a different response had become a mainstream issue, indeed one of the most pressing issues, within children's safeguarding ... albeit one without any simple answers.

Tensions within children's safeguarding and their relevance to young people at risk

The Independent Review of Children's Social Care and the subsequent government response (Department for Education 2023b) echoed the need for an enhanced response to exploitation and extra-familial harm, calling for a 'bespoke pathway' (Independent Review of Children's Social Care 2022). However, this approach runs the risk of dislocating extra-familial harm from wider safeguarding structures, especially with the proposed creation of specialist child protection units for those facing harm in the family (Child Safeguarding Practice Review Panel 2022). Furthermore, in asserting that children's social care workers lack the specialist expertise to work with the complexity of harm outside the home, this narrative underplays the existing expertise within social work, youth work, and advocacy groups and misses an opportunity to build on current strengths of the system. As is common within policy rhetoric, proposed solutions are largely focused on structural or service-level reform – such as 'bespoke pathways' and specialist teams (Department for Education, 2023b). However, a coherent approach is needed to whole system reform that connects, rather than separates, young people with the rest of the population, and consciously seeks to build on and strengthen existing capabilities in order to nurture confidence across the multi-agency partnership and communities. One of these reviews also noted that future revisions to statutory safeguarding guidance should ensure this bespoke approach for extra-familial harm allows 'for plans to continue beyond 18 where necessary' (Independent Review of Children's Social Care 2022, p 78), which is the position the sector has been arguing for years. It is unfortunate that the government response includes no such intention (Department for Education 2023b).

There are a number of tensions within safeguarding practice and policy worth exploring in order to design a system that is fit for purpose for young people and their safeguarding needs. One such example is the awkward fit between the rights of children to have their wishes and feelings taken into account, as legislation statutory guidance requires (HM Government 2020),[1] and the pervasive culture of child protection in which children are too rarely heard (Munro 2011). While few would argue against children having the right to be heard, in practice this is tempered by 'a paternalistic approach that seeks to eradicate and avoid risk, rather than a participative approach that empowers the young person' (Cocker et al 2021, p 147). This issue of ensuring participation within safeguarding or child protection activity relies on the quality and depth of relationship between the child or young person and the professional in their lives (Cossar et al 2016), and this insight has implications for safeguarding young people in two key ways. First, much of the literature regarding participation within safeguarding has focused on child protection practice in the context of intra-familial harm, and so the influencing role of parents and their participatory engagement is key. This dynamic can play out very differently for young people, most of whom are likely to be developing a stronger sense of relational independence (Hanson and Holmes 2014) and some of whom may be rejecting parental influence as a result of being exploited (Firmin 2020). Secondly, the coercive nature of exploitation – which affects teenagers significantly more than younger children – makes participatory practice even more crucial in order to counter the impact of this harm (as discussed in Chapter 2). For those young people who have experienced or are experiencing control and coercion, as is a common feature of exploitation, it is vital that the safeguarding response is one that affords them a sense of choice and empowerment (Hill and Warrington 2022; Warrington 2016). Such an approach can be undermined, however, if professionals are constrained by the 'rescue' paradigm in which protection from risk is privileged over participation and rights (Shemmings 2000).

Against a backdrop of increased political and public concern (reflected in the afore-mentioned Child Safeguarding Practice Review Panel review), and growing evidence that young people are facing tragic consequences in a child protection system beset with 'complexity and challenge' (Brandon et al 2020), it is not hard to see why practitioners might err on the side of paternalism, relegating participatory approaches in favour of decisive action. The use of secure out of area placements for young people facing extra-familial harm is one such example which has invited critique; research found worried professionals feeling they must 'do something', however restrictive, suggesting physical safety sometimes outweighs psychological and relational safety in professional decision making (Firmin et al 2020).

For young people whose harmful circumstances are perceived to be related to behaviour and choices, especially those positioned at the awkward interface of safeguarding and justice systems, the tension between protection and participation might manifest differently. Young people facing abuse in the home are already seen as 'imperfect victims' (Rees and Stein 1999); if abuse is perceived as being due to 'lifestyle choices' and where the young person becomes in conflict with the law, they face a different barrier to participation. Here, they may be conceptualised not as too passive or vulnerable to have their voices heard but rather as too culpable or deviant to deserve either a participative *or* a protective response. Although prominent national agencies have argued for a 'child-first approach' in which young people are seen as children not criminals (Youth Justice Board 2021), victim-blaming attitudes are still evident and police colleagues concede some young people continue to face prosecution despite clear evidence of exploitation (Ofsted 2018).

These punitive approaches disproportionately affect already minoritised groups, such as Black young men (Bateman 2017; Child Safeguarding Practice Review Panel 2020), and research has highlighted the inequitable approach to surveillance and intervention within safeguarding (Featherstone et al 2018; Wroe and Pearce 2022). As understanding of extra-familial harm increases, more issues are added to the list of harms that children's social care may feel underequipped to deal with. These issues include peer-on-peer violence, 'county lines' drug trafficking and gang association; the response to which usually involves more surveillance (Wroe and Lloyd 2020) and often expands state intervention in ways that are highly racialised (Williams and Clarke 2016). The proposals to reform young people's safeguarding by creating a distinct pathway (Independent Review of Children's Social Care 2022) are well-intended but lacking in structural analysis and risks a two-tier approach to child protection replicating existing inequities. In addition, the response to young people facing exploitation and extra-familial harm is significantly affected by law enforcement agencies and education settings, and some extra-familial harms are not universally accepted as even constituting a child protection concern. It is therefore rather illogical for proposed solutions to be located within proposed new frameworks for children's social care (Department for Education 2023b) that have no mandate to reform other agencies. That is not to say that children's social care cannot play an important part in the solution. Though there is a tendency, not least within the reviews mentioned earlier in this chapter, to assert that social workers lack the specialist skills required, it could be argued that the *generic* skills of social work are vital to creating a more effective system response. There are few, if any, professional groups better placed than social workers to ensure that anti-oppressive practice underpins the professional response to young people facing harm, given the regulatory standards for social work in England,[2] and the global definition of social work,[3] make clear that promoting human rights, challenging discrimination, and respecting diversity are all a core function of the profession. Crucially, in terms of Transitional Safeguarding, social work is a unified profession serving adults and children in accordance with underpinning values and ethics; any reform agenda for young people's safeguarding must consider those over 18 and so social work has an essential contribution to make here.

Exploring key innovations within children's safeguarding

Several new approaches to safeguarding children and young people have been developed in recent years. Some of these are specifically intended to better respond to young people facing harm outside the home, while others are broader in focus and aim to change how children and families are supported in general. While not an exhaustive list, these examples have been chosen because they are widely recognised within the children's sector in England and may offer potentially relevant learning for the development and adoption of a Transitional Safeguarding approach.

The first approach to consider is Contextual Safeguarding,[4] a term coined by Professor Carlene Firmin, which has been developed over several years through a structured research programme in multiple local authorities. Contextual Safeguarding is described as 'an approach to understanding, and responding to, young people's experiences of significant harm beyond their families' (Firmin and Lloyd 2020, p 3). It is based on three core ideas: 1) it is possible to change the nature of contexts where harm has occurred, 2) a commitment to and centring of anti-oppressive practice, as inequality is both a cause and consequence of extra-familial harm and each young person's journey to safety is unique, and 3) that harm occurs through interaction between individual choice and structural/environmental constraints, so trying to change young people's choices/behaviours without changing the contexts in which choices are made is not compatible with Contextual Safeguarding (Firmin and Lloyd 2020). Contextual Safeguarding offers a framework comprised of four 'domains': targeting intervention; applying the legislative framework; developing partnerships; and measuring outcomes. Contextual Safeguarding advocates for a safeguarding and child protection approach which identifies, assesses, and intervenes with the contexts in which abuse occurs, rather than targeting only the individual young person. It argues for harm outside the home to be addressed through child protection and child welfare legislation and processes instead of these being viewed through the legislative lens of community safety and/or policing. Developing and embedding such an approach requires partnerships to be inclusive of those agencies or people who work where young people spend their time, such as education settings, transport services, retail centres, and public spaces. A safeguarding system operating in this way must then measure impact within the contexts in which young people were facing harm instead of measuring change in the behaviour of young people (for a more detailed description, see Firmin and Lloyd 2020). Although Contextual Safeguarding has, to date, focused on the safeguarding of young people under 18, it connects with Transitional Safeguarding in its explicit focus on young people and the nature of harms they face, and in its blending of person-centred approaches coupled with attention to structural inequity and exclusion.

Another approach intended to respond to the specific issue of exploitation and extra-familial harm is that of Complex Safeguarding. This is a term used and described by the Manchester Safeguarding Partnership as 'criminal activity (often organised), or behaviour associated with criminality, involving children and adults, where there is exploitation and/or a clear or implied safeguarding risk. This includes, but is not limited to, sexual exploitation, criminal exploitation, modern slavery, including trafficking' (Manchester Safeguarding Partnership 2020, p 4). The term is also used to describe the hub and spoke approach to service delivery that has been developed across the ten Greater Manchester local authorities, with a Complex Safeguarding hub designed to support consistency of practice and promote learning across the ten local areas. The initial aim of the approach was to reduce the number of young people being relocated by managing the risks, in collaboration with young people, in their local communities. Multi-agency Complex Safeguarding teams (the 'spokes') in each local authority area aim to bring together social workers, youth justice, police, health, and voluntary sector partners. The Complex Safeguarding hub works closely with other agencies and initiatives focused on addressing organised crime and with the Violence Reduction Unit, which also operates to a Greater Manchester footprint. The practice within Complex Safeguarding teams aims to be strength based, trauma informed, and flexible. In relation to Transitional Safeguarding, some local

Complex Safeguarding teams are working with adult services to develop a response to the Complex Safeguarding for adults (Firmin et al 2019) and the previously mentioned Manchester Safeguarding Partnership Complex Safeguarding Strategy applies to adults as well as children.

Turning attention beyond extra-familial harm to wider safeguarding innovations, another approach which has gained traction in a number of local authorities in England is that of Family Safeguarding. This approach to child protection was pioneered by Hertfordshire County Council and was funded through the Department for Education Social Care Innovation Programme.[5] Family Safeguarding brings together the professionals working with a family into one team, aiming to keep children safely within their families, with a particular focus on addressing the needs of families affected by domestic abuse, parental substance misuse, and parental mental health. Motivational interviewing is a core aspect of the Family Safeguarding practice model, emphasising a strength-based approach with families. Evaluation of the work in Hertfordshire found the use of child protection plans had reduced by a third over just 15 months, generating significant cost savings (Forrester et al 2017). This success led to Family Safeguarding being scaled up across a number of other authorities, with a further independent evaluation finding significant reductions in the use of care and child protection plans, a reduction in police call-outs and in unplanned mental health contacts among the adults in families being supported, and a strong financial case for Family Safeguarding (Rodger et al 2020). The use of specialist adult services practitioners to support children's safeguarding offers a connection with Transitional Safeguarding; both call for multi-disciplinary expertise in order to respond to people's needs and strengths in a less siloed way. This bringing together of different disciplines and expertise in order to improve outcomes is a core principle of the 'Think Family' approach, as championed by government (Cabinet Office 2008). That said, unlike Transitional Safeguarding, Think Family maintains the boundary between children's and adults' safeguarding in the sense that it is applied to children (that is, those aged under 18) in families. Young adults without children or wider family are not primary beneficiaries of Think Family, and researchers argue that 'a policy focus that emphasises the need to protect children primarily from the harms posed by their parents' actions or inactions' can actually undermine family-focused approaches' (Tew et al 2016 p 3).

Through the same DfE innovation fund accessed by Hertfordshire, Leeds City Council introduced restorative practice as a core tenet of their work with children and families in an initiative called Family Valued. Restorative practice is a strengths-based approach which focuses on doing 'with' families rather than doing 'for' or 'to' and eschews punitive approaches in favour of participatory learning and decision making (Wachtel 2003, 2013). It is described within Leeds as 'behaviours, interactions and approaches which help to build and maintain positive, healthy relationships, resolve difficulties and repair harm where there has been conflict ... enabling those who work with children and families to focus upon building relationships that create and inspire positive change. Creating change sometimes requires challenge as well as support' (Leeds City Council, no date). In the first round of funding, Leeds developed and delivered a comprehensive workforce development programme for professionals across children's services and wider partners to build confidence and skills in restorative practice, and centred family group conferencing as a core approach to working with families. In the second round of funding, seven Restorative Early Support teams were introduced to create a new layer of intervention between early help and social work. In addition, further work was undertaken to embed restorative practice across services in order to promote a consistent approach to restorative practice (called the Leeds Practice Model). An independent evaluation found that families achieved 84 per cent of all goals and only 12 per cent led to a referral to the area social work team, and reported significant savings as a result of reducing care entrants (Harris et al 2020). The focus on strengths-based and relationship-based practice is the obvious link between restorative practice and Transitional Safeguarding.

Lastly, an approach which – like restorative practice – existed previously but found prominence within children's services in England through DfE innovation funding, is that of Signs of Safety. This approach to child protection was developed in Western Australia. It is described as being focused on how workers can 'build partnerships with parents and children in situations of suspected or substantiated child abuse and still deal rigorously with the maltreatment issues' and aims to 'expand the investigation of risk to encompass family and individual strengths, periods of safety and good care that can be built upon to stabilise and strengthen a child's and family's situation' (Signs of Safety, no date). The model includes a specific format for assessing risks and strengths/safety which is known as a mapping, comprising three elements: what is working well, what child protection services are worried about, and what needs to happen. The model operates under licence, with organisations paying to use the tools, supported by trained implementation leads. An adapted version of Signs of Safety was already being applied, at least in part, in a large number of local authorities evaluated in the first and second round of the DfE innovation fund, with the stated aim of addressing the significant gaps in evidence regarding its effectiveness (Baginsky et al 2020). One study found greater levels of empowerment among families and a reduction in care entrants, alongside enhanced clarity for professionals (Idzelis et al 2013). However, the mixed-methods quasi-experimental evaluation of its implementation in nine English local authorities reported minimal impact. The evaluation report was blunt in its appraisal: 'None of the different strands of analysis found significant and robust improvement across outcomes in relation to practice, staff well-being and retention, or the removal of children from their homes … [and] found no moderate or high strength evidence that Signs of Safety positively affected the outcomes for children and families. Furthermore, the qualitative work found that the visible changes observed seem to be down to good leadership rather than the programme itself' (Baginsky et al 2020, p 7). Further critique included the highly variable implementation across sites, the increasing level of prescription within recording and process, and concerns that the levels of expenditure required may not be realistic and sustainable over the longer term (Baginsky et al 2020). These findings echo those of a systematic review published by the What Works Centre for Children's Social Care, which found no evidence that Signs of Safety is effective in reducing the need for children to enter care, and no evidence of its cost-effectiveness (Sheehan et al 2018). A tenuous connection could be made between the strengths-based ethos of Signs of Safety with the key principles of Transitional

Safeguarding, though as the former is a licensed model intended for use within intra-familial child protection there is not a great deal of commonality between the two.

Transitional approaches outside of safeguarding

The idea that some young people need support as they make the transition to adulthood is not new; several examples of policy initiatives and legislation intend to address the 'cliff edge' that exists beyond the realm of safeguarding. One of these, as noted in Chapters 2 and 7, is the provision for young people leaving care, which were introduced in the Children and Social Work Act 2017. This new duty required local authorities to offer personal assistant support to all care leavers up to age 25; previously, this support ended at 21 unless the young person was in education, training, or employment. The same Act included two related new duties on local authorities: to consult on and publish a 'local offer' for care leavers, setting out care leavers' legal entitlements and the additional discretionary support available, and to have regard to seven 'corporate parenting principles'[6] in how the local authority provides its services to children in care and care leavers. The rationale offered within the statutory guidance (Department for Education 2018) includes a recognition that 'each care leaver will reach [independence] at a different age', an understanding that support should 'taper over time, in recognition of growing maturity', and that there are 'care leavers aged 21–25 who may be continuing to struggle with the transition to independence and adult life' (Department for Education 2018, p 6). Of course, all of these points can equally be applied to other young people *not* in care. It appears that policy rightly attempts to smooth one sharp boundary, the eighteenth birthday, only to reinforce another, that of legal care status. Limiting entitlement to those leaving care might seem logical in terms of resource management, but it is important to remember that many young people who have faced very significant harm and trauma are never taken into care – partly because the legal framework was never designed to contend with extra-familial harm (Firmin and Knowles 2022). While this transitional support is much needed, it does not address the cliff edge in support that too many young people in society face.

As discussed in Chapter 7, another area where young people's entitlements to support post-18 is reasonably well established is that of special educational needs and/or disabilities (SEND). The Children and Families Act 2014 introduced several changes, set out in the accompanying statutory guidance, including an extension of the code of practice to encompass children and young people aged 0–25 and an emphasis on supporting those with SEND to make a successful transition to adulthood (Department for Education and Department of Health 2015). There is much within this guidance that complements the intentions of Transitional Safeguarding, for example the definition for SEND 'provides a relatively low threshold' (Department for Education and Department of Health 2015, p 6); there is an explicit emphasis on participation and choice for young people; expectations placed on agencies to collaborate and co-commission services; a focus on inclusive practice and anti-discrimination; and efforts to foreground the transitional needs of young people. That said, this guidance does not address the wider needs of young people needing support to be safe as it is limited only to those with identified SEND, excluding, for example, those with neurological difficulties due to trauma. Despite welcome mention of young people with SEND in youth custody, the provisions exclude those serving their sentence in the community, those detained in Young Offenders Institutions aged 18–21, and those in the adult estate. As noted in Chapter 7, this is clearly problematic given evidence that many in the youth and adult justice system have learning needs and are neurodivergent (House of Commons Justice Committee 2016) and that such needs often go undiagnosed (Parole Board 2021). Tellingly, in relation to transitional support the guidance repeatedly emphasises the goal of 'independence and employability' rather than wider safety and well-being; and where safeguarding is mentioned, the guidance defers to the binary safeguarding protocols for children and adults, with little recognition of the gap between these two systems. The implementation of these duties has also been problematic; the government review of the SEND system concluded that experiences and outcomes for children, young people, and their families remains below-par, and acknowledged that required expenditure outstrips funding and the system is therefore not financially sustainable (HM Government 2022).

Drawing the learning together

Despite some clear differences, each of these policy developments and practice innovations offers some insight that is useful to the development of the Transitional Safeguarding approach.

To avoid the reactive proceduralism described earlier, it is important to resist locating the argument for Transitional Safeguarding solely in the many tragic stories found within safeguarding reviews (see Chapter 8). These form part, but not the entirety, of why Transitional Safeguarding is needed. The ambitions for young people leaving care and those with SEND are broadly aligned with the intentions of Transitional Safeguarding, however they fall into the same trap of delineating between young people based on legal status and eligibility, rather than responding to dynamic and contextual need. This is not surprising given the fragmented nature of policy making, with different divisions responsible for defined cohorts rather than cross-cutting outcomes. This suggests that policy support for Transitional Safeguarding must be distributed across divisions and departments to avoid siloed definitions and implementation. That neither policy initiative has achieved its stated intentions – evident in the 2022 SEND Review and in the problems regarding leaving care services outlined in the review of children's social care (Independent Review of Children's Social Care 2022) – suggests that system change requires more than legislative impetus. This is important to bear in mind within Transitional Safeguarding discourse, where the focus can easily fall on inadequacies with the legal frameworks (Cocker et al 2021). Introducing duties without sufficient resource attached is not only ineffective, it can also be directly counter-productive as it may fuel cynicism and even resentment among professionals tasked with achieving the impossible. This has implications for the proposed revisions to statutory safeguarding guidance mentioned earlier (Independent Review of Children's Social Care 2022; Department for Education 2023b): any move to extend support for young people facing extra-familial harm beyond 18 must be fully funded. Furthermore, consideration should also be given to those with experience of intra-familial harm in order to avoid redressing one boundary only to reinforce another.

Learning from Family Safeguarding reminds us that the seemingly obvious – in this case bringing different disciplines together to create a coherent team that can work across boundaries – can constitute radical positive change in an otherwise fragmented system. The most important learning from the implementation of Signs of Safety comes from the designers of the adapted model applied in England, who published two linked pieces titled, 'You can't grow roses in concrete', (Munro et al 2016, 2020). They highlight the imperative for whole system transformation, ongoing implementation support, and a focus on enabling system conditions in order to reap the benefits of changes to practice. All of these are important messages for us in promoting a Transitional Safeguarding approach to attend to, as it develops. A clear message from the implementation of restorative practice is that adopting a whole system approach and changing culture means not simply delivering a different intervention to citizens, but also changing how professionals behave with each other. The strengths-based practice approach and commitment to participative and collaborative working within restorative practice offers a clear connection with the core tenets of Transitional Safeguarding. Figure 2.1 in Chapter 2 draws on the Social Discipline Window that underpins the philosophy of restorative practice (Wachtel 2003) to show how protective and participative practices must be held in balance as part of a Transitional Safeguarding approach.

In terms of Contextual Safeguarding, the iterative approach to generating knowledge and testing ideas is very different to the reactive development of crisis-driven policy, and reminds those of us trying to develop and embed Transitional Safeguarding to seek investment in research alongside arguing for changes to practice. The enthusiasm for Contextual Safeguarding, together with the inclusion of the term within statutory safeguarding guidance (HM Government 2020), seemingly contributed to some agencies claiming they were 'doing Contextual Safeguarding' without a full understanding of the approach. This prompts those advocating for Transitional Safeguarding to ensure definitional clarity and highlights that careful custodianship of the concept will be essential as it continues to be developed. A particularly resonant insight comes from a blog from one of the Contextual Safeguarding research team, which emphasised that adopting a

Contextual Safeguarding approach is not simply about rolling out a new set of practices, but rather: 'It also requires an interrogation of the systems and attitudes that have allowed adolescents to be criminalised, blamed and made responsible for the harm they have experienced. Contextual safeguarding is not simply about expanding the remit of child protection systems, but about asking difficult questions about the systems that already exist.' (Wroe 2021). This important reflection reminds us that a zemiological analysis – one in which the harmful impacts of practices and structures are considered alongside the harms facing, or being caused by, people – is a key aspect of designing a Transitional Safeguarding approach (Wroe 2022).

Conclusion

Reflecting on how the current children's safeguarding system evolved and exploring lessons from related policy initiatives and innovations in recent years offers much useful learning for the development of Transitional Safeguarding. While the concept is new, the problems it seeks to address are not; successful implementation of the concept will rely on a curiosity and willingness to learn from all that has come before.

6

Learning from safeguarding adults for Transitional Safeguarding practice

Introduction

This chapter explores learning from safeguarding adults' policy and practice, particularly from the Making Safeguarding Personal (MSP) approach. It complements Chapter 5, which focuses on learning from safeguarding children's practice, to inform our thinking about Transitional Safeguarding. It highlights how the legal and policy frameworks for safeguarding adults determine the ways in which practitioners and local systems respond to the safeguarding needs and risks faced by young adults over the age of 18. The Care Act 2014 provides the primary statutory framework for safeguarding adults and the accompanying guidance (Department of Health and Social Care 2021) describes how duties are to be delivered. The powers, as well as duties, which agencies can draw on, can enable proactive safeguarding prevention activity and work with young people who do not meet the criteria for statutory duties to make adult safeguarding enquiries leading to intervention and protection. There are also assessment duties regarding young people who may have care and support needs in the transition into adulthood. However, these are not always fully understood or delivered, often due to resource constraints (ADASS 2022).

MSP is an approach to adult safeguarding practice that prioritises the needs and outcomes identified by the person being supported and focuses on what they want to achieve to be safe (Cooper et al 2018). It is underpinned by a risk-enabling approach; enabling appropriate risk-taking in the context of becoming an adult is core to preparing for adulthood (see Chapter 7). MSP for young adults involves strength-based practice, requiring a relational partnership between the person and practitioner, where a focus on needs and deficits is counterbalanced with recognition of the resilience and assets that someone has. In this way practice can deliver a Transitional Safeguarding approach.

As described in Chapter 2, safeguarding practice still operates within a child/adult binary and neither safeguarding system currently adequately meets the needs of young people. Transitional Safeguarding advocates an approach to working with young people that is relational, developmental, and contextual; it is also participative, evidence informed, and promotes equity, equalities, diversity, and inclusion. This chapter argues that MSP provides a way of working with young adults that can adapt to their personal developmental needs, ensures their active participation, and provides an inclusive safeguarding response (see Cocker et al 2021).

There is a raft of legislation that supports safeguarding adult activity generally (Spreadbury and Hubbard 2020) and specifically, depending on the type of harm or abuse (Braye and Preston-Shoot 2017a). As well as the Care Act 2014, the Mental Capacity Act 2005 and Human Rights Act 1998 provide key frameworks for safeguarding adults' practice in terms of responding to risk and protecting rights. Legal literacy and appropriate application of the law support Transitional Safeguarding practice. 'Drawing down' from all this learning helps to address the safeguarding needs of young adults who experience the safeguarding 'cliff edge' at 18.

Safeguarding adults under the Care Act 2014

In England, the legal framework and statutory guidance for safeguarding adults developed over the last three decades. Initially driven by concerns about 'elder abuse' during the 1990s, adult protection mainly focused on the safeguarding needs of older people (Institute of Public Care 2013). 'No Secrets', published in 2000, was a government memorandum for practice in adult protection, which provided a framework for safeguarding adults, however it was not underpinned by statute (Department of Health and Home Office 2000). As with safeguarding children (see Chapter 3), safeguarding adults' policy has been influenced by several tragedies, particularly abuse in institutions such as hospitals and care homes. For example, the Panorama programme in 2011 exposed abuse in Winterbourne View, a private hospital for people with learning disabilities, and was one of the drivers for the inclusion of safeguarding adults in the Care Act 2014 (Norrie et al 2014). Drivers for reform also included the weaknesses in the existing legal framework, the Law Commission's Review on adult social care, changing demographic trends, and the funding crisis in adult social care (Braye and Preston-Shoot 2020a).

The Care Act 2014 provided the first statutory framework for safeguarding adults. The definition of safeguarding adults in the statutory guidance is:

> people and organisations working together to prevent and stop both the risks and experience of abuse or neglect, while at the same time making sure that the adult's well-being is promoted including, where appropriate, having regard to their views, wishes, feelings and beliefs in deciding on any action. Adults sometimes have complex interpersonal relationships and may be ambivalent, unclear or unrealistic about their personal circumstances. (DHSC 2023, para 14.7)

Central to this definition is consideration of the person's well-being alongside the risks or experience of abuse or neglect. 'Well-being' is a core element of the Care Act 2014 and the statutory guidance states that 'local authorities must promote well-being when carrying out any of their care and support functions in respect of a person. This may sometimes be referred to as 'the well-being principle' because it is a guiding principle that puts well-being at the heart of care and support.' (Department of Health and Social Care 2023, para 1.3) This duty applies to children, their carers, and young carers when they are subject to transition assessments (Department of Health and Social Care 2023, para 1.4). Further, the guidance acknowledges that:

> 'Well-being' is a broad concept, and it is described as relating to the following areas in particular: personal

> dignity (including treatment of the individual with respect); physical and mental health and emotional well-being; protection from abuse and neglect; control by the individual over day-to-day life (including over care and support provided and the way it is provided); participation in work, education, training or recreation; social and economic well-being; domestic, family and personal; suitability of living accommodation; and the individual's contribution to society. (Department of Health and Social Care, 2023, para 1.5)

Significantly, the concept of 'well-being' therefore includes safeguarding within its remit. The guidance emphasises that professionals and other staff should not be advocating 'safety' measures that do not take account of individual well-being, as defined by the Act. When safeguarding young people, balancing safety and well-being is essential to tailoring appropriate support. (See Chapter 3 for the similarities and differences between principles in the legislation relating to adults and children).

The statutory guidance describes six principles that should underpin all safeguarding practice: empowerment, proportionality, prevention, protection, partnership, and accountability.[1] These are expanded into 'I statements' to ensure that the principles are put into practice in ways in which the people we work with can understand them (Department of Health and Social Care 2023, para 14.13).[2] The principles are helpful, whether applied in practice at an operational level by practitioners working with citizens (Department of Health and Social Care 2022), or at a strategic level for system leaders to support improvement and change. They can help guide practice and decision making in work with young adults; they can inform a Transitional Safeguarding approach.

The core safeguarding duty under Section 42 of the Care Act 2014 is for the local authority to make enquiries, or require others to undertake them, into circumstances of abuse 'where it has reasonable cause to suspect that an adult who has care and support needs (regardless of whether those needs are being met) is experiencing, or is at risk of, abuse or neglect and as a result of those care and support needs is unable to protect themselves from either the risk of, or the experience of, abuse or neglect'

(Department of Health and Social Care 2023, para 14.2 and 14.100). This duty to enquire applies to any form of abuse or neglect (ADASS 2019). There are ten categories described in the statutory guidance: physical abuse, domestic violence, sexual abuse, psychological abuse, financial or material abuse (including scams), modern slavery, discriminatory abuse, organisational abuse, neglect and acts of omission, and self-neglect (Department of Health and Social Care 2023 para 14.17). However, this list is not considered exhaustive and 'local authorities should not limit their view of what constitutes abuse or neglect as they can take many forms … exploitation, in particular, is a common theme' (Department of Health and Social Care 2023, para 14.17). This is helpful when considering the various types of exploitation that young people may experience, which may not fit into the other categories. Unfortunately, because the ten categories named in the guidance are used in most systems for recording, data collection, and performance information, someone at risk of, or experiencing, exploitation may not be seen as requiring a safeguarding intervention.

The safeguarding enquiry aims to establish whether any action needs to be taken to prevent or stop abuse or neglect, and if so, what and by whom, and enable the person to achieve resolution and recovery (Department of Health and Social Care 2023, paras 14.93–94; LGA/ADASS 2019a, 2020). As such, it is a significant process, which brings professionals and agencies together with the person and their carers and family members to understand risks and plan how to mitigate them. There are also duties to provide advocacy for people during safeguarding work who would experience 'significant difficulties' in participating in the process, which might be very relevant for a young person (Department of Health and Social Care 2023, para 7.24).

Anyone can raise a safeguarding concern with the local authority about someone who they think might be experiencing abuse or neglect. Following this, the first stage of the process is to gather information from relevant people, professionals, and partner agencies to establish whether a safeguarding enquiry is required, as well as from the person themselves. Critically this is the stage of the process where alternative interventions and support can help the person mitigate and manage risks, information and advice can be provided, and abuse or neglect prevented (Department of Health and Social Care 2023, para 14.37 and 14.15; LGA/ADASS 2019a, 2020). Indeed, prevention is a key theme running through the Care Act 2014 (Section 2). This is the stage in the safeguarding process when people at risk of, or experiencing, abuse or neglect, who do not meet the eligibility criteria for a safeguarding enquiry, can be supported, for example if they are experiencing domestic abuse.

In summary, the Care Act 2014 helpfully introduced a statutory process for safeguarding activity but limited its remit to people with care and support needs that prevented them being able to keep themselves safe. Further, these duties constitute a process of enquiry and protection planning; adult safeguarding is a verb or adjective not a noun. For some young people who have had safeguarding support as children, this can mean that there is a 'cliff edge' when they become 18. This is because they are not considered to have care and support needs that prevent them being able to keep themselves safe, despite the enabling preventative powers of the Act (see Chapter 2).

Tensions in safeguarding young people: exploring the 'cliff edge' at 18

Statutory safeguarding adults' duties apply to people with care and support needs unable to protect themselves from the risk or experience of abuse or neglect due to those needs. The Care Act 2014 describes 'care and support needs' as 'arising from, or are related to, physical or mental impairment or illness. These can include conditions as a result of physical, mental, sensory, learning or cognitive disabilities or illnesses, substance misuse or brain injury'. The remit for adult safeguarding intervention therefore is narrower than the remit of safeguarding children's work, which can apply to any child at risk of harm; this creates the safeguarding 'gap' or 'cliff edge' for some young people, not deemed eligible for a safeguarding enquiry (Holmes 2022a; see Chapter 2).

How 'safeguarding adults' is understood and interpreted varies. While it is helpful that these words are more widely used and recognised than they used to be, they mean different things to different people. Public perception about safety and who may need to be safeguarded can differ from the statutory safeguarding duties that apply to people with care and support needs. This is evident regarding people 'on the edge of care and support' who may be vulnerable but not have care and support needs that affect their ability to protect themselves. What constitutes a 'care and support need' can be misunderstood. There may be different perceptions or limitations regarding how 'vulnerabilities' may be seen or expressed. For example, the needs of young people who are care-experienced, homeless, traumatised by experience of childhood abuse, sexually or criminally exploited, or using drugs or alcohol may not be understood, or their behaviours can sometimes be seen as 'lifestyle choices'. Substance misuse may not be recognised as a means of responding to previous trauma and/or managing emotional and mental difficulties. For young people the boundaries between 'recreational usage' and 'misuse' of alcohol and drugs can be difficult to identify and fluctuate. The impact of substance misuse in terms of mental and emotional ill-health, as well as links to self-neglect, may be challenging to understand and assess. Similarly, how this might impact on the young person's mental capacity, especially executive mental capacity, may be hard to accurately assess (see later). Some mental health needs may not be considered serious or have a diagnosis that meets the threshold for adult mental health specialist services and also go unrecognised as 'care and support needs'. Further, the very definition of 'safeguarding' itself may exclude the harms that a young person might face, for example, peer-on-peer abuse (Holmes 2022a). So, while all children under 18 can be protected, only specific groups of adults must be safeguarded.

Even if young people have care and support needs, these may not be considered to impact on their ability to protect themselves from abuse or neglect and therefore they are deemed ineligible for a safeguarding enquiry. There are various aspects to consider in this context, including how the information gathering stage of the safeguarding process might be utilised to provide preventative support and how an assessment is made of the capability of the person to protect themselves if they have care and support needs. There are various ways in which young people can be supported to mitigate the risks in their lives, particularly those young people at risk of sexual or criminal exploitation, such as gaining access to education, alternative employment, and safe housing.

The statutory guidance states that safeguarding enquiries can be made even when there is not a section 42 duty, 'if the local authority believes it proportionate to do so and it will enable the local authority to promote the person's well-being and support a preventative agenda' (Department of Health and Social Care 2023, para 14.44). Section 2 of the Care Act 2014 to 'prevent, reduce or delay the development of needs for care and support' provides generic flexibilities that practitioners can use to ensure that someone is safe and well even when the statutory safeguarding duties do not apply (Department of Health and Social Care 2022; 2023). This means that safeguarding work can be undertaken with someone who may not meet the criteria for a section 42 enquiry but where help is needed in order to manage risks and prevent abuse or neglect. Young people whose experiences or trauma mean that they may need support but do not have formally defined care and support needs under the Care Act 2014 can be assisted in these circumstances (OCSWA/RiP 2021). This provides flexibility for practitioners but is not necessarily consistently understood, depending on the level of legal literacy, or applied in practice due to a range of pressures on, and limited capacity of, adult social services. The eligibility criteria for safeguarding adult support therefore can be described as a 'floor target' not a 'ceiling' in this context.

Further, there are core generic duties for local authorities under the Care Act 2014 which include care assessment, provision of prevention services, information, and advice. These may be relevant when someone may not be eligible for a section 42 enquiry and exercising these duties could prevent or reduce risks or experience of abuse or neglect (Braye and Preston-Shoot 2020b). There are also wider responsibilities for system partners, in prevention and risk reduction. For example, providers of services have duties to ensure that their services are not only safe but good quality; when care and support are inadequate and poor quality, there may be safeguarding risks, abuse, or neglect. Regulated providers have responsibilities to address safeguarding issues (see also Department of Health and Social Care 2023, para 14.68–69). Commissioners have responsibilities to ensure that the care and support commissioned is safe, seeking assurance that the staff providing services are adequately trained to provide safe services and any indications of poor-quality care are tackled, as this can lead to safeguarding risks and harms. These responsibilities sit alongside their duties regarding the use of safeguarding procedures, whether local authority, health, or other commissioners (see also Department of Health and Social Care 2023, para 14.73–74). This should ensure that, for those young people using commissioned care and support services, these should meet their needs and provide a safe environment. Unfortunately, as Safeguarding Adults Reviews demonstrate, this is not always guaranteed (see Chapter 8). The police have responsibilities to protect people from crime and disrupt criminal behaviour. This can be relevant to safeguarding practice with young adults when they are involved in exploitation.

The ability of a young person to protect themselves may not be fully appreciated by all practitioners, for example if they are experiencing mental health problems, substance misuse, or other issues that may impact on their mental capacity and ability to look after themselves and lead independent 'adult' lives. Self-neglect was a new category of abuse and neglect included in the Care Act 2014, which previously had been inconsistently addressed in safeguarding adults' work. It is different to all the other categories insofar as there is no external person who is the 'abuser'; the person is harmful to themselves. It continues to be an area for ongoing learning, as is evidenced by being the most common abuse type identified in a national analysis of over 200 Safeguarding Adults Reviews (Preston-Shoot et al 2020). For young people the ability to self-care may be affected by their emotional or mental ill-health, experience of trauma, or personal developmental stage. Understanding self-neglect during this period of life, when taking responsibility for being independent and becoming an adult is still developing, may be tricky for professionals to assess (see Chapter 4). Therefore, several factors may impact on the judgement that is made to undertake a safeguarding enquiry regarding whether a young person's care and support needs are affecting their ability to look after themselves and protect themselves.

There are huge ongoing resource and financial pressures on adult social care services (ADASS 2022), and a funding gap for adult social care of at least £2.1bn was estimated just to conduct 'business as usual' in the context of an ageing population (Health

Foundation 2021; House of Commons Health and Social Care Committee 2020). A subsequent Commons Select Committee added that a lack of investment in public health services and prevention was stopping people receiving support at an earlier stage and estimated a need to allocate more funding to adult social care, 'at least £7 billion' a year (House of Commons Levelling Up, Housing and Communities Committee 2022, p 24). In this context, lack of adult social care service capacity and limited resource availability affects how safeguarding concerns about young people are responded to, capacity to deliver preventative services and ability to extend support to those young people on the 'edge of care and support'. The criterion for safeguarding enquiries is then in danger of being used as a 'threshold' for rationing safeguarding adults' services, rather than a tool for managing processes and enabling preventative responses.

Making Safeguarding Personal

The MSP approach has many of the same features that provide the pillars of the Transitional Safeguarding approach (Holmes 2022a; see Chapter 2). It advocates safeguarding practice that focuses on the needs and outcomes that the person experiencing or at risk from abuse or neglect has themselves identified so it is an essentially 'participative' approach (Cooper and White 2017). MSP built on the 'nothing about me without me' mantra of the disability rights movement (Charlton 2000). Critical to delivering MSP is a person-centred approach: involving the person throughout, asking simple questions so that the process is driven by their wishes and aspirations, and ensuring that they define the outcomes to be achieved (Lawson 2017; Department of Health and Social Care 2023, paras 14.94, 14.96, 14.104)

Being person-centred, the impact of structural inequalities on the person, and any aspect of equity, equalities, diversity, and inclusion, should be acknowledged and considered in the safeguarding work with them. MSP is 'contextual and ecological' in its approach to risk assessment, enabling risk taking as well as responding to and managing risks (White 2017), while supporting resolution of the safeguarding issues and recovery from any trauma experienced by the person (Cooper et al 2018).

A personalised approach should ensure that the impact of context is acknowledged and any developmental needs are considered.

MSP promotes an approach where safeguarding is done 'with' and not 'to' people, emphasising interpersonal skills (Cooper and White 2017). It relies on positive relationship building by practitioners with the person to achieve their outcomes of resolution, recovery, and protection (Lawson 2017, pp 35–37; Cooper 2019). Building mutual trust and understanding with them is essential to MSP practice and emphasised in the guidance issued by the Chief Social Worker in 2022 (Department of Health and Social Care 2022). This speaks to the 'relational' requirements of the Transitional Safeguarding approach.

The journey of MSP has also addressed issues regarding strategic transformation as well as operational delivery. Like Transitional Safeguarding, MSP has required system change and system leadership (see Chapter 10). The MSP national programme was a joint initiative led by safeguarding leads from the Association of Adults Services and LGA from 2009, with other partner agencies and colleagues across many local authorities. It was developed in response to identified weaknesses in safeguarding practice at that time; safeguarding practice was not embracing the personalisation agenda in adult social care services. Adult protection work was dominated by processes to establish whether harm was 'substantiated' or 'not substantiated', rather than what the person themselves wished to achieve in terms of their own safety and well-being.

Following research about what already existed regarding safeguarding adults, the MSP toolkit was developed to bring together several frameworks and methods that could be used to achieve a more person-centred and outcome-focused approach for safeguarding adults. A sample of these was tested in a small number of local authorities (Klee and Williams 2013) before being piloted by a much larger group of local authorities and externally evaluated (Pike and Walsh 2015). The process of developing the MSP programme was therefore 'evidence based'.

The MSP toolkit has been updated four times, with the most recent version containing key resources and specific practice tools, which can be downloaded and printed for use by individuals in supervision, team meetings, and other learning forums (LGA/ADASS 2018a). The toolkit includes a case example on Transitional

Safeguarding with reflective questions to prompt discussion and learning (LGA/ADASS 2018b, no 15). Prior to this, MSP resources included two publications of case studies to illustrate good safeguarding practice. These include descriptions of safeguarding work with young people in a range of situations (LGA/ADASS 2014, case study 17; LGA/ADASS 2019c, case studies 5 and 9).

Other resources have been developed to support improvement in safeguarding practice and are accessible through the LGA website.[3] These resources to support change and improve practice were developed over several years. They provided the 'how', which was needed to deliver the 'what' of MSP, once it was understood 'why' MSP was needed. The resources were developed to be used by strategic leaders and practitioners across relevant sectors and organisations. The learning from this for Transitional Safeguarding is that a similar broad range of resources may be required to support culture and system change as 'sector-led improvement' in safeguarding adults' practice (Local Government Association 2012).

The Care Act 2014 changed the status of the MSP approach to safeguarding adults from 'good practice' to 'statutory practice', by incorporating it in the statutory guidance (Department of Health and Social Care 2021).

> MSP means it should be person-led and outcome-focused. It engages the person in a conversation about how best to respond to their safeguarding situation in a way that enhances involvement, choice and control as well as improving quality of life, well-being and safety. (Department of Health and Social Care 2023, para 14.15)

The guidance acknowledges that 'people have complex lives and being safe is only one of the things they want for themselves. Professionals should work with the adult to establish what being safe means to them and how that can be best achieved' (s.14.8). It states that 'the adult should be involved at the beginning of the enquiry, and their views and wishes ascertained' (Department of Health and Social Care 2023, paras 14.77, 14.78) and 'safeguarding plans involve joint discussion, decision making and planning with the adult for their future safety and well-being' (Department of

Health and Social Care 2023, para 14.90). The MSP approach is consequently threaded through statutory guidance.

The MSP Voluntary Return collates data from local authorities on engaging people in defining and achieving the outcomes from safeguarding processes and shows that most of the practice achieves this in the majority of cases in most local authority areas (NHS Digital 2022a). Unfortunately, the safeguarding adults' datasets are not broken down by age, apart from 18–65 and over 65, so there is no national picture of how MSP is being used with young adults.

Over the years, there has been some misunderstanding in practice when delivering an MSP approach, for example, focusing solely on the person's wishes to the exclusion of assessing the range of risks to them or others, particularly if someone refuses support and help. This has been summarised as a 'myth' – 'MSP means "Walking away when people say 'no'" (LGA/ADASS 2019b). This is one of several 'myths and realities' explored to demonstrate how MSP should not be interpreted simplistically but understood in the context of the complexities of safeguarding practice (LGA/ADASS 2019b). Rather than 'walking away', adopting the MSP approach means that professional curiosity and relationship-based practice needs to be used to understand why someone is rejecting help if they are experiencing or are at risk of abuse or neglect. Further, it is acknowledged that there are situations when someone's wishes can and should be overridden, such as if a person lacks the mental capacity to decide, if there are issues regarding duties of care, public interest, or if a criminal offence has or may have been committed, if a child is being affected and there are risks to others to be considered.

The Care Act 2014 provides the power to carry out assessments under section 11 if the adult is experiencing, or is at risk of, abuse or neglect, regardless of their wishes so practitioners can act in these circumstances. MSP does not mean ignoring the full range of safeguarding duties and responsibilities. It requires practitioners to have safeguarding literacy and legal literacy to act appropriately and proportionately in these circumstances. This is relevant to safeguarding work with young people as they may be apprehensive or ambivalent about professional support or intervention in their lives and they may avoid or refuse help, even when they are at risk of or experiencing abuse or neglect. The young person may not acknowledge that they are being abused, as illustrated in an MSP case study (LGA/ADASS 2019c, no 9).

Putting MSP into practice means applying the six safeguarding principles from the Care Act 2014 (Lawson 2017) and utilising strength-based approaches to practice. A strength-based approach to front-line practice requires a personalised and relational partnership between the person and practitioner where a focus on needs and deficits is counterbalanced with recognition of the resilience and assets that someone has (Department of Health and Social Care 2019). MSP can be delivered using a range of different tools, models, and methods to achieve someone's outcomes (Department of Health and Social Care 2017, 2019).

Restorative justice approaches, where work is undertaken with the 'victim' and the 'offender' to move on through mutual understanding with a facilitator, can be a useful means to deliver the MSP approach (Gunner 2017). The MSP case study from Herefordshire highlights this approach to working with two young people with learning disabilities who were in a relationship together where there was alleged sexual abuse (LGA/ADASS 2019c).

Family Group Conferencing (see frg.org.uk) is another model that has been used in some local areas to deliver the MSP approach. It was piloted in Greenwich and Central Bedfordshire during the development stage of the MSP programme (Manthorpe et al 2014). In this model, an external facilitator supports the 'family' to support the person to make decisions about keeping themselves safe (Taylor and Tapper 2017). It is a model used across children and adults' services and could be helpful in delivering a Transitional Safeguarding approach as well as MSP.

While different localities have piloted and tested some of these approaches in delivering MSP, they have not been fully evaluated or reported on, so the effectiveness of these interventions and approaches is unknown. Further, the relative effectiveness of these models with young people remains unexplored.

Human rights, mental capacity, and equalities: legal literacy in safeguarding adults

Although the Care Act 2014 describes the key statutory safe-guarding duties and powers, other significant legislation regarding human rights, mental capacity, and equalities is critical to informing good practice in safeguarding adults.

A Human Rights perspective should underpin all safeguarding practice; this assumes that all adults (and children) have rights under the Human Rights Act 1998, however, some of these rights are qualified, they are not absolute, and there is a very high threshold for when these rights have been breached. Specific rights relevant to safeguarding include Article 2 – right to life; Article 3 – freedom from torture and inhuman or degrading treatment; Article 5 – right to liberty and security; Article 8 – right to respect for a private and family life; and Article 14 – right not to be discriminated against. In safeguarding adults' practice 'Human Rights' provide both a legal framework and a values-based perspective for practice (Spreadbury and Hubbard 2020, p 21). In practice, this means that practitioners need to be aware of any potential breaches of someone's human rights and the implications when abuse violates someone's rights or freedoms. For young people this would mean consideration of their human rights in respect of the risks that they are experiencing.

Mental capacity affects someone's ability to make informed decisions, understand and take risks, mitigate unwanted risks, and prevent harm, all of which are critical to keeping safe from abuse or neglect. Working with risk is key to safeguarding and is critical in safeguarding practice. Adult social services have adopted a 'risk enabling' approach, working with adults to support their understanding of risk and enable them to make decisions about keeping themselves safe (Lawson 2017; White 2017). This approach has developed over time, as adult safeguarding emerged from a paradigm focused on protection and risk elimination to one which enabled positive risk taking or risk enablement (McNamara and Morgan 2016).

Before the Care Act 2014, Faulkner (2012) explained that the language used in adult safeguarding to describe risk was influenced by social workers' attitudes and assumptions; the absence of service users' voices meant their concerns were not acknowledged and therefore their views on risks in their lives not considered. Practice has changed since the Care Act 2014, influenced by MSP, with an expectation that people are at the centre of decision making about their lives and their views inform the safeguarding process and, specifically, their approach to risk (Cooper et al 2016). Assessing someone's mental capacity as part of the safeguarding process helps to evaluate whether their wishes and views are reliable and executable. This is particularly relevant when there are complex dynamics regarding the person's ability to care for themselves (self-neglect) or keep themselves safe in a relationship (domestic abuse).

Fundamental to both enabling risk taking and reducing risk is establishing that the person understands risk and can make and act on their decisions. Therefore, assessing someone's executive mental capacity is critical to decision making about risk and safety. The Mental Capacity Act 2005 applies to anyone over 16 years of age. Their mental capacity will determine the extent to which they are involved in decision making about risks in their lives. This Act provides a framework, principles, tests, and checklists for professionals to support people to make decisions when they may be unable to do this, due to mental illness, learning disability, substance misuse, etc, and to ensure that any decisions about them are made in accordance with their best interests. Under the Mental Capacity Act 2005, mental capacity should be assumed unless it is proved otherwise. Assessing mental capacity, including executive mental capacity, is essential since, should the person not be able to make decisions, then professionals can make decisions, including those regarding limiting someone's liberty, in their best interests (under the Deprivation of Liberty Safeguards/Liberty Protection Safeguards processes). Evidence from Safeguarding Adult Reviews (SARs) shows that mental capacity assessment remains an area of practice weakness (see Chapter 8 and Preston-Shoot et al 2020). Consequently, it is essential that practitioners understand and can assess someone's ability to make and execute decisions about risks in their lives in all safeguarding work.

Exploring new experiences and enabling young adults to take risks can be argued as age appropriate. However, there is a danger that 'risky activities' are perceived as 'lifestyle choices', resulting from capacitous decision making and the harms misunderstood (Cocker et al 2022b, p 210). In areas of abuse such as criminal exploitation, sexual abuse, domestic abuse, county lines, and modern slavery, the young person may be subject to coercion and control by others, influencing them and affecting their ability to make independent and capacitous decisions about risk taking and execute those decisions. Additionally, there are a number of factors that can affect someone's mental capacity and decision making regarding risk, for example physical and mental health issues, or substance misuse. For young people experiencing or at risk of abuse or neglect, these can significantly affect their ability to make informed decisions about risk and go unrecognised. Balancing the practitioner's duty of care and the young person's self-determination/autonomy can be challenging and is essential in risk assessment work. These factors have been highlighted as common factors in poor mental capacity assessments (Preston-Shoot et al 2020).

The Equalities Act (2010) articulates duties to protect people from discrimination because of 'protected characteristics', which include age. While this is generally interpreted as ensuring that older people are not discriminated against, it is challenging to raise the question, are adult safeguarding processes and services age-discriminatory in terms of young people? Generally, it is significant to note that discriminatory abuse is a very under-reported and recorded area of safeguarding activity, whether by individuals or organisations (Mason et al 2022; Spreadbury and Hubbard 2020, p 37). Acknowledging discrimination and structural inequalities and the impact on a young person's life is essential to understanding their personal experience and the impact this has on their resilience and ability to keep themselves safe. Someone may have more than one protected characteristic and will have responded to this in their own individual way. Promoting equity, equality, diversity, and inclusion are key and underpinning principles of Transitional Safeguarding (Holmes 2022a, p 11). For practitioners this means developing their knowledge, understanding, and competence to work with young people with any protected characteristic(s) or experiences of exclusion. It means encouraging recognition of discriminatory abuse more widely and recognition of the potential for safeguarding activity in itself to collude with discrimination and social exclusion. As well as the protected characteristics, other experiences, such as state care or prison, may be relevant; the concept of 'multiple exclusion', helpful in understanding the lives of people who become street homeless, is relevant here (Mason et al 2017/18).

A human rights approach situates safeguarding practice within a broader ethical framework. Similarly, a positive approach to equity, equalities, diversity, and inclusion situates safeguarding within a broader values base. Ethics and values are key to safeguarding practice with young adults experiencing harm or abuse, for example enabling exploration of experiences that have led to self-harming behaviours, or understanding how their experiences may affect the ability of a young person to make informed choices about addressing their safeguarding risks and needs.

As well as the Care Act 2014, which defines adult safeguarding duties, and legislation mentioned earlier regarding human rights, mental capacity, and equalities, there is specific legislation relevant to the different categories of abuse: physical abuse, domestic violence, sexual abuse, psychological abuse, financial or material abuse, modern slavery, discriminatory abuse, organisational abuse, neglect and acts of omission, and self-neglect. There is also legislation related to areas of need such as housing and homelessness or environmental health that may be relevant in safeguarding work. The range of legal powers and duties that can assist practitioners to support and protect someone is vast; legal literacy and access to legal advice are key to effective safeguarding practice.

In considering the safeguarding needs of younger adults, depending on the type of abuse or exploitation they are experiencing or at risk of experiencing, there may be powers and tools useful to enable young people to be supported and protected, for example being homeless and accessing appropriate accommodation. Practitioners need to be legally literate, not as lawyers, but aware of what may be helpful in terms of achieving protection, resolution, or recovery for the person they are supporting, and know where to go for specialist help. For young adults, this can be particularly challenging due to the different age thresholds that apply to different legal frameworks (see Cocker et al 2021).

Conclusion

In conclusion, existing legislation and guidance regarding safeguarding adults can support a Transitional Safeguarding approach. Legal literacy and safeguarding literacy are critical for practitioners working to safeguard young people effectively. The 'cliff edge' exists for those young people not eligible for a formal safeguarding response because they do not have recognised care and support needs. However, they can be supported if resources are available as the Care Act 2014 is permissive; lack of staffing capacity and resources appear to limit its delivery. The common interpretation of the criteria for a section 42 enquiry as a 'threshold' drives the unintended consequences of stressing the deficits – care and support needs – rather than the assets someone has. As such this contradicts the strength-based approaches to practice promoted in many localities. This tension can be challenging for practitioners to navigate when working with young people.

The MSP approach provides a way of addressing the six pillars of Transitional Safeguarding, ensuring personalised support to enable a young person to achieve safety and well-being in their lives. The evidence is that the MSP approach is widespread and applied to those people who meet the criteria for safeguarding enquiries, however there is limited evidence to date of its use with young people.

7

Transitional Safeguarding and transitions[1]

Introduction

Transitional Safeguarding is often confused with transitions and transitions planning. They are not the same thing. However, there are connections between the two – not least that poor transitions/transfer can create or worsen risks for a young person. We will explore the differences and intersections in this chapter, using case examples to show good practice in local authority transitions work, and discuss the potential safeguarding risks that can occur in this work. In particular this can happen when young people are struggling with issues like homelessness, poor physical or mental health, substance misuse, and financial (in)stability.

The chapter begins with a brief overview of definitions of 'transitions' and how they differ from Transitional Safeguarding. This is followed by an exploration of the legislative landscape around transitions planning. This is substantial, which is why it is included in this chapter and is not part of Chapter 3. The case studies we include later in the chapter demonstrate the differences between Transitional Safeguarding and transitions work and how these approaches, concepts, and practices interact with each other.

What is the difference between 'transitions' and 'Transitional Safeguarding'?

A transition refers to a process an individual goes through to move from one situation, state, condition, or age to another (Johansson 2021).

The word 'process' is important here, as a transition is not a single event. Munro and Simkiss (2020) describe transitions as 'the process of moving from a child focused system to an adult orientated system' (p 175) and there are clear legislative and social policy frameworks in place to assist with transitions planning for young people. There are various life stage transitions which are often referred to in the child development literature, such as moving from primary school to secondary school (a life stage event); moving from childhood to adulthood (a life stage that in many western nations is defined legally at age 18 years); or moving from school or university into employment (another life stage event). Other disciplines also reflect on transitions, for example education, child and youth studies, geography (Valentine 2003), and sociology (Giddens and Sutton 2021), noting that the boundary between childhood and adulthood is difficult to define (Valentine 2003), and context is important to understanding the meaning of transitions for individual young people (Johansson 2021). These ideas are discussed further in Chapter 4, exploring the term 'emerging adulthood' (Arnett 2000).

Becoming an adult tends to be a challenging time, with biological, social, emotional, psychological, and cognitive changes during this part of the life course journey for young people. However, it is not a 'level playing field'. Many young people will have the support of their immediate family, extended family, neighbours, friends, and community members during this time. Some young people face additional adversities, such as health or mental health difficulties, or have experienced trauma and so they may need additional support. Some will have this readily available and others will not.

Additionally, transitions are neither a one-off nor a one-way process and there are distinct limitations with normative models of transition that measure transitions to adulthood by activities such as gaining employment, getting married, or other 'conventional measures of autonomy' (Valentine 2003, p 49). Racism, sexism, and homophobia towards young people are known to structure and exacerbate inequalities in health throughout the lifespan (Krieger 2020). Structural inequalities will also affect young people and their experiences of transition, particularly those who face additional hurdles in childhood, such as experiences of abuse and neglect. However, 'many of those who might be defined as vulnerable or on the margins of society demonstrate great resilience in successfully attaining lifestyles of stability, productivity and well-being despite difficult childhood circumstances' (Valentine, 2003, p 49).

Transitional Safeguarding is concerned with safeguarding young people across the 'cliff edge' of 18 years. In Chapter 3 we explained that it is the age of 18 years that determines the difference between the legal safeguarding frameworks for children and adults. However, a key element of the Transitional Safeguarding approach is the need for fluidity, recognising the developmental nature of becoming an adult (Holmes and Smale 2018), because a safeguarding response being determined simply by age and not need has serious human costs and represents poor value for public money.

The Transitional Safeguarding approach includes activity that currently lies outside of what is usually understood by both 'transitions' and 'safeguarding' remits and it is important to acknowledge the differences. For many young people already known to social care and health services, 'transitions' most often refers to 'transitions planning' (for example, from being in care to then being out of care as a 'care leaver' or planning for young people with physical disabilities, learning disabilities, or autism) moving between children's and adults' social care, health, and education services, that is planning how services will be commissioned and function to support that young person over this time period (see later). The term 'safeguarding' through this lens is understood as limited to statutory safeguarding enquiry duties (see Chapter 6). In transitions planning work, any safeguarding risks should, and hopefully would, be explored. However, there is a danger that 'safeguarding' becomes 'a threshold to be reached' (Holmes 2022a, p 9), for the person becoming 18. Their eligibility for adult safeguarding support is dependent on them having care and support needs and not being able to be safe because of these (see Chapter 6).

The limited eligibility for adult safeguarding enquiry and support then raises issues about what happens to those young people who do not meet the required threshold, 'despite their safety being undermined' (Holmes 2022a, p 9):

> a person over 18 facing harm may not receive a safeguarding response if they do not meet the criteria set out in the Care Act 2014. So, it is 'not safeguarding' if the person does not receive a safeguarding response, and they do not receive a response if their situation is understood in procedural terms to be 'not safeguarding'. This self-reinforcing loop, with terms defining actions that in turn prescribe the terms, undermines the sector's ability to adapt and refine its response to emerging need and evidence. (Holmes 2022a, p 9)

This is particularly relevant, given the dominant focus of children's safeguarding on intra-familial abuse in children's services (Firmin 2020) compared to adults' safeguarding and is explored in more detail elsewhere (see Chapter 5).

Transitional Safeguarding is still an emergent approach to safeguarding young people and a developing concept, as discussed in Chapter 2. It provides a language to describe a complex area of practice and policy concerned with supporting young people to be as safe as possible in a way that meets their developmental needs. It is not a prescribed model that can or should be replicated identically across geographical or service areas, rather it is an approach where local areas can innovate; health, social care, and voluntary sector services are encouraged to work together to prevent and meet the safeguarding needs of young people in their locality and in a way that reflects the dynamic processes of transition (Cocker et al 2022a).

Figure 7.1 describes groups of young people who may have safeguarding needs that many agencies involved in supporting young people already know about before they become 18 years old. One group includes young people who have physical or learning disabilities or difficulties, autism, or mental health problems. Someone's disability does not automatically make them vulnerable to abuse, but there is a high likelihood that these young people will already be known to statutory health, education, and social care services. As such, these services will be aware of and should be supporting those young people to manage any safeguarding risks in their lives as they become adults. Additionally, some young people who have had experience of the care system may require ongoing support to keep safe.

Figure 7.1: Mind the gap: young people who may have Transitional Safeguarding needs

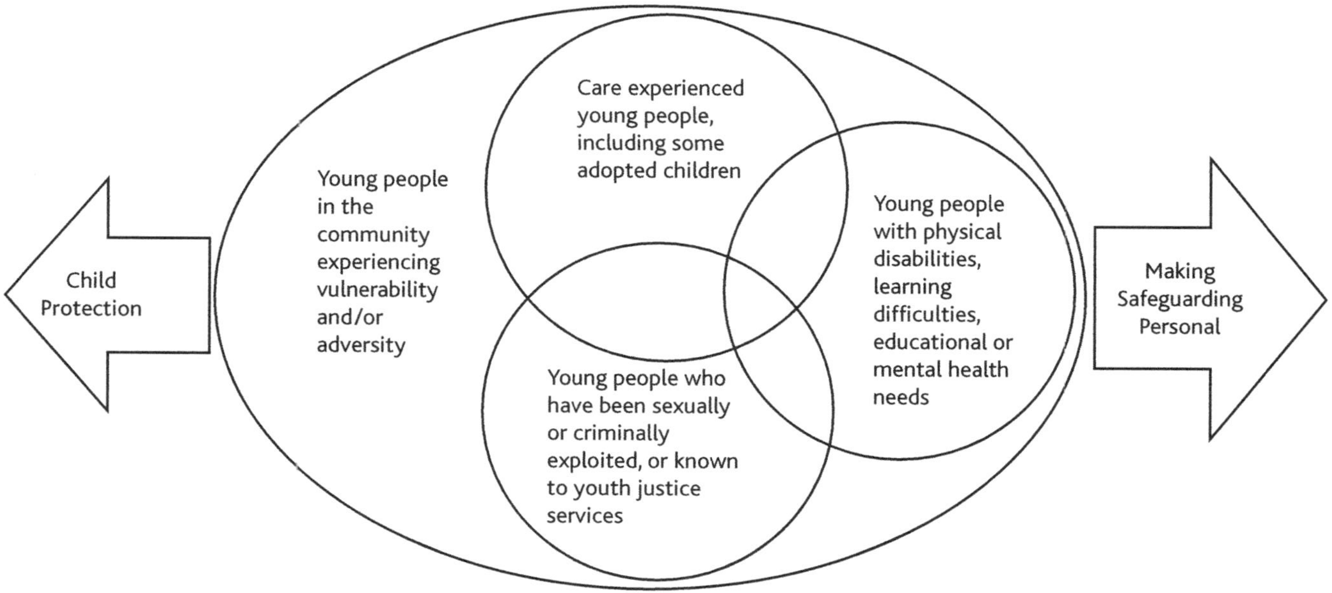

Source: Cocker et al 2021, p 157.

These young people have personal adviser support until they are 25, to also help manage becoming adults (Cocker et al 2022a). A further group of young people may be known to YJS, including young people involved in county lines, criminal exploitation, or modern slavery (Cocker et al 2021). Some of these young people will also be supported when they are over 18 and may have ongoing safeguarding needs if they have care and support needs and are eligible for adult social services. Young people involved in the justice system face a range of challenges as they approach the transition to adulthood, and much improvement is needed in terms of transfer to adult services and wider transition to adulthood (Harris and Edwards 2023).

There is evidence of very high levels of needs – particularly due to mental ill-health, neurodiversity, and health-harming behaviours – among the youth and young adult custody population, alongside the under-identification of such needs (Lennox 2014). As explored in Holmes and Smith (2022), there are practice and policy initiatives within the justice system that do attend to transitions. These include the National Transitions Protocol, which guides professionals in the effective transfer of young people between YJS and probation (HM Government 2021), and sentencing guidelines that aim to respond to the particular needs of 18–21-year-olds (Parole Board 2021). As with transitions activity within health and social care, such initiatives do not comprise a Transitional Safeguarding approach in themselves, but they do offer a useful basis upon which to build.

There will be some young people whose needs do not become apparent until they are in this transitional phase of their lives. For example, we know that most adult mental health problems begin in adolescence (Jones 2013); 50 per cent of mental health problems are established by age 14 and 75 per cent by age 24 (Kessler et al 2005). Some young people face homelessness during this period (Neinstein and Irwin 2013; Preston-Shoot 2020), and there are those young people who do not have diagnosed disabilities, who are particularly at risk of falling through the gaps (Cocker et al 2021). In addition, too many young people in the adult custody population do not have their learning and/or mental health needs identified until they are incarcerated (House of Commons Justice Committee 2016).

To summarise, there is a difference between Transitional Safeguarding and transitions and also a difference between young people requiring Transitional Safeguarding support and those requiring support with transitions planning, although there will be some overlap (see later).

Guidance and legal requirements for transitions planning

There is a great deal of guidance available to support timely transitions planning. We highlight several salient pieces of guidance to outline current legal requirements in England, where the state has legal duties and responsibilities regarding transitions planning.

National Institute for Health and Care Excellence (NICE) guidance

In addition to primary legislation, NICE has produced two guidance documents that set out quality standards for transition from children's to adults' health and social care services (National Institute for Health and Care Excellence 2016a) and transition from children's to adults' services for young people using health or social care services (National Institute for Health and Care Excellence 2016b). The key principles underpinning transitions planning are that young people and family members are involved in planning (section 1.1.1), the process is developmentally appropriate (section 1.1.2), support is strengths based (section 1.1.3), and is person centred (section 1.1.4) (National Institute for Health and Care Excellence 2016a). This document does not mention safeguarding. Crucially, both guidance documents are ostensibly about the transition to adulthood, but they focus on those young people who are already deemed eligible for adult health or care services and so are going through 'transition' in the service-jargon sense. This differs from Transitional Safeguarding which is broader than the transition between children and adult services. This broader focus is necessary because many young people need support services during this transition and do not get it because they are not seen as 'eligible'.

The NICE guidance indicates that planning for transitions should start early in Year 9 when a young person is aged 13–14, or if they come to the notice of children's services after Year 9 then transitions planning should begin immediately. For those young people covered by health and social care or education legislation, including young people with EHCPs, early transition planning is already a legal requirement (National Institute for Health and Care Excellence 2016b). There should be a particular focus on the young person's ambitions and goals post-16. These duties include young people with EHCPs up to the age of 25 if they remain in education. The NICE guidance mentions the need to ensure that transitions planning is not based on a rigid age threshold and that it should take place at a time of relative stability for the young person (National Institute for Health and Care Excellence 2016a, p 8).

The second NICE guidance includes references to safeguarding roles and responsibilities. It cites 'information sharing regarding safeguarding issues' as a key principle; specifying that every service involved in transitions planning should take responsibility for sharing safeguarding information with other organisations (National Institute for Health and Care Excellence 2016b, section 1.1). Following the young person's transition this NICE guidance suggests that any non-attendance or non-engagement by the young person should be addressed within safeguarding protocols by adult services; practitioners should contact family members and others to support the process (National Institute for Health and Care Excellence 2016b, pp 14–15). Further, the guidance emphasises that practitioners and managers need to know the legal context and frameworks relating to consent and safeguarding (National Institute for Health and Care Excellence 2016b, p 25).

Special Educational Needs and Disabilities (SEND) Code of Practice

Partnership working is critical to successful transition planning, particularly for young people with SEND. The SEND code of practice (Department for Education and Department of Health 2015) describes the duty placed on education, health, and social care to work together to plan and jointly commission services for young people with special educational needs and/or disabilities with or without EHCPs. These duties are set out under the Children and Families Act 2014, the Care Act 2014, and the National Health Services Act 2006. The code of practice sets out that:

> local governance arrangements must be in place to ensure clear accountability for commissioning services for children and young people with SEN and disabilities from birth to the age of 25. There must be clear decision-making structures so that partners can agree the changes that joint commissioning will bring in the design of services. This will help ensure that joint commissioning is focused on achieving agreed outcomes. Partners must also be clear about who is responsible for delivering what, who the decision-makers are in education, health and social care, and how partners will hold each other to account in the event of a disagreement. The partners must be able to make a decision on how they will meet the needs of children and young people with SEN or disabilities in every case. (Department for Education and Department of Health 2015, paragraph 3.25)

The SEND code of practice mentions safeguarding issues referencing children's safeguarding statutory guidance, such as 'Working Together to Safeguard Children'. In the section on 16–17-year-olds, the code of practice reminds practitioners that children's safeguarding legal duties apply up to the age of 18 ((Department for Education and Department of Health 2015, p 127). In the section on EHCPs, the document reminds practitioners that if the young person is over 18, safeguarding adults' duties should apply. Local authority child safeguarding colleagues should be involved if the young person is already known to them, among others ((Department for Education and Department of Health 2015, p 139). In the section on the use of Direct Payments, safeguarding is mentioned as a consideration if the person lacks mental capacity or is more vulnerable ((Department for Education and Department of Health 2015, p 184).

The relevant transitions guidance does remind practitioners of the legal frameworks for safeguarding children and adults, but they do not draw out the differences in how safeguarding risks may be perceived, deemed eligible, and managed. And again, there is a mismatch between the eligibility or qualifying criteria for adult services, so this guidance excludes the great number of young people who have some needs but receive no statutory support post-18 or 25 years (see Chapter 2).

Youth Justice and transitions guidance

There are also levels of need in the youth custody population. However, the SEND code of practice excludes older young people in the justice system. Section 10 includes children and young people with SEND who are in youth custody, but section 10.61 says, 'This section does not apply to children and young people serving their sentence in the community, to persons detained in a Young Offenders Institution for 18–21-year-olds or to persons detained in the adult estate,' (Department for Education and Department of Health 2015, p 223) so is only partly transitions focused. This approach does not reflect the intersectionality of young people's lives and separates some young people in conflict with the law from their peers.

As mentioned previously, there is a national protocol for managing transitions between young people moving from Youth Offending Teams (YOT) to the National Probation Service (NPS) (HM Government 2021). This guidance sets out the responsibilities for each of the organisations that are involved in the transitions planning for young people. It refers to the Youth Justice Board Case Management Guidance,[2] which details the supporting principles of transition from YOT to the NPS and good practice for working with children in the youth justice system, and the Youth to Adult Transitions Framework Process Map 2021.[3] Despite these requirements, research notes that 'young people turning 18 while in contact with the justice system face a steep cliff edge, leaving them at risk of harm and continued contact with the criminal justice system' (Harris and Edwards 2023, p 4).

Figure 7.1 highlights the crossover between different groups of young people poorly served by the current binary approach. Care-experienced young people in custody are one such group. The Farmer Review (Farmer 2017) highlighted the over-representation of care-experienced young people in prison and the significant adversities they face (Farmer 2017). This led to the creation of the Ministry of Justice Care Lever Covenant and the creation of a toolkit to support prison establishments in working with care-experienced young people (Barnardo's 2019).

Care-experienced young people

Care-experienced young people are another group of young people where the state has statutory responsibilities to provide support to them after 18, delivered by a range of agencies including local authorities. Concerns about the state's failure to support care-experienced young adults are not new (see Stein 2004, 2006a, 2006b), despite significant legislation and guidance in place to address this. The Children Act 1989 (s24) states that all young people qualify for advice and assistance from the local authority to promote their welfare when they cease to be looked after. The Children Leaving Care Act (CLCA) 2000 strengthened this by creating a duty to assess and meet the care and support needs if eligible,[4] relevant,[5] and for former relevant young people.[6] They must have a pathway plan until they are at least 21 and in some cases 25, covering education, training, career plans, and support.

There are three principles for transition set out in the Children Act 1989 guidance for young people leaving care, which should govern practice when talking to the young person and when making any decision about them. These are: 'is this good enough for my own child?; providing a second chance if things do not go as expected; is this tailored to their individual needs, particularly if they are more vulnerable than other young people?' (Department for Education 2010, p 9).

Finally, the Children and Social Work Act 2017 states that personal adviser support can continue to 25 for all care-experienced young people, not just those in education and employment. The duties on agencies to cooperate to improve young people's well-being and to safeguard and promote their welfare (Children Act 2004 ss.10 and 11) apply to young people aged 18 and 19 receiving 'leaving care' services.

An example of a situation where transitions practice for a care-experienced young person was poor and led to safeguarding issues is Mr D (Morgan 2019):

> Mr D has a learning disability. At the age of 11 Mr D was removed from the family home due to neglect and his parents' inability to support his nutritional needs. At this time he weighed 16 stone 7 lbs and required oxygen at night as a result of his obesity. Mr D appears to have experienced stability of placement through his seven years in care, with just two placements, and the second placement being with respite carers from the first. He successfully lost weight through a maintenance eating plan and at the age of 16 he was discharged from Paediatric Outpatient Services as he no longer required oxygen at night. He also started attending college. ...
>
> Mr D remained in foster care until the age of 18 when he was deemed to have the capacity to choose to return to the family home. On leaving care he weighed 15 stone 4 lbs and was no longer obese. Foster carers and professionals expressed concerns about his mother's behaviour and her capacity to change. Over the next three years, Mr D's weight increased to 29 stone. ...
>
> In September 2017 Mr D was admitted to hospital on an emergency basis, with a grade 4 pressure sore and osteomyelitis. He required surgery for debridement of the wound. It was deemed by all professionals that it was not safe for Mr D to return home. Mr D was judged to lack capacity to make informed decisions regarding his health needs. Mr D was discharged to a residential placement. (Morgan 2019, pp 2–3)

The SAR found that, 'all the agencies involved with Mr D failed to identify the need to raise a safeguarding concern with the local authority at an early enough stage' (Morgan 2019, p 6) and that, 'the Adult Multi-Agency Safeguarding Hub did not initiate a s42 Enquiry as required by the Care Act 2014 when it received a safeguarding concern relating to Mr D' (Morgan 2019, p 6). This illustrates a lack of attention to safeguarding issues in transitions planning for Mr D and it surfaces some interesting questions about how mental capacity is understood and assessed. Mental capacity should be assumed unless assessed as otherwise, but capacity can fluctuate, is decision specific, and, as Mr D's narrative illustrated, it changes over time. In addition, it is important to assess someone's executive mental capacity functioning to be assured that they understand the decision they are making and are able to act on it. Insight into this aspect of executive mental capacity needs to be weighed up alongside their wishes, particularly in terms of any 'unwise decision' (see Chapter 6, where we note the participation/protection 'both/and' issues that Transitional Safeguarding seeks to address).

The Care Act 2014 and transitions planning

The Care Act 2014 is the primary legislation affecting social care with adults in England and provides the statutory framework for adult social care. The duty under Section 58 requires the local authority to carry out a needs assessment for a young person before they are 18 to identify whether they have care and support needs. If they do, there should be careful planning to meet their care and support needs as they transition into the adult world at 18. The statutory guidance (Department of Health and Social Care 2023) states that an assessment should be carried out if a young person is 'likely to have needs', not just those needs that will be deemed eligible under legislation. The eligible needs are those requiring care and support arising from or related to a physical or mental impairment or illness. This includes any condition resulting from physical, mental, sensory, learning or cognitive disabilities or illnesses, substance misuse, or brain injury, but not needs caused by other circumstantial factors, for example, trauma or exploitation, hence the need for Transitional Safeguarding.

The guidance also defines a reciprocal duty for relevant partner agencies to cooperate, for the purposes of supporting transitions work:

> Local authorities should have a clear understanding of their responsibilities, including funding arrangements, for young people and carers who are moving from children's to adults services. Disputes between different departments within a local authority about who is responsible can be time consuming and can sometimes result in disruption to the young person or carer. (Department of Health and Social Care 2023, para 16.43)

The ethos of the Care Act 2014 is that assessments should be needs-led and not restricted by available services. A lack of clinical diagnosis should not act as a barrier to support. Additionally, courts take a dim view of internal wranglings between different local authority and health services about jurisdiction and finance getting in the way of a young person receiving necessary and timely services.

Responsibilities across boundaries

For those young people with SEND who reside or are educated away from home, specific mention is made in the NICE guidance document of the need to begin transitions planning early for those young people in 'out-of-authority' placements (National Institute for Health and Care Excellence 2016b, p 7). This is important to know as there can be confusion about which local authority is responsible for taking action to safeguard or support young people who are living out of the area responsible for them. There are many occasions where services from different local authority areas are involved in supporting a young person and it is important to emphasise that there are duties for organisations to cooperate in transition planning to support young people across geographical boundaries (Department of Health and Social Care 2023, para 16.43)

However, this is a complex area and who is responsible for what can be confusing, not least for the young person and their family. There are two key tests that apply to different duties for health and social care when young people move across local authority boundaries: 'ordinary residence'; and 'physical presence'. Ordinary residence describes the place that a person 'has adopted voluntarily and for settled purposes as part of the regular order of his life for the time being, whether of short or long duration.'[7] However, this does not apply when a child is accommodated by the local authority under its duties under the Children Act 1989, the person is in hospital, or placed in 'specified accommodation', which includes a specialist residential unit provided under the Care Act 2014 or as part of a package of s117 aftercare. The person's 'physical presence' means that responsibility sits with the area where the person is physically located at the time of an incident or an admission into a health setting.

The local authority that is responsible for meeting a person's needs under the Care Act 2014 is the one where the person is 'ordinarily resident'. If they have no settled residence, the test is 'physical presence', and the local authority carrying out the assessment has responsibilities for arranging an advocate if they need one, to engage with the assessment, and for organising an Approved Mental Health Practitioner if required. The local authority where someone is physically present (even if only temporarily) is responsible for carrying out any safeguarding inquiry under s47 of the Children Act 1989 or safeguarding enquiry under s42 Care Act 2014 and arranging an advocate if needed.

For services to meet someone's needs under s117 of the Mental Health Act 1987, the local authority where the person was 'ordinarily resident' at the time they were detained under the Mental Health Act is responsible, even if they have subsequently moved to a new area after discharge from hospital. Similarly, the local authority where the person is ordinarily resident is responsible for carrying out a best interest assessment and authorising a Deprivation of Liberty Safeguards (DOLS) application under the Mental Capacity Act 2005, appointing an independent mental capacity advocate, making accommodation decisions, and instigating care reviews.

An example of poor practice in exercising responsibilities across boundaries, Care Act 2014 assessments, and transitions planning between children and adult services is Madeleine (Bateman and Cocker 2021):

Madeleine was of mixed parentage (White British/Black Nigerian), she was 18 years old when she died, and was well known to many services. She had a long history of mental health support (CAMHS) from a very young age, including being an inpatient when she was 9. At 16 her parents were told that CAMHS had 'tried everything' so they should ask for help from social care.

Madeleine had a diagnosis of Autistic Spectrum Disorder, 'emotional dysregulation', and Obsessive-Compulsive Disorder. She had an EHCP but, despite this, had been excluded from schools because of her behaviour, which was described as challenging. She was first assessed by social care services when she was 12 and at 16 she was taken into care. She experienced eight different placements in five months and was then placed in secure accommodation in Scotland. Shortly before her eighteenth birthday she moved from there to an independent living placement in Croydon. Despite having reached adulthood, coordination of her care needs remained the responsibility of LB Wandsworth's Children's Social Care.

On the evening of 13 August 2020, while at her placement, Madeleine took ketamine. Staff called 111 for advice. A short time later, staff found her suspended from her door. She was taken to hospital and died on 16 August 2020. (Bateman and Cocker 2021, pp 3–4)

For Madeleine, multi-agency support was not robust in either transition planning or in mitigating Transitional Safeguarding issues. This also included management decisions, service structures, and local thresholds, which also played a part. In complex cases, transition planning requires careful multi-agency working and this was lacking with Madeleine, particularly around her mental health and placement provision. The Transitional Safeguarding issues across the children's and adult's divide and between social care and health were not fully understood for her. In situations like this, practitioners should not walk away and close down involvement when support is declined (which is what happened here) but should remain curious and tenacious in seeking ways to engage young people, particularly where there are complexities, such as mental health and substance misuse, which compound their experience of services.

Transitions panels

One of the criticisms about transitions planning from adult services staff is that they do not hear soon enough about young people with care and support needs who are turning 18 (Cocker et al 2022a). Many local authorities use transitions panels as a useful process to bring partners together, scrutinise, and approve the transition plans for young people. This process enables senior managers from different services to review the support planning for young people as they move on and consider how this will be delivered, including the commissioning and funding arrangements. All partner agencies can consider how they manage or commission services to bridge the transition from children's to adult support services by designing bespoke services for young people 16-plus, extending children's services post-18, or joining waiting lists for adult services pre-18.

An example of this process is outlined in Wallace and Cocker (2022), where a local authority's response to the death of Ms A, a care-experienced young person (Preston-Shoot 2017), was to set up a transitions panel, a multi-agency planning forum comprising representatives from Children's Social Care, Adult Social Care, Health Foundation Trust, police, and the Department for Work and Pensions. This is explored later. Its stated aims and objectives include creating opportunities 'through which information is shared to influence safe planning, options considered, and a learning environment promoted for all' (Dooley 2019, p 2). The panel meets monthly to enable discussion of three to four young people. An indication of its effectiveness is that, in the first 18 months of the panel's existence, there had been no evictions of care-experienced young people. This is significant, given that one third of young people leaving care are reported as experiencing homelessness within two years of leaving (Stein and Morris 2010).

To facilitate transition planning in mental health, partners should agree a joined-up approach across the wider partnership too, which may involve a transitions panel or identifying a lead practitioner to coordinate the professional network, to enable the young person's needs and choices to be met during and post-transition. A number of NHS foundation trusts are now investing in transitions posts (for example, South London and Maudsley adolescent and young adult mental health specialist) and/or developed mental health transitions frameworks (Richmond and Wandsworth Safeguarding Adults Board 2020).

What matters in transitions planning

The evidence base about transitions planning has been slow to evolve, with little data about what is effective (Willis and McDonagh 2018). Much of the literature exploring transitions planning is health focused (for example, Suris and Akre 2015; Campbell et al 2016; Kerr et al 2020) but there is a growing database of literature about transitions planning for young people leaving care services (for example, Butterworth et al

2017; Munro and Simkiss 2020). However, safeguarding issues are not highlighted in these discussions about transitions, again indicating that service transfer/transition is not the same as Transitional Safeguarding.

Care Quality Commission review

In 2014 the Care Quality Commission (CQC) undertook a piece of work to examine transitions planning and processes for young people likely to need health and social care support after turning 18; they found a significant shortfall between different policies and the realities of practice (Care Quality Commission 2014). Their findings included: that the process of transition was not clear or well understood by young people, their families, or carers (p 18); nor by some professionals delivering the care (p 18); guidance and protocols for transition were often in place but were not always being used; and some professionals were unaware of their existence (p 18). In terms of the system, it was often fragmented and parents and young people reported having to tell their story repeatedly to numerous professionals across health and social care (p 18). The process of transition had rarely begun in accordance with guidance at age 14 (p 18) and planning often started late, which sometimes delayed decisions and caused gaps in care (p 30). There were often no transition plans at all; where they did exist, they were of variable quality (p 30). Some young people were left without equipment, services, or respite during transition because of a failure to agree funding responsibilities (p 26). Health assessments were often out of date and there was a lack of a regular review (p 30). There were many examples where support plans did not include young people's wishes and views (p 34) and records of capacity to make decisions were generally very poor (p 34). There was generally a lack of coordination across children's and adult health services with regard to planning for the future. Health professionals in adult services were not routinely involved in planning transition to adult services, they only became involved after age 18 (p 42).

The CQC concluded that, 'there is a general lack of provision for, and knowledge of, the specific needs of the young adulthood developmental phase. This is worse for young people with complex health needs' (Care Quality Commission 2014, p 66). While more services are recognising the needs of young people as they move into adulthood as a distinct part of the life course, there are gaps, as illustrated by the CQC critique. This is happening despite the existence of a robust legislative and policy framework that sets out duties and responsibilities for agencies and professionals working with young people.

There is also a gap in most transitions planning documents and guidance identifying safeguarding issues. In the CQC review, safeguarding is referenced in respect of personal health budgets and the agencies' responsibilities to conduct or organise DBS checks on staff (Care Quality Commission 2014, p 28). Another point was raised about consent and mental capacity issues:

> Staff in acute hospital trusts told us that basic training in the Mental Capacity Act was included in training on safeguarding, but it was clear that there were gaps in their knowledge. This created a lack of confidence on a practical level in decision making and best interest processes as the young people moved into adulthood. However, although patchy, where we did see recording of consent between ages 14 and 18, this was generally undertaken by adult health professionals rather than other professionals. (Care Quality Commission 2014, p 38)

Mental capacity

Mental capacity relates to a young person's ability to make a specific decision, not just a generic statement about decision-making potential. The Mental Capacity Act 2005 applies to 16-years-olds, however some practitioners working with children may not be aware of this. As such, young people over 16 years old do have mental capacity unless assessed otherwise and can make 'bad' or 'unwise' decisions. Some practitioners can over-rely on this to then consider that young people have made 'lifestyle choices' when they may be actually facing harm or experiencing abuse, including exploitation. Applying an understanding of executive mental capacity and how adverse childhood experiences, trauma, and 'enmeshed' situations can affect decision making, including making 'unwise' decisions, is essential when considering need for protection alongside upholding their rights. There is a danger of 'victim blaming' here, in terms of making 'poor' or 'risky' choices. NICE guidance (National Institute for Health and Care Excellence 2018) advises assessments should take into account observations of the person's ability to execute decisions in real life situations, highlighting the situational aspect of decision making. Where there is evidence that, outside of an assessment environment, the person is not able to understand or weigh up information to enact a decision, this should be thoroughly explored. The presumption of capacity under section 1 of the MCA does not override professional and statutory duties to ensure that young people or adults with care and support needs are safe from abuse, neglect, or exploitation. 'There is a difference between someone who has an appreciation of risk and yet goes on to take the risk – albeit unwisely – and someone who … lacked awareness of the risk and sufficient problem-solving ability'.[8]

Capacity can also change over time, or depending on different circumstances (for example, when under the influence of substances). Where young people are approaching 18, mental capacity assessments may need to be carried out before the young person turns 18 to assess whether they have the capacity to choose where to live and in what type of accommodation, carry out key life skills independently, and recognise and take steps to mitigate risks.

Transitions and safeguarding prevention

This section provides two examples that explore the intersections between transitions and Transitional Safeguarding and how two different local authorities have responded to the needs of their local community to develop services for young people. The information is taken from two articles included in a special issue about Transitional Safeguarding.[9] The first example illustrates how a service was developed to undertake transition planning and support young people through this, which could address their safeguarding needs appropriately. The second example shows how recommendations from a SAR led to the establishment of a multi-agency resource for care-experienced young people, co-produced with young people and a transitions panel which provides ongoing oversight of transition planning.

Norfolk Preparing for Adult Life (PfAL) service

The PfAL service in Norfolk County Council is funded by both children's services and adult social services (ASSD), led by the latter and working with young people from age 14 to 25 years. It is designed to support young people moving from children's to adults' services. In 2017 Norfolk Council commissioned a review of its existing transitions services, which resulted in establishing the PfAL service. The council used the NICE guidance (National Institute for Health and Care Excellence 2016) to benchmark their services. Common themes identified in the review included an inconsistent transition experience for young people, with a lack of support and uncertainty about the process of preparing for adulthood, echoing the CQC findings described earlier. Johnson and Avery note that the existing system:

> was based on those individuals who had special educational needs (SEN), those with an EHCP, and other pathway plans for looked after children and in health (Department for Education and Department of Health (Department for Education and Department of Health 2015; National Institute for Health and Care Excellence 2016). This system helped identify some categories of young people who were likely to need support from ASSD but did not include information in relation to young people likely to need support as adults from a Mental Health (MH) team, with an additional issue identified around the lack of information sharing from MH services for people under 18. Some of these individuals were not known to children's services, and in some cases were being supported out of county in a residential school and had complex needs and vulnerabilities that demanded an earlier Transitional Safeguarding approach. As a result, ASSD led on making links with the MH Trust and children's services as part of establishing an improved information sharing protocol around transition. It was also agreed that the PfAL service would include support for individuals with MH needs, to provide a

> more inclusive approach and extend the range of safeguarding oversight around transition. (Johnson and Avery 2022, p 53)

In terms of managing safeguarding concerns and issues and promoting greater inter-agency cooperation, adults' services provided 'Better Working Together' workforce development sessions. These clarified professionals' roles and responsibilities across children's services, education, adults' social services, health services, and the voluntary and community sector. PfAL adopted the 'MSP' approach as part of transition planning, with the focus on promoting well-being and empowering the young person to have 'choice and control' and be at the centre of the decision-making process from the start (Department of Health and Social Care 2023, s.14.15). As a service, PfAL ensures that safeguarding goals are understood by all; 'the emphasis on supporting young people in transition should be on "preparing" them rather than just keeping people "safe" '. (Johnson and Avery 2022, p 56)

Emerging impact

In its first 18 months, the PfAL service supported 493 young people, with over 225 of these identified as 'new referrals' and not previously predicted as likely to need transition support, demonstrating the visibility and accessibility of the new service. Of these referrals, 398 people received an assessment, with 60 per cent of young people having a Care Act assessment and care and support plan agreed before they reached 17.5 years. Initially, the team prioritised support for individuals who were already 17 but extended their services to support people from 14 years to ensure the transition assessment is completed at the point of most significant benefit to the young person.

> As a centrally managed team, there has been greater oversight of safeguarding concerns and management in partnership working with relevant teams as part of providing a shared approach in managing the safety of individuals and identified benefit of an ASSD led risk assessment practice. (Johnson and Avery 2022, p 57)

Havering Cocoon service for care-experienced young people

In 2017 the London Borough of Havering (LBH) published a Safeguarding Adult Review concerning a care-experienced young adult, Ms A, who was receiving leaving care services at the time of her death at the age of 20 (Preston-Shoot 2017). One of the recommendations was for the council to develop and strengthen services for young people in transition from children's services into adulthood, particularly care-experienced young people. This required children's and adult social care services to work closely together. Following a successful funding bid to the Department for Education, LBH made significant investment in its transition services, co-producing these with young adults themselves in conjunction with a mental health charity. This work resulted in the creation of the Cocoon, a new 'one-stop shop' onsite multi-agency service provision for care-experienced young people, and the transitions panel, a new multi-agency planning forum (Wallace and Cocker 2022, pp 61–62).

The Cocoon is a hub for specialist multi-agency services to be provided to care-experienced young people, creating opportunities for them to meet with key workers and progress their personal development. Agencies involved in operational delivery include children's services, housing, police, mental health services, and the Department for Work and Pensions (Wallace and Cocker 2022, p 62). The development of the Cocoon involved co-production with care-experienced young people who named the space, created the branding, designed the layout of the premises, and led on planning decisions. A Youth Management Board meets monthly to discuss and plan young people's input into areas such as policy and group-based activity (Bostock et al 2020, p 35). This has influenced a style of professional practice at the Cocoon that involves 'a commitment to co-produce pathway plans with young people based on mutually agreed goals and co-created solutions' (Bostock et al 2020, p 22; Wallace and Cocker 2022, p 63).

The monthly transitions panel is an ongoing collaboration with multi-agency engagement, discussion, and planning aiming 'to improve the shared responsibility, joint working and collaborative practice' required to deliver effective transitions services' (Dooley 2019, p 1, cited in Wallace and

Cocker 2022, p 64). Benefits from the transitions panel include improved cross-agency communication and joined-up thinking. Benefits for young people include reduced evictions (Dooley 2019, p 8, cited in Wallace and Cocker 2022, p 65).

Emerging impact

In terms of safeguarding issues for care-experienced young people, the Havering approach has been preventative, addressing a range of needs that they may have and aiming to improve a range of outcomes.

> the developments in Havering can be considered as contributing to preventing safeguarding risks through addressing a range of needs of care-experienced young people. These are a key group who may have a range of general safeguarding needs, due to their experiences of care and the reasons why they have been in care, compared to other people of the same age and can therefore fall through the 'safeguarding gap' when leaving care services are provided (Holmes and Smale 2018). However, many care-experienced young people may not have needs that are eligible for care and support under the Care Act, and as a consequence not be able to access ASC safeguarding services under section 42(2) of the Act. (Department of Health and Social Care 2020)
>
> Local Authorities do have broader powers regarding prevention of safeguarding risks, however a lack of resources and capacity can affect the ability of local authorities to respond to young people's safeguarding needs. Recommendations from the Ms A SAR highlight the issue of young people appearing not to meet thresholds, suggesting a broader and more flexible approach to interpreting the Care Act and safeguarding adult duties that does not focus solely on eligibility criteria. (Wallace and Cocker 2022, pp 66–67)

Conclusion

As Transitional Safeguarding is a relatively recent approach, many of the guidance and policy documents pertaining to transitions planning do not specifically mention Transitional Safeguarding. More fundamentally, the guidance and policy documents adhere to the eligibility-led construct of transitional support; they focus on improving service transfer for those young people who will qualify for services post-18. This is different to the needs-led/person-specific of a Transitional Safeguarding approach. Although they may reference safeguarding, they do not specifically refer to safeguarding challenges and issues or understand these within a developmental or relational context. A Transitional Safeguarding approach should be incorporated into transitions planning work when young people are moving between services as they reach 18. Unfortunately, safeguarding risks for these young people are sometimes not managed effectively; they are often not recognised or are misinterpreted as young people making capacitous but 'unwise' decisions. Cross-geographical border issues about who takes responsibility for what can also be barriers to supporting young people to keep themselves safe.

There are examples of poor transitions planning and critical failures in safeguarding in various Safeguarding Adult Reviews (SARs) that have been written about young people, many of whom have SEND, mental health, learning disabilities and autism, and experience of care. The two SARs cited in this chapter illustrate how young people can fall through the cracks. The examples from two local authorities show how they have responded to Transitional Safeguarding challenges in their areas and developed different services. Chapter 9 provides more examples of local initiatives to improve transitions work as part of whole systems Transitional Safeguarding transformations. Each local area will know the needs of their young people, consider most service redesign options, and understand pressures on capacity and resources. Regardless, there is compelling evidence that better use needs to be made of the guidance already in place to improve transitions work with young people, and this can help address their safeguarding needs.

8

Learning from Safeguarding Adult Reviews, Serious Case Reviews, and Child Safeguarding Practice Reviews about care-experienced young people

Content warning: this chapter reports general findings from cases where young people have died from abuse and neglect.

Introduction

Although Transitional Safeguarding seeks to highlight the needs of all young people, including those for whom there are no service entitlements post-18, there are particular groups of young people whose very specific needs warrant close examination. Care-experienced young people are one such group where the state has duties, powers, and obligations after they turn 18. There is a considerable documented history which shows how these young people are failed by the support offered to them (for example, Stein 2004, 2006b). As part of our work on Transitional Safeguarding, we examined 59 Serious Case Reviews (SCRs), now called Child Safeguarding Practice Reviews (CSPRs), and Safeguarding Adult Reviews (SARs) that were written in England following the death or serious injury of care-experienced young people aged between 15 and 25. This chapter presents the rationale for this work, outlines the framework used to analyse the data and discusses the themes identified from these reviews.[1] The learning from these individual reviews highlights where practice and systems need to change. Some of these themes may also apply to other young people with safeguarding needs who are not care-experienced and further research would evidence the similarities and differences.

Rationale for work

In Chapter 3 we referred to the way in which public inquiries, SCRs, and SARs have influenced public policy around safeguarding in England over the past 50 years. This effect continues with the publication of a report investigating the deaths of Star Robson and Arthur Labinjo-Hughes (Child Safeguarding Practice Review Panel 2022) who were both killed by caregivers during the COVID-19 pandemic lockdowns in the UK in 2020. Both children were young and not in care and the report recommended a fundamental change in safeguarding systems for children. There is useful learning from specific cases where things have gone wrong, but there are limitations of this approach being the major factor to influence system change. During the COVID-19 lockdowns a number of teenagers and young people also died; some at the hands of their parents and carers, such as Sebastian Kalinowski (Vinter 2022). Other young people have died for different reasons, including knife crime and so-called gang-associated activity (Wright 2021). A number of national reports about adolescents and extra-familial harm have also been published over recent years, including criminal exploitation and sexual exploitation (Child Safeguarding Practice Review Panel 2020; Joint Targeted Area inspection 2016, 2018; Commission on Young Lives 2022), with a number of government policies published as a result.[2]

In addition, the prevalence rates of young people with serious mental health problems continues to rise. The most recent survey of young people and mental health showed that 22 per cent of young people aged 17 to 24 years had a probable mental disorder. In young people aged 17 to 19 years, rates of a probable mental disorder rose from 1 in 10 (10 per cent) in 2017 to 1 in 6 (16.7 per cent) in 2020. Rates were stable between 2020 and 2021, but then increased from 1 in 6 (16.7 per cent) in 2021 to 1 in 4 (25 per cent) in 2022 (NHS Digital 2022b). This rise is concerning, particularly given the difficulties of Child and Adolescent Mental

Health Services (CAMHS) and adult mental health services in meeting the needs of those young people referred for help and support (Children's Commissioner 2023; Health and Social Care Committee 2021).

Why have we focused on reviews regarding care-experienced young people? As a group they have experienced considerable adversity in their lives. While the care population is heterogeneous and each child and young person is unique, outcome statistics over many years show that there is an ongoing gap in their attainment and achievement in education and employment compared with other young people. The author of the latest independent children's care review examining children's social care in England commented that, 'the disadvantage faced by the care-experienced community should be the civil rights issue of our time' (Independent Review of Children's Social Care 2022, p 10).

The state is heavily involved in the lives of this group of young people and significant financial resources are invested in their care. Improvement in the care system is needed, however improvement requires political commitment, financial investment, and market control as these affect what is possible to deliver in practice. Various researchers have responded to critiques of the care system as an abject failure as simplistic (Stein 2006b) and research studies examining outcomes do not always take into account pre-care experiences or acknowledge the positive impact care can have for some children and young people (Forrester et al 2009; Sebba et al 2015). Care can offer children and young people access to resources in education (Sebba et al 2015) and mental health support (Luke et al 2014). General outcomes can be better when comparing children in care to a similar demographic of children in need but not in care (Forrester et al 2009).

Although legally adults at 18, for many care-experienced young people, their earlier adversities can affect the way in which they approach adulthood and are supported through it. Specifically, they can experience the worst of both worlds: they are not given the support that other 18-year-olds can usually expect from their families. Independence can begin as early as 16 with young people being moved into supported accommodation that will not be regulated until at least October 2023 (Department for Education, 2023). However, these young people are also simultaneously subject to professional scrutiny in ways that curtails their freedom to make unwise decisions.

Concerns about the state's support of care-experienced young people are not new, despite a comprehensive legislative and policy agenda developed over the past 40 years to support them (Preston-Shoot and Cocker forthcoming; Stein 2004, 2006b). Leaving care at 18 has always been known as a 'crunch point' where young people who require additional support are forced to leave care too soon (Ofsted 2022). The legal requirement for local authorities to provide support to care-experienced young people after leaving care at 18 years up to the age of 25 has meant that care-experienced young people have contact with personal advisers and some financial support. Examining the service provision for the small number of care-experienced young people where things had gone tragically wrong or died aimed to identify whether there were any Transitional Safeguarding issues that were addressed or not met by the range of services with statutory responsibilities to support them.

Transitional Safeguarding framework for SAR analysis

For many years the Department for Education has conducted regular biennial and latterly triennial reviews of SCRs and CSPRs (Brandon et al 2008, 2009, 2010, 2012, 2020; Dickens et al 2022; Sidebotham et al 2016), whereas the first national review of SARs 2017–19 was published in 2020 (Preston-Shoot et al 2020). There are thematic reviews of SARs, for example on adults with learning disabilities (referred to as SCRs (Manthorpe and Martineau 2015)), self-neglect (Braye et al 2015; Preston-Shoot 2021), homelessness (Martineau and Manthorpe 2020), care homes (Manthorpe and Martineau 2017); dementia care (Manthorpe and Martineau 2016), and a review was completed of a sample of SCRs involving adults (Manthorpe and Martineau 2011). These reviews identify key themes and lessons for practice, but the vital issue is how sustainable change is enabled through implementing the recommendations from these reviews. Similar themes arise, indicating the complexity of the problems at a practice, organisational, multi-agency, and strategic level.

In their analysis of studies of SCRs, Brandon and colleagues used a whole system model (Brandon et al 2011). This model was also used in the national SAR analysis (Preston-Shoot et al 2020). Teenagers are mentioned in a number of the biennial and triennial SCR analyses (Research in Practice 2020). Drawing on specific learning for this group of young people has been helpful in identifying specific knowledge for how and why safeguarding practices should work differently with young people. Their developmental needs cannot be ignored. Neither can their context (Firmin 2020). In making a case for Transitional Safeguarding, Holmes (2022a) provided an examination of literature from adolescent development studies, health research, youth justice research, sociology, and social work research. The work of Holmes and others has then been used to develop a framework for analysing practice where SARs concern young adults (Preston-Shoot et al 2022). It uses the same domain framework found in the many thematic adult safeguarding reviews and the national analyses of children and adult reviews (Preston-Shoot 2019; Preston-Shoot et al 2020).

The whole systems model has been applied to develop an evidence base from the existing literature to describe what constitutes evidence-informed practice in relation to Transitional Safeguarding. This was done so that, when undertaking a SAR, the author could use this information in their analysis to explore what facilitated good practice and to identify the barriers or obstacles that led to practice shortfalls. The features of evidence-informed Transitional Safeguarding practice in each of the four domains is described in detail later.

The model was first used by Braye, Orr and Preston-Shoot (2015) in their analysis of SARs featuring self-neglect and was also used in the first national analysis of Safeguarding Adult Reviews 2017–2019 (Preston-Shoot et al 2020). That approach was itself modified from a framework used in thematic reviews commissioned by the Department for Education (Brandon et al 2011).

The first domain of the four stages of the whole systems model is 'the evidence base for direct practice with the young person'. Good practice features an orientation towards the young person within their lived reality; their context and history are important,

Figure 8.1: The whole systems model

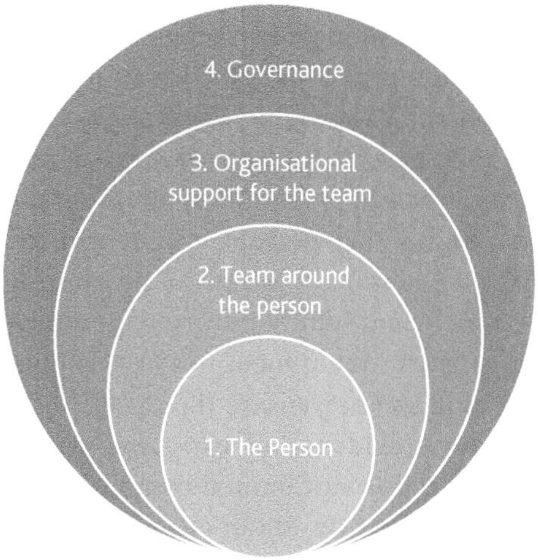

Key:

Domain 1: Direct practice with the young person

Domain 2: The team around the young person

Domain 3: Organisational support for the team working with the young person

Domain 4: Governance

as is understanding where they are within the developmental boundaries of their stage of development, recognising that there are tensions within the socio-legal framework that governs practice but seeks to overcome these (Cocker et al 2021). Practice with the young person should be personalised, relational and participative, tenacious and curious, needs-led, person-centred, and rights-based: all aspects of their situation are taken into account in the safeguarding process, including structural inequalities (Preston-Shoot et al 2022, pp 92–93). Practice should be trauma-informed, strengths-based, and outcomes focused, aimed at promoting safety and well-being (Holmes and Smale 2018) in order to promote prevention, protection, and recovery. The approach should be holistic, working with the whole person, not just defining a young person in relation to their needs and eligibility criteria. Other factors relevant to good practice with young people include: recognising (in)equalities and their impact, including unconscious bias in practitioners; identifying exploitation and challenging assumptions about lifestyle choices (Holmes and Smale 2018); and acknowledging the importance of mental capacity, and practitioners demonstrating a legally literate understanding of the Mental Capacity Act 2005 (Preston-Shoot et al 2020). Assessment and planning are important here; they must be timely and fulfil statutory requirements. Assessments of care and support should focus not just on eligible needs but also on well-being and prevention (Preston-Shoot et al 2022). Good practice shows evidence of early and proportionate planning (Holmström 2020), not limited by a focus on eligibility criteria and thresholds (Preston-Shoot et al 2020). Finally, it is important that services are meeting needs; there is wrap-around support aimed at meeting needs and also enhancing physical and mental well-being and supporting young adults into training and/or employment. Options are offered and considered, with adherence to the young person's preferences unless contraindicated (Preston-Shoot et al 2022).

The second domain is, 'the evidence base for the team around the person'. This domain looks at how the team of professionals work with each other to support the young person. Agencies working together across service and geographical boundaries should offer an integrated system of planning and support; given the interconnected nature of harms and risks, working in siloes is unhelpful (Holmes and Smale 2018). Information sharing is vital; there should be early and proportionate sharing of information about risk and the range and level of support required (Holmström 2020). Legal literacy, safeguarding literacy, and knowledge are robust, with less focus on eligibility and more on preventative work and well-being. Advice and support should be sought to address the inconsistencies in age in the legal, policy, and service frameworks regarding young people's transitions to adult services (Cocker et al 2021). Good practice is characterised by the use of multi-agency, and/or multi-disciplinary meetings to share information, identify needs and risks, and agree a coordinated plan, with a lead agency and key worker clearly identified and a recording of decision making (Preston-Shoot et al 2020). This includes clear recording of the reasons for decisions, including mental capacity assessments and best interest decisions (Holmström 2020).

The third domain is 'the evidence base for organisational support for the team members'. This domain examines the support available for the team of people working with the young person, including policies and procedures (Preston-Shoot et al 2020) and practice guidance in relation to Transitional Safeguarding (OCSWA/RiP 2021) and supervision. Practitioners should be offered reflective, trauma-informed supervision, to enable them to manage the emotional impact of the work and explore any unconscious bias. Supervision enables practitioners to maintain a person-centred approach in complex cases where a young person's engagement may be ambivalent (Preston-Shoot et al 2020). Training should be available to practitioners and managers to develop their knowledge and skills of Transitional Safeguarding. This includes understanding the developmental needs of young people, proportionate risk taking, legal literacy, mental capacity, trauma-informed practice, and development of skills of professional curiosity and enquiry into young people's lived experiences (Preston-Shoot et al 2020). It may also be necessary for practitioners and managers across services to have access to specialist advice and guidance, for instance from lawyers and mental capacity and mental health specialists (Holmström 2020). One of the important, yet undervalued activities that supports good practice in this area is co-production, involving young people in co-designing relevant services (Wallace and Cocker 2022). Commissioning the right services for young people by health, housing, and social care jointly is also vital; services that are not bound by rigid age-determined boundaries and offer flexible support. Regular needs analyses and reviews of available services will identify any gaps in provision, ensuring that planning is responsive and evidence-informed (Preston-Shoot et al 2020, 2022).

The Transitional Safeguarding approach requires whole systems change (see Chapter 10) and senior managers have an important role in demonstrating leadership that spans boundaries, setting a clear vision across different service areas (Cocker et al 2022a).

Staff also require support to encourage the development of relationship-based practice as it is a key principle of Transitional Safeguarding (Holmes and Smale 2018).

The fourth domain is 'the evidence base on governance'. SABs work closely with Community Safety Partnerships and Children's Safeguarding Partnerships (CSP). These are important strategically and have a role to play in the development of Transitional Safeguarding policy and practice locally. Good practice includes quality assurance mechanisms, such as case audits of transitional arrangements to identify areas for learning and improvement (Holmes and Smale 2018). Taking forward recommendations and learning from SARs and CSPRs involving young people provides local systems with road maps for improvement, and monitoring the impact of these provides assurance.

There is a further fifth domain: 'National legal, policy, and practice issues'. SAR authors may identify national legal frameworks, policy areas, and financial contexts that create barriers or obstacles for safeguarding young people. These may appear as common threads across a number of reviews. There is now a process by which SABs can escalate concerns about the impact of this national context to the Department of Health and Social Care, Ministry of Justice, Home Office, and DWP, as appropriate, through the national network of Safeguarding Adults Boards (SABs) Chairs.

The evidence that falls into the domains provides key features of good practice. Taken together, this becomes a framework for analysis which then invites a further set of questions regarding the conditions for practice: 'what has enabled best practice, where this is identified and what have been the obstacles or barriers to best practice, where these are also found?' (Preston-Shoot et al 2022, p 92). Preston-Shoot et al (2022) then apply this to inform the structure and content of SARs about particular young people, each of whom will have experienced a unique set of circumstances. This framework can also be used to interrogate practice with young people who are not the subject of SARs, as it sets out the current body of research that underpins Transitional Safeguarding practice.

The next section provides an overview of the key themes that emerged from the analysis of 59 reviews about care-experienced young people. In order to ensure anonymity, direct quotes have not been referenced to specific reviews as some of the reviews were not published and were shared with the review team on the basis that they would remain confidential.

Themes from the analysis of reviews involving care-experienced young people

There were common features regarding young people's experiences of services. Too many young people did not have a comprehensive plan for when they turned 18, including where they would be living and what services would be supporting them. For example, the 'rush' to semi-independent living did not take into account M's history and ability. A was 'catapulted into adulthood and adult services, where she was expected to have responsibility for herself and her behaviour without any preparation or support.' Therefore, there was an emphasis in the reviews' recommendations on the importance of early planning and preparation for transitions and independence.

In relation to transitions planning, referrals were often sent through to adult mental health and adult social care services late, which meant that transition funding issues for many of these young people were not identified and resolved in a timely manner. Often children's services continued to fund placements after a young person turned 18 while these issues were resolved. For Y, the movement from child mental health services to adult mental health services showed no sign of pre-planning or awareness of Y's earlier experiences. Many reviews commented on a lack of pathway planning. Sometimes this meant the young person had to move back home. D's review discusses how lack of pathway planning with his family meant that D's birth mother was uninformed how to cope when he moved back into the household. Assessments were also noted to be poor in many cases. For example, the SCR commented on P being treated as an 'adolescent' with all the negative connotations of that label, rather than treated as either a young person in need of support, or an adult subject to exploitation.

There was a lack of young people's voice expressed within the plans. For example, for L, the idea of transition to adult services filled her with anxiety. Better planning and taking L's views into consideration could have assuaged her anxiety. A was another young person who had a lot of worries about turning 18 and what would happen to them.

Young people's risks and vulnerabilities were not recognised, particularly when involved in exploitation. Young people were treated as an 'offender' and criminalised rather than as a 'victim' and worked with under a safeguarding umbrella. This was particularly the case for young people over 18 years old. An example of this is young person I; not enough priority was given to safeguarding issues and the primary focus was on his criminal activity.

For young people with complex needs, many different professionals and services were involved in their lives. These added layers of complications, particularly when professionals did not talk to each other, share information, or respond appropriately to the young person. For one 19-year-old who murdered another young person, one of the primary failures identified was the failure to keep adequate and full records of prior behaviour and the sharing of these records and information with other agencies, including the police. This was even more pronounced when young people were placed out of area and services were working across country or service borders. This complicated how support was provided to young people with complex needs and where there were safeguarding concerns and disclosures. For example, Q (age 16 when he died) moved regularly between different local authorities. Effective transfer of records and information would have enabled authorities to react quickly to Q's challenging behaviour. Child C moved between geographical areas, and when he returned to his originating borough he could not access CAMHS because he was over the age of 16. This cut-off point did not reflect his needs, only his age.

We know from other studies that frequent changes of staff working with young people, changes in services that occur around 18, and changes in placements are problematic (Preston-Shoot et al 2020). This must be recognised and addressed to ensure that the system and services are focused on the young person (Munro 2011). Further, professionals generally focused on individual crises rather than considering underlying causes or reasons for behaviours. This meant staff were firefighting, moving from one crisis (for example, a placement breakdown or a further missing episode) to another; M had 12 placement moves in six months. Holmes and Smale

(2018) argue that this is not the best time for services to cease or providers to change. In addition, inequalities issues also impacted on young people's experiences of services. Adultification was an issue identified by the review about how the police treated young person I (mentioned earlier). He was viewed as an adult rather than as a young person supported by care services.

One other problem was that when responding to young people in a time of crisis, procedures were not always followed, particularly with 'missing' episodes, which meant that young people were not kept safe from harm. M (mentioned earlier) had 66 referrals to police over a six-month period because of 'missing' episodes. Another young person, Q, frequently came to the notice of the police through numerous missing episodes and their behaviours led to frequent moves from one carer to another. During the latter period, incidents were noted almost on a weekly basis which resulted in agencies responding to the presenting issue and they were not able to address one incident before another was highlighted. D was involved in several police investigations including alleged stabbings, drug possession, and criminal damage and was listed in police records at various times as being 'wanted' and a 'person of interest', rather than as a missing care-experienced child.

There was often a lack of understanding about complex safeguarding needs, which were perceived as 'lifestyle choices' (for example, substance misuse, alcohol misuse, CCE, CSE). For example, the day before C's death, they were found collapsed on a train having consumed alcohol and prescription drugs. They were taken to A&E but was discharged from the hospital later that day. C then visited a friend's house, drank two small bottles of vodka, and was found at 2am in bed and unresponsive.

In addition, safeguarding problems at transition points also meant that services were not always responsive, particularly between children and adult local authority services and CAMHS and adult mental health services. One SAR recommended that 'Children's Social Care and Adults Social care should develop protocols together to address the safeguarding needs of young people aged 18 or over who are assessed as vulnerable or at risk, particularly at transition and specifically for care leavers and ensure that social work staff have a clear escalation process if there are disagreements between children's and adults' services about safeguarding young people and adults' (Vinall, 2020, p34). Having escalation policies within agencies and between agencies that are effective was a recommendation made in many of the reviews.

Poor legal literacy was reported in reviews as a major problem, with practitioners in children's services not always cognisant of mental health and mental capacity legislation; this affected social workers' and personal advisers' ability to advocate for young people, particularly after CAMHS involvement ceased and young people were referred to adult mental health services.

Some SABs had undertaken more than one SAR about Transitional Safeguarding between 2014 and 2021. Individual reviews picked up some trends about Transitional Safeguarding and made specific reference to national issues in their report. For example, 'There are strong parallels between J's case and the case of S in respect of the challenges in providing effective transition pathways, which are reflected in many SARs nationally, and it is important to consider why these problems continue to arise to enable real changes to be made to systems to prevent future tragedy'(Williams 2020, p 9).

Discussion

Almost all of the 59 reviews mentioned 'transitions planning' or 'transition between services', but this is not the same as Transitional Safeguarding (see Chapter 7 where this is explored further). Planning for transition for care-experienced young people before age 18 involves education, housing, employment, and health. It also involves transitions between services delineated by age, for example social services and mental health services. For an individual young person, there are contextual aspects of their life that may be protective or contribute to the risks they experience, for example, homelessness, substance misuse, and mental illness. Transitional Safeguarding focusses on these risks of harm and abuse and this is different to transitions planning, although there may be links between them.

Many of the situations that young people faced were complex. Camillus (2008) uses the term 'wicked problem' or 'wicked issue' to describe such circumstances. These occur when organisations face constant change or unprecedented challenges. Such problems thrive within a context of organisational or multi-agency disagreement. Confusion, discord, and a lack of progress are the all-too-common signs of a 'wicked' issue. Transitional Safeguarding is one such issue. However, there are no easy answers with wicked issues. If there were easy answers, the questions raised about Transitional Safeguarding and the gaps in provision for young people would no longer be relevant.

In Chapter 2 we examined the six key principles underpinning Transitional Safeguarding (Holmes 2018). These are used now to discuss the results from the study of the 59 reviews.

Contextual/ecological

Any assessment should include the context in which a young person experiences harm or abuse, be personalised, and consider the issues important to them (Cocker et al 2021) otherwise the accuracy of any assessment is limited. It should include their history, important relationships with family members, friends, and significant others within their local community (youth groups, school, other professionals) (Preston-Shoot et al 2022). Given the shortcomings identified in many of the reviews about assessments, particularly when young people were placed out of area, there is room for improvement. Geographical location can add complexities and delays around referral systems and processes, meaning young person's needs are not addressed quickly.

The other contextual factor often reported in the reviews was that adult services staff (in the main but not exclusively) failed to take into account the young person's adverse childhood experiences and the long-term impact of adversity, poverty and abuse, and other negative experiences on their ability to adapt and grow into adulthood. Keeping a person at the centre of their care planning is a central tenet in adult social care, including safeguarding (Cocker et al 2021) and so supporting the workforce to develop skills, knowledge, and confidence in working with young people who have experienced adversity and have Transitional Safeguarding needs is important. This requires working across agency boundaries and age boundaries and staff sharing skills and knowledge. Using a 'risk enablement' approach is important in terms of understanding someone's strengths and protective factors, but this should not be done without understanding ongoing risks as well.

A key aspect of Contextual Safeguarding (and of this principle) is that it requires an expansive understanding of partnership as the goal is to create safer spaces/places/contexts and not just focus on the individual and their 'choices'. Firmin (2020) provides a number of excellent examples of how this works in practice, involving staff from fast food restaurants and from local authority parks service in safeguarding planning. This type of contextual activity should not be limited to safeguarding young people under 18. In a further example, Calderdale included community safety wardens in Halifax town centre, the security guard at Sainsbury's, and the manager of McDonald's in a SAR about homeless men (Cullen 2020).

Transitional/Developmental

In terms of transitions planning, the age of the young person was seen as the most important factor affecting the services they received and their eligibility for services changed according to their age rather than needs. However, we know that 'harm and the effects of harm do not stop at age 18. Therefore, the response to harm, taking into account adolescent development and the external risks that young people can experience, means that safeguarding services need to be fluid across arbitrary boundaries, such as age,' (Cocker et al 2022a, p 1291).

Holmes (2022a) notes research that suggests adolescence usually involves young people experiencing an increasing sense of independence and autonomy. Taking a 'developmentally-attuned response' (Holmes 2022a, p 11) acknowledges the ongoing impact of trauma, something which was often missing in the approaches taken by professionals when working with young people in this study. Terms like 'TIAs' (trauma-informed approaches) or 'relationship-based approaches' can be overused in practice, and not understood in the depth required in order that practice can be truly transformational (Asmussen et al 2022). Often the reviews noted that multiple protective interventions were focused around addressing a young person's behaviour, but these were not understood within a context of the young person struggling with being an adolescent or young adult alongside experiencing other traumatic events. Ensuring that young people have a sense of choice and agency is a developmentally appropriate response (Holmes 2022a), however when practitioners are solely focused on the risks and consequences of behaviour rather than understanding the developmental impact of living with heightened anxiety and violence, practice can become limited to addressing behaviours. It was evident from the reviews that practitioners sometimes did not understand and address the young person's needs and behaviours within a developmental context. This may mean their practice was constrained to an individualistic approach, due to the way services had been designed and the way thresholds/criteria were applied locally.

Relational

A relational and person-centred approach is critical to working with young people; relationships are central. Howe (2005) believes that 'if relationships are where things developmentally can go wrong, then relationships are where they are most likely to be put right' (p 278). It is essential that any work also recognises the ongoing impact of trauma on a young person (Lefevre et al 2017), and that organisational practices allow for this focus on relationships, particularly where changes in social worker or support worker may have a disproportionate effect on a young person. The issue for practice is how relationships can be put first within systems so that there is a continuation of the strongest relationship with the person who knows the young person the best throughout their transition to adulthood. The leaving care system is geared towards having one personal adviser who helps young people work with different people responsible for separate parts. This begins with pathway planning in most local authorities at age 16, at the very time that most young people are moving from secondary school to sixth form or college, and in the midst of school exams. Once a young person turns 18 then they are seen as responsible enough to manage relationships with professionals independently. Many young people manage this with support, but some young people are not able to engage the support they need at this age. There are many reasons why this might be the case, for example, because they are being coerced, or are experiencing a mental health crisis. Being left to manage these relationships only works for those who are generally safe and does not work for those who are unsafe. Some of these issues are explored further in Chapter 1.

There were gaps identified by the reviews in relational practice management throughout the organisational systems. Systems can be a source of stress and dysfunction too. At the practice level repeated mention was made in the reviews of high staff turnover and poor supervisory practices that did not allow for reflection. Where there were problems and issues (and there always will be problems that need airing and resolving within professional networks), the escalation processes which should be in place to unlock blocks at strategic levels within and between agencies were not working effectively. Chapter 2 described how relational working has to be modelled at the leadership level in inter-agency partnerships. If organisational relationships begin to mirror problems in practice relationships, then there is an increased likelihood that communication throughout organisations will be affected, as will leadership, management approaches, and cultures within organisations (Hafford-Letchfield et al 2014). Practice then becomes focused on outputs and outcomes rather than processes that concentrate on keeping a young person at the centre of any intervention.

Participative

Young people's participation in determining their own future is key. Too often decisions were made about young people without their involvement, or their views and wishes were not taken into consideration when drawing up care plans, particularly during transition to leaving care services and beyond. This added another source of anxiety for young people, who did not always understand their care plans. Practice responses should ideally focus on outcomes agreed with young people and be personal to that young person (Lawson 2017).

According to Kellett (2009), participation has been historically linked to ideas about promoting and understanding active citizenship (Arnstein 1969). There are many different ways in which participation is addressed by agencies in their work with young people. Hart's (1992) ladder of participation is a frequently used and widely critiqued model. There are other approaches that have built on Hart's ladder. Treseder (1997) took the top five levels from Hart's ladder and arranged them in a circle, and in-so-doing changed the power relations between each rung so they are not sequential, demonstrating instead that they are different but equal forms of good participation (Kellett 2009).

There are reasons why a professional might take the lead in safeguarding enquiries and investigations. It is entirely reasonable that a young person might not initiate their own safeguarding process; they might not see what is happening to them as being abusive. But co-production has a place, particularly in adult safeguarding, unless there are clear reasons why it cannot happen (for example, a person lacks mental capacity). Although the legal principles underpinning children's safeguarding in the Children Act 1989 include young people being involved in safeguarding processes according to their age and understanding, this is patchy. With adult safeguarding concerns and referrals, the person's consent and cooperation is almost always obtained (Cocker et al 2021). The evidence from the reviews suggests that the more complex a young person's issues are, the more likelihood the manner of working with the young person will move away from a participative approach to one which is about 'controlling risky behaviours'. In addition, there is evidence that practitioners viewed certain types of behaviours as 'choices' and so decisions made by young people were considered 'unwise' rather than being explored more deeply, particularly where there were serious mental health and drug dependency issues. This can potentially be a 'worst of both worlds' situation; simultaneously the young person is presumed to have agency and choice and at the same time denied agency and choice. Good knowledge of the Mental Health Act 1983/2007 and the Mental Capacity Act 2005 by all children and adult practitioners in health and social care agencies is essential to counter such practices.

Equalities informed

Holmes (2022a) reminds us that, 'just as harm doesn't stop at 18, neither do the structural disadvantages that can disproportionately affect certain groups of young people' (pp 13–14). Diversity data about the young people (apart from gender and age) were not available in the reviews. Authors may have been aiming to avoid identification of the young person and their family, however, this means that equalities, diversity, inclusion, and equity issues were not taken into consideration for each young person in the reviews and recommendations. This is a gap already identified in SARs that has been recommended to be addressed (Preston-Shoot 2020). Another factor that is not commented on in the reviews was how poverty and the ongoing structural disadvantage that this causes might have affected the young people who died (Lister 2021).

The effects that racism and homophobia can have on young people is well known. Black and minoritised people and LGBT+ people experience discrimination and prejudice over their life course and there is a significant cumulative effect of discrimination, stigma, and marginalisation on physical and mental ill-health (Kneale et al 2021). Meyer's minority stress model (Meyer 2003) captures the differences and tensions between the values of a minority group and the dominant culture or society and its impact. Age and gender biases and constructs also affect how young people are viewed. There were examples in the reviews of inappropriate assumptions of maturity regarding young people over 18, where vulnerabilities were not fully acknowledged, illustrated in some instances by a change in the language used to describe a young person (from 'victim' to 'perpetrator'). Some young people were not seen as vulnerable but instead as culpable. This has been further developed by Davis and Marsh (2020, p 255) who explain the term 'adultification' as, 'how preconceptions of children (specifically Black children) may lead to them being treated and perceived as being more adult-like (Goff et al 2014). If Black children are seen as less vulnerable and more adult-like, services may overlook their needs and disregard their legal rights to be protected, supported and safeguarded.' More recently the report on 'Child Q' specifically cites 'adultification' as a key factor which affected how professionals worked with her (Gamble and McCallum 2022).

Constantly checking assumptions made about young people in assessments, including our own unconscious biases, is an essential part of ensuring that equality, equity, diversity, and inclusion are prominent in the thinking and action of staff and of organisations. The debate about Child Q reminds us that structural inequalities distort perceptions of young people, and that there is a considerable deficit in multi-agency practice that needs to be addressed.

Evidence informed

Finally, taking an evidence-informed approach to working with young people with complex needs is essential. Often the term 'complex needs' is applied to young people who have a range of disabilities or health conditions. However, in the context of this study, complex needs refer to the interplay of young people having experienced some of the following: mental health problems or a diagnosis, drug and alcohol issues, multiple exclusion homelessness, criminal history/exploitation, and a history of sexual exploitation (see Introduction).

There are challenges as some of the evidence is weak about what effective working with young people with complex needs might look like, particularly with young people who have co-morbidities or multi-morbidities or issues as described;[3] and the research base regarding extra-familial harm is constantly changing (Firmin 2020). Smith et al (2013) suggest that the limited evidence for specific interventions with people who have multi-morbidities is a challenge. However, there is evidence of a link between multi-morbidities and socio-economic deprivation; people from lower social-economic backgrounds develop co and multi-morbidities 10 years before people who are more affluent (Smith et al 2013).

Highlighting one issue, mental health, we know that many young people with mental health problems (a feature in most SARs included in this study) face additional issues, and some studies report conflicting treatment outcomes for children and young people with multiple conditions (Riosa et al 2011). We need to understand this better. The rate of mental illness for care-experienced children and young people is more than four times that of those in the general population (Meltzer et al 2003). There are problems with the current systems of monitoring (missing data) and inadequate referrals into CAMHS to support care-experienced young people (Cocker et al 2018). This is an issue for mental health practitioners, social workers and other staff working with care-experienced young people. Solutions are not straightforward and require organisations to work together to address funding and thresholds for services.

Conclusion

This chapter has presented the key findings from a research study undertaken to look at Transitional Safeguarding in 59 reviews of care-experienced young people aged between 15 and 25 who have died or been seriously injured because of abuse or neglect. The majority of these reviews identified issues with 'transitions planning' or 'transition between services', but this is not the same as Transitional Safeguarding. There is a growing awareness of Transitional Safeguarding and more recent reviews did identify it as a key concern.

Many of the messages for agencies working with care-experienced young people reflect those from other studies where children and adults have died as a result of abuse and neglect. These messages include a lack of young people's views being taken into account; a lack of timely planning for young people as they approached adulthood; weak acknowledgement of the complexity of lived experience so that safeguarding needs were seen as 'lifestyle choices'; a focus on individual circumstances instead of looking at structural issues affecting young people; poor legal literacy across the system; failure of multi-agency communication – professionals not talking to each other; poor links between Child and Adolescent Mental Health and adult mental health services; and frequent changes of staff. There are multiple challenges for all practitioners and agencies in addressing practice and strategic issues to better prevent the tragedy of deaths continuing. Part III of the book now moves on to consider innovations in Transitional Safeguarding that might address these complexities.

PART III

Innovations

9

Innovations in Transitional Safeguarding

Introduction

One of the key tenets of the Transitional Safeguarding approach is that local areas use the key principles to develop their response according to local needs. We have been encouraged to see the proliferation of responses in relation to Transitional Safeguarding and the many ways in which local areas have developed their own Transitional Safeguarding workstreams. This shows how they have had to think deeply, juggling this development activity among a plethora of demands and priorities across organisations and partnerships in their own areas.

This chapter describes a range of examples from localities across England where Transitional Safeguarding is being taken forward through initiatives aiming to improve the safeguarding experience of young people. These are showcased to prompt and inspire others to consider how their local area or service might be able to do things differently, in order to ensure that young people can be and feel as safe as possible. No one area has the complete solution, and all are on a journey with this work. Some of these examples have been able to access modest funding to augment existing resources; others have reconfigured their resources. The current pressures on public sector services needs to be acknowledged; people are driving and creating change using whatever power and influence they have in their professional roles, because 'doing nothing' is not an option. They are creating solutions, working together across boundaries, and leading change with young people.

These examples provide a picture of what is emerging locally to put the principles of Transitional Safeguarding into action. The way in which change happens is a process, not a single transformative event. To try to make sense of the range of initiatives that currently exist, we have developed four typologies which help situate and understand each of the examples within the system transformation that needs to be achieved. There are common themes, blocks, and barriers as well as enablers, that come from reviewing these initiatives, which we discuss towards the end of the chapter. Chapter 10 then explores the aspirational whole systems change that Transitional Safeguarding aims to achieve; the examples in this chapter help us begin to visualise what this might look like.

Collecting examples of Transitional Safeguarding work

Using a range of networks, we approached local agencies and partnerships with a request to share with us what they were doing to take forward Transitional Safeguarding in their area. It is important to stress that the examples used in this chapter are not exhaustive. There is considerable activity being undertaken in relation to Transitional Safeguarding in many different places across England, including briefings, blogs, training sessions, and learning events. This includes publishing local seven-minute briefings (see: Norfolk Safeguarding Adults Board 2021).

We developed a pro-forma for people to use to record their activities and the information from this has been used in some of the examples in this chapter and in Chapter 7. Further relevant examples are in 'Bridging the Gap' (OCSWA/RiP 2021), the Practice journal's special issue on Transitional Safeguarding (Griffiths 2022; Johnson and Avery 2022; Wallace and Cocker 2022; Walker-McAllister and Cooper 2022) and in the NHS padlet.[1]

Typology for examples of local initiatives

The examples of the initiatives that we received have been clustered into four typologies to draw out learning from work done to date, to inform thinking about what activities might be possible locally to progress a Transitional Safeguarding approach.

Each of the examples, except one, describes activities in part of a system in a specific geographical location. One example is of work undertaken nationally in the health sector. Most examples highlight work in a specific service and some are about work across or within sectors in that area. The initiatives were developed in response to local needs and circumstances or sector requirements, so there is no universal 'model' or 'template' for development and delivery.

Figure 9.1 shows the four typologies and their inter-relationships. Typology 1 is whole systems change, referring to multiple organisations within a locality aiming to change the systems, and the interplay between systems, including culture, and

Figure 9.1: Typologies of systems reform for Transitional Safeguarding

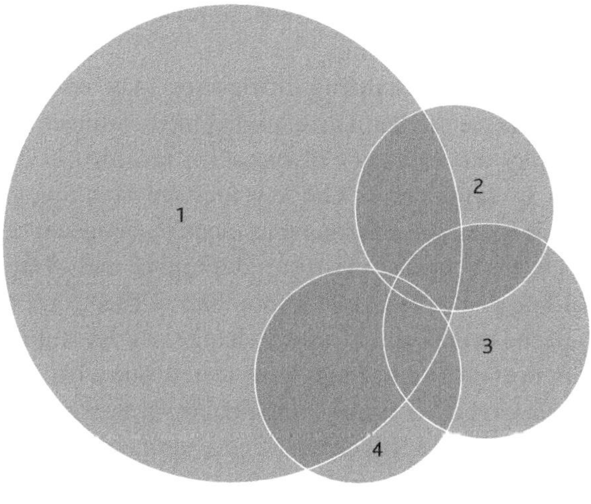

Key:

1. Whole systems reform
2. Issue specific reform
3. Operational reform across multiple services in one locality
4. Sector specific reform

collective vision that determine and impact on the safeguarding of young people. The two examples cited later show how organisations are starting to lead and influence change across and in-between the systems, at all levels from strategic leadership to front-line delivery of services.

Typology 2 is where localities or organisations have selected a particular area affecting the safeguarding of young people to focus their efforts on transformation. Our examples include a focus on exploitation of young people, which is an emerging and increasingly significant area of safeguarding adults work.

Typology 3 is where operational reforms occur across multiple services in one locality. The example we include in this section illustrates an organisation leading change across a range of pathways within the organisation and between services in one locality.

Typology 4 illustrates sector-specific reform, which contributes to progressing the Transitional Safeguarding approach, for example in health services. The other example illustrates how one voluntary sector organisation has transformed its offer to young people with substance misuse issues, applying the key principles of Transitional Safeguarding.

Transitional Safeguarding initiatives may overlap these typologies, hence the Venn diagram has inter-connecting circles. For example, the voluntary organisation included in Typology 4 also fits in Typology 2. The key message that emerges from our analysis is that local partnerships need to design an offer that best meets local needs, ensuring alignment with Transitional Safeguarding principles while responding to their local context. Although the overall aim is system change, service improvement can be important as a starting point to test out what works and how to work together with young people on service and system redesign. Incremental change can achieve joint ownership, support culture change, and demonstrate effectiveness.

Examples of Transitional Safeguarding initiatives

The first group of examples illustrate localities that are working towards **whole system reform**.

The key principles of 'being evidence-informed' and 'relational' (see Chapter 2) are particularly evident in their approach.

Haringey

The council's chief executive brought together a range of Haringey partners at a local Transitional Safeguarding event to start their journey. Subsequently, the local authority Assistant Directors of Children and Adults Services attended one of the national Research in Practice Transitional Safeguarding workshops facilitated by Christine and Adi in 2018. Following the death of a young person who had left care, a local multi-agency learning review suggested the need for a Transitional Safeguarding protocol to be introduced across Haringey. The Haringey Safeguarding Adult Board and Haringey Children's Safeguarding Partnership agreed to develop a Transitional Safeguarding programme of work as a joint strategic priority. This joint strategic leadership has ensured continuity and commitment across all partner organisations in Haringey working with young people to improve their safeguarding practice and processes. The two independent chairs have continued to ensure that both boards meet together bi-annually to review the work undertaken and support and engage all partners.

As part of this work, the local authority undertook an audit of 16 case files of young people in receipt of care and support and other acute services, looking at their experiences of these services over time, including the contact that just over half of these young people had with services where they were deemed not to be eligible for ongoing support. Although this audit had the benefit of hindsight, there was valuable learning in considering whether earlier intervention may have prevented some of the later service needs. This learning review provided evidence that was shared with the joint boards and informed the development of the Transitional Safeguarding protocol. This was developed jointly by officers from children's and adults' services and has included engagement with all partners through both boards' representatives. The associated action plan and 'partnership pledges' set out the commitment of partners to reduce the 'cliff edge' experiences for young people, and move practice away from a concrete application of eligibility criteria based on age, to an approach that acknowledges the vulnerability and unpredictability of human experience, recognising the importance of strengths-based relational practice.

Young adults and family members have been engaged in developing the Transitional Safeguarding work in Haringey. In July 2022 an event was held with workshops to explore what co-production meant and how it could work. At this event young people presented, led workshops, and constructively challenged professionals. The output from this event informed the development of the Transitional Safeguarding protocol. The respective directors of children's and adults' social services model positive joint working and productive relationships across their respective directorates and this demonstrates the importance of the relational principle of Transitional Safeguarding at a strategic level.[2]

There has been a specific focus on work with the following groups of young people moving into adulthood: care-experienced young people, including some adopted young people; young people with physical or learning disabilities, autism, educational or mental health needs; and young people who have been sexually or criminally exploited, or who have been previously known to the Youth Justice Service. The protocol also recognises and includes young adults at risk who may not meet service criteria. It emphasises the six safeguarding principles and key practice approaches: person-centred practice; strengths-based approaches; trauma-informed practice; consideration of structural inequalities; and mental capacity regarding decision making and consent. As one of the most deprived areas in the country, with a very diverse population, the considerable challenges that young people face are recognised.

Emerging impact

One of the 'tests' for the Transitional Safeguarding protocol involved a care-experienced young person from another local authority who had been placed with a semi-independent provider in Haringey one month before his eighteenth birthday. On his birthday the provider asked the young person to leave, rendering him homeless. The two local authorities agreed to work jointly to prevent him becoming homeless by jointly commissioning the provider to continue to work with the young person. The commissioning priorities for Haringey were re-examined to consider modelling a lifelong links approach to avoid the 'cliff edge' at 18 years. Some work was done with social housing colleagues to consider a shared housing resource with onsite tenancy support for vulnerable young people. Finally, senior managers reprioritised funding to enable recruitment of a dedicated Transitional Safeguarding post based in Haringey's Care Leavers service.

Wiltshire

At an early stage in their Transitional Safeguarding journey, Wiltshire Council examined data from a group of young people who were engaged in or vulnerable to exploitation, who displayed highly chaotic risk-taking behaviours. The aim was to determine how the partnership could work with this cohort to effect the best possible outcomes. One of the major findings from this piece of work was the high level of mental health needs that these young people were experiencing. Other key issues affecting this group of young people included substance use, alcohol use, criminal involvement/ exploitation, and self-harm.

Partners involved in Transitional Safeguarding include Wiltshire Police, who chair the project group, as well as probation, children's social care, adult social care, adult mental health, children's mental health, children's substance use, adult substance use, council commissioning, integrated care system commissioning, community health council housing services, and the voluntary sector. All share ownership and responsibility and contribute to the agenda of work for Transitional Safeguarding. The partnership wanted to create a sustainable model for system-wide change, embracing leadership, culture, and practice change that would improve young people's safety, well-being, and long-term outcomes. They did not want to simply create a new specialist service, but create a practice approach that can embed across all teams and systems.

Wiltshire has created a dedicated Transitional Safeguarding co-ordinator post. This post ensures that Transitional Safeguarding activities are firmly located in the partnership transformation agenda.

Emerging impact

Wiltshire is part-way through driving forward an approach based on maximising multi-agency engagement that involves learning from all stakeholders, crucially including young people themselves. It is not just a local authority project, but a system-wide partnership agenda.

The development and implementation of a Creative Solutions Board is at the heart of gaining insight into existing system constraints and driving change at practice, policy, and strategic levels. The introduction of a multi-agency outcomes framework enables robust monitoring and impact assessment.

The partnership has reinforced its understanding from young people, lead professionals, and practitioners that relationships are crucially important and at the heart of what young people want and value. This information has resulted in the commissioning of a new mentoring provision for young people. In addition, the partnership is clear that it is not just relationships between young people and their workers that are important, but also the relationships, trust, understanding, and commitment between partners. This is an approach to Transitional Safeguarding where relationships are valued and centred on the key principle of 'being relational'. The key message is that Transitional Safeguarding is complex, and Wiltshire's Families and Children's Transformation partnership is on a journey of culture, practice, and system change.

The second typology is **issue specific reform**. This is where reform within and across systems and organisations is based on a specific aspect of safeguarding work that has created the need for change in a locality. The example illustrates that Transitional Safeguarding is a flexible principles-led approach rather than a prescriptive model. Earlier in the book we have cited other examples of Transitional Safeguarding initiatives that have focused on a specific area of service development: Chapter 4 includes the Dorset Transitions Service and Newham Hub, and Chapter 7 shares the Havering Cocoon service for care-experienced young people and transitions panel and Norfolk's service to support young adults preparing for adulthood.

Solihull's work to develop all age exploitation procedures focuses on one area of safeguarding young people. This is an area that others have worked on too. In Newcastle there has been ongoing work in this area since Operation Sanctuary (Spicer 2018; Dearden

2018). Other areas have developed protocols and policies regarding all-age exploitation, for example, West Midlands and Southend, Essex, and Thurrock.[3]

Solihull

A Safeguarding Adult Review about 'Rachel' in 2019 identified the need to take a consistent and multi-agency approach to exploitation and led to the development of an All-Age Exploitation Reduction Strategy and Delivery Plan. Rachel had been a victim-survivor of sexual abuse as a child and had a history of mental health difficulties and self-harming behaviours. She was also a victim-survivor of sexual exploitation and trafficking from the age of 17 onwards. In October 2016, at the age of 20, she was found deceased in her bedroom at the supported accommodation where she had been living. Following a coroner's inquest, the cause of death was recorded as drug related.

The All-Age Exploitation Strategy and Plan was produced in 2020. At the same time an 'Adult Exploitation Reduction Lead' post was created within the Adult Social Care Directorate to provide additional capacity for strategic coordination of Solihull's All-Age Strategy and to lead on the progression of the delivery plan from an adult perspective. This role also focused on developing links with Solihull Council's Children's Exploitation and Missing Team, who provide consultation and advice to other teams within Children's Social Care. The role is built on relationships with police and NHS partners, in order to develop transitions pathways for young people who had either been exploited prior to 18 years or where concerns remained that they were continuing to be exploited.

Support is now offered to all adults regardless of age. Previously, for individuals whose care and support needs did not meet the Care Act 2014 eligibility criteria, even if they were victims of exploitation, there was limited support after age 18 and Children's Social Care stopped working with them.

In recognition of this gap, in March 2021 All-Age Exploitation Reduction Multi-Agency Safeguarding Procedures were launched. These procedures set out all processes, including how Transitional Safeguarding is applied for young people who continue to be exploited after 18 but do not have any care and support needs. This has involved Solihull Adult Social Care

Directorate executing powers and interpreting use of the Care Act 2014 to offer support to any person over 18 who has been exploited as a child or adult, or where there are concerns that they are currently being exploited.

The process for offering this ongoing support has been built on existing processes within Children's Social Care, namely the Multi-Agency Child Exploitation meeting process to discuss any child or young person where there are exploitation concerns and to develop support and disruption plans. The development of the All-Age Procedures has involved renaming this process the Multi-Agency Adult/Child Exploitation meeting to reflect consistency across children and adult social care and to provide a consistent response for individuals.

Underpinning the Adult Exploitation Reduction Team's approach and in keeping with the key principles of Transitional Safeguarding, there is an emphasis on strengths-based and trauma-informed approaches (TIAs), where time is spent building trusted relationships. The team also helps with employment, housing, benefits, providing foodbank vouchers, providing emotional support, and signposting to other agencies. There is no time limit on this support offered to individuals.

The Adult Exploitation Reduction Team are co-located with the Children's Exploitation and Missing Team. Co-location helps to build strong working relationships between directorates and supports information sharing with a focus on timely and person-centred support.

Emerging impact

The learning from Solihull is that this way of working requires commitment from all partner organisations both in terms of operational support but also at a strategic level to develop policies and procedures. There are challenges in terms of agencies prioritising post-18 support including meeting attendance and embedding new processes and ways of thinking. This is a culture change for all partners, including adult social care services. Multi-agency workshops have been held to address this and to identify solutions, including the aspiration to hold daily triage/information sharing meetings between Solihull Children's Social Care, adult social care, and the police. There have been some early successes and the positive impact on the lives of the individuals supported is significant. Those who have been willing to share feedback with the team have talked about the importance of feeling in control, being listened to, and being valued as individuals. The team has supported individuals who were at risk of exploitation and now are in employment or education and are settled in accommodation.

The third typology is **operational reforms across multiple services in one locality.** This looks like a number of different changes across a range of pathways led by an organisation. This can lead to whole systems change, though is not necessarily whole system change in itself. This should not underplay the importance of this type of organisational change. Whole systems change takes time; by introducing reforms across different service areas within an organisation, culture change can be influenced, which supports longer term systems change.

Northumberland

At a strategic level, the Children and Adults Safeguarding Partnerships were integrated in 2022. Transitional Safeguarding was a strategic priority; this aligned with a Think Family/Life course approach. Local drivers came from several joint (children and adult) learning reviews, which identified areas of learning and improvement such as:

- the need for a Transitional Safeguarding protocol;
- joint workshops to help people understand each other's roles and responsibilities;
- improving legal literacy of practitioners;
- early identification and response to trauma.

There are several initiatives already available within Northumberland to support good transitions planning. This includes an all-age strategic exploitation sub-group; exploitation training on a number of different approaches; a Joint Transitional Safeguarding protocol which sets out pathways for young people, particularly those not known to child protection services; collaborative Mental Capacity Act/Deprivation of Liberty Safeguards (DOLS) training for children's social care staff; a transitions policy; a transitions panel that reviews the support for young people who were 14-plus and who may or may not require care post-18; early referrals and joint working between the Adolescent Service and adult social care that include joint visits and a focus on handover; Transitional Safeguarding workshops; staff briefings and seven-minute guides; and CARE (Caring about Adversity, Resilience, and Empowerment) Northumberland. CARE provides a multi-agency approach to trauma-informed, resilience-focused services and communities; a learning framework for training and communication; and multi-agency awareness raising and resources.

In looking at what further work was required, an audit of case files concerning young people with Transitional Safeguarding needs was carried out. The aim of this was to understand how unresolved trauma could increase risks in later adult life if not responded to appropriately in early adulthood. The learning from the audit showed that trauma and adversity needs to be considered in assessments and planning at every stage. For young people moving between children and adult services, separate assessments and plans were not always joined up at the point of transition. Co-working was also needed to support transition. This also highlighted the challenges of different information systems in children's and adults' services, including the issue of consent – how it is viewed and how different agencies approach and manage consent issues.

Emerging impact

The learning so far includes the need for strategic 'buy-in', as this enables access to resources and to build capacity. Starting with small steps is important. Transitional Safeguarding requires creativity, collaboration, and culture change; it is an ongoing journey. The challenges identified through this work included restrictive Care Act eligibility around 'care and support needs' resulting in 'screening out' young people.

Northumberland Adolescent Services work with young people to age 25. The 14-plus social work team uses a multi-agency transition protocol to ensure smooth transition at 18 where young people are identified who need adult support, who are at risk of harm or abuse, and continue to be at risk into adulthood. Key meetings include quarterly transitions panels and individual transition meetings with children and adults' staff. Substance misuse services hold monthly consultation meetings to identify young people who require ongoing support and treatment after 18 and the assertive outreach worker engages with the young person. Probation has a direct link with the Youth Justice Service and has a 'transition discussion' about who is best placed to work with young people on offending orders after 18. Adult housing services attend care leavers accommodation and support protocol meetings or joint housing protocol meetings to explore accommodation and support needs for care-experienced young people post-18.

The final typology is **sector specific reform**. Several resources for specific sectors regarding Transitional Safeguarding have been developed. For example, 'Bridging the Gap' the Chief Social Worker (Adults) Briefing is aimed at social workers and adult social care leaders, with key messages for other partners on taking forward the Transitional Safeguarding approach. An Academic Insights Briefing on Transitional Safeguarding has been developed for the probation sector (Holmes and Smith 2022). Chapter 4 includes the Newham Hub initiative as an example from the criminal justice sector.

This section includes an example from the NHS to illustrate a sector-specific initiative that promotes Transitional Safeguarding, covering both the work of a national group promoting Transitional Safeguarding in the NHS as well as an example of how it can be delivered through the work of a dedicated Transitional Safeguarding nurse (West Sussex).

The second example is the Hope project in Oasis (Brighton). This example illustrates how Transitional Safeguarding can be taken forward in the voluntary sector, where it inspired the organisation to shape a new service to meet the needs of 18–25-year-olds with substance misuse issues.

Transitional Safeguarding in health

National work – safeguarding adults national network Transitional Safeguarding task and finish group

This group was commissioned by the NHS Safeguarding Adults National Network to work on Transitional Safeguarding. They talked to the different

National Networks for Designated Professionals for Children and Looked After Children. The group had a wide membership spanning the life course and sector; including people working in mental health, learning disability services, transition services, doctor and nurse representatives, as well as the Royal College of Nursing. The group undertook a resource mapping exercise and identified a gap, which resulted in a padlet being created for professionals to access.[4] The padlet is a live resource and is curated by the group. They also produced a Transitional Safeguarding Rapid Read which can be used in training and provides information about Transitional Safeguarding, principles, definitions, and links to other resources.

The ethos of the group was that individual members are stronger together; they believe that creative collaborative and courageous thinking is what makes the difference.

Transition between paediatric health and adult services, as explored in Chapter 7, is not the same as Transitional Safeguarding, however they are interlinked. NICE guidelines define transition as moving from children's to adults' services and includes planning between services and support throughout, involving the young person. Transfer of care is between one health service and another. However, there may be transition or transfer of care between many services and the impact on a young person experiencing many 'transfers' in conjunction with safeguarding concerns requires consideration. A Transitional Safeguarding response requires more than addressing abuse or neglect in these transitional or transfer processes. There are also safeguarding risks in terms of intra and extra-familial abuse or neglect. Transitional Safeguarding cannot be reduced to care pathways or flow charts because these can exclude some young people.

In terms of influencing and using non-statutory levers in health, this is ongoing work. Schedule 32 of the NHS Standard Contract refers to safeguarding responsibilities for all providers of NHS services. It does not include reference to Transitional Safeguarding. However, the Safeguarding Accountability and Assurance Framework, which fleshes out Schedule 32, does include reference to Transitional Safeguarding and this provides a reference point for all NHS providers.

The 'Intercollegiate Documents' (children, young people, looked after children, and Adult 'Roles and Competencies for Health Care Staff') set the standards for safeguarding training in the NHS. They outline the learning outcomes and competencies for training health professionals. These are now due for review and Task and Finish Group members are involved in work to include Transitional Safeguarding in these documents in the future, which will mean that training of the NHS workforce will include reference to Transitional Safeguarding.

The NHS long-term plan means that the NHS should be thinking 'transitional by design'. It states that by 2024 at least 345,000 children and young people, 0–25, will be able to access support by NHS mental health services. A complete system redesign will change eligibility criteria and should improve access; the current 'cliff edge' for mental health services for that age group would be addressed.

Safeguarding in health services can take a binary approach to young people over and under 18; dedicated safeguarding roles exist of 'named' and 'designated professionals' working with children or adults. In some places dedicated roles have been created for people who have responsibilities for safeguarding both age groups in the NHS and independent health providers, who can identify, understand, and apply the Transitional Safeguarding approach. Having colleagues and structures that bridge the gap, that can offer colleagues the opportunity to better support those crossing the boundary from adolescence to adulthood, is welcomed and should be harnessed and developed.

Transitional Safeguarding nurse – Role of Deputy Designated Nurse Safeguarding Transition in NHS Sussex Integrated Care Board

This deputy designated nurse role leads on transition and Transitional Safeguarding in NHS Sussex. The first steps were to map processes and network across the organisation locality and nationally. A key aim was to share knowledge and practice, working together with safeguarding partners in the area. By working with commissioners, providers, and safeguarding partners the aim is to bring Transitional Safeguarding into transition planning from paediatric to adults' services. Data are collected and collated to identify themes to then escalate to safeguarding boards, meetings, and subgroups.

Work over two years has included supporting other areas in health to develop their roles and portfolios; giving a voice to Transitional Safeguarding in health; role modelling the way forward; and developing a Transitional Safeguarding training package to help change thinking about safeguarding young people. The role provides Transitional Safeguarding specialist supervision to help others. Multi-agency policy review work has been undertaken with partners regarding transition arrangements. The transition aspects of serious incidents, Safeguarding Adult Reviews (SARs) and Child Safeguarding Practice Reviews (CSPRs) have been highlighted and reported on. The specialist nurse role has contributed to work on becoming a trauma-informed organisation and has begun to influence culture change.

Oasis Project (Brighton and Hove) – Hope Service

The Oasis Project is a voluntary sector substance misuse service. Inspired by the concept of Transitional Safeguarding and the specific needs of 18–25-year-olds, Oasis Project launched the Hope Service to deliver specialist support to this group of young people. It was created within existing resources which were reallocated. Internal restructuring enabled the development of the service.

The Hope Service responds to the developmental and transitional needs of 18–25-year-olds when addressing substance use, rather than offering a 'one-size fits all' service. This response has been implemented out of moral and ethical concerns; young adults should receive services early to prevent harm and entrenched substance use in later adulthood. Drawing on existing trauma-informed, relationship-based practices embedded within the Oasis Project, the Hope Service responds to the needs of young people by recognising that their needs may be different from older adults. The service's approach involves listening to young adults and using their strengths to ensure safe and informed practice. A dedicated multi-disciplinary team of practitioners with passion and expertise of working with this age group delivers both psychosocial drug and alcohol treatment and psychotherapy. This approach has received 'buy-in' from existing funders and has attracted new investment from both local authority children/family and adult directorates via delivery of the Office for Health Improvement and Disparities (OHID) Government drug strategy.

There are cultural practice differences between local authority youth substance services and non-statutory adult treatment services. Oasis Project is largely a project-based service reliant on a person's motivation and choice to access support. This has been recognised as a difficult transition for young people who are not used to having to attend services for support.

Emerging impact

There is evidence of relationship building, responsive support; and positive change occurring in young adults' lives. The service has received an increase in referrals both from individuals and from partner professionals. The separate service provision limits a young adult's exposure to older adults with entrenched substance use who may also pose risk of harm, for example, exploitation. Relationships with partner agencies and professionals are now well established, providing an opportunity to advocate for the needs of young people and develop joint working protocols. Drug and alcohol patterns within this age group are different from older adults. Younger adults' drug trends tend to lean towards patterns of substance use including cannabis, alcohol, and other non-opiates like cocaine and ketamine, so much lower rates of opiate use than older adults (Office for Health Improvement and Disparities 2023). Treatment monitoring and KPIs for services are also predominantly targeted with abstinence-based outcomes, whereas for young adults, lifelong abstinence is too big a goal to consider and they have hopes around reduction and harm minimisation. Sector knowledge and systems are well established and designed to respond to the needs of older adults. This impacts on the readiness of skill set within drug and alcohol treatment and professional/organisational confidence to respond to the needs of young people. We are re-working models and implementing new approaches to support young people.

When young adults are listened to, organisations and practitioners can hear about and respond to the harm they are experiencing and think with young people about how systems could be better designed to work for them. Common barriers include accessing adult social care statutory safeguarding support when it is difficult to show how they meet the eligibility criteria. The 'prevention principle' within Care Act 2014 is not always recognised, especially within an overstretched social care system placing emphasis on eligibility to manage constrained resources. Young people also feed back difficulty in accessing mental health support; young people feel they are viewed as too old to access youth mental health services but considered too young by medical professionals to be provided with certain clinical treatment, with alternatives not being offered. Young adults often report self-medicating their mental health needs with illicit substances, but substance use then becomes a barrier to accessing mental health support. Dual-diagnosis approaches are required. Staff can currently feel they are left holding risk and worry, and that the issues are often outside their own expertise of substance use.

Reflections on the examples

In this chapter we have provided a sample of what people have been doing in their local areas or sectors to adopt a Transitional Safeguarding approach. Unfortunately, we have not been able to include every initiative that was shared with us, nor have we included all the information we have been given about the examples in this chapter. The response and commitment to Transitional Safeguarding has been wonderful to observe. Some places have focused on a specific practice area (see Chapter 7); some have seen this change snowball across other services (for example, Northumberland). Others were particularly ambitious and so are grappling with embedding whole system change, prompting opportunities to pause, rethink, and adapt (for example, Wiltshire). Although we have clustered the examples into typologies, there are multiple overlaps between them and common patterns within them.

The most common theme across the case studies we received is that change is difficult because it challenges the way systems work and how people practice within and across them. Senior leadership buy-in and support are crucially important pre-requisites to enable the change to happen and bed-in. Having effective escalation or resolution routes to unblock problems at strategic levels helps to support learning and change. For example, eligibility criteria for adult social care services can be interpreted in ways that exclude some young people; revisiting the consequences of this and emphasising some of the prevention requirements in the Care Act legislation and guidance requires senior leadership support and collaboration. To say that change is difficult may seem obvious, but the emotional, intellectual, and practical effort required can sometimes be underestimated. Several of the contributors expressed their frustrations in trying to change approaches and several noted that sharing frustrations was important. This helped to build the positive relationships between practitioners, partners, and agencies which helped to progress their local initiatives. Three of the key principles of Transitional Safeguarding are particularly relevant here: Firstly, being evidence-informed involves drawing on the expertise of practitioners and people using services – collaboration from the outset can help to create a culture where change is a shared goal. In addition, using evidence of what makes innovation successful is a key aspect of the change process. Secondly, adopting a contextual/ecological approach in practice means engaging wider partners and stakeholders across the system. This inclusive approach can make the change process more complicated, but the broadening of expertise and talent available to support that change is worth its weight in gold. Thirdly, the principle of taking a participative approach is significant. The more that young people and those who care about them are engaged in the change process, the more vividly we see the need for change. When change feels too hard, young people will remind us that we must keep going.

Another important theme is the need to talk about money and resources, because the last decade has seen unprecedented cuts in local authority and public sector services across the board, creating a huge funding gap in social services (ADASS 2022; Health Foundation 2021; House of Commons Health and Social Care Committee 2020; House of Commons Levelling Up, Housing and Communities Committee 2022). Each of these early adopters has begun a change programme in their locality or agency, utilising whatever capacity existed at a particular point in time. For some this has involved redistribution of available resources and capacity, while others have benefitted from additional investment. Some of the organisations referred to have reallocated resources (for example, Oasis Hope Service), with a commitment to changing culture and ethos mirrored across organisations and between partners.

It is important to acknowledge the impact of COVID-19 and the lockdowns, years of austerity, and more recently the cost-of-living increases, which create challenges for any innovation and development work. That said, resource constraints also act as a driver for innovation. As noted in Chapter 2, the current binary system can mean that a focus on eligibility comes at the expense of prevention. Transitional Safeguarding, designed well, offers an opportunity for local partnerships to provide support before problems become entrenched in later adulthood, and so contributes to later cost avoidance. Attending to the key principle of 'being evidence-informed' is an important means of managing the tension between innovation and resource constraints. By taking time to deeply understand local needs, and considering the evidence underpinning particular interventions (say, mentoring schemes), local areas can thoughtfully target the resources available to best effect and can strengthen cases for investment.

Another common theme is that of boundary-spanning leadership and infrastructure. Efforts to develop Transitional Safeguarding in local partnerships and agencies appear to be more effective when there is engagement and leadership across children and adults' systems and wider partners. The importance of joint governance for leadership can be seen in the integration of boards or meeting jointly in some areas. Leadership by the statutory Safeguarding Adults Board and Children's Safeguarding Partnerships is critical to support whole systems reform as well as validate change within organisations, pathways, and services. In order to ensure a developmentally-attuned approach (another of the key principles of Transitional Safeguarding), there needs to be ways in which expertise from children's and adults' sector colleagues can be shared. Local leaders and governance groups have a key role to play in creating a coherent joined-up vehicle for collaborative learning, collective vision, and shared accountability. There are some good examples of joined-up strategic leadership (for example, Bath and North East Somerset as described in Walker-McAllister and Cooper 2022). When the governance arrangements work across the binaries, there is the potential to support Transitional Safeguarding via joint systems leadership, but this structural join-up is only a starting point. Modelling partnership working and authentic collaboration between children and adults' services at a strategic level can influence the practice that organisations want to see on the ground; this can be transformational (for example, Haringey, Wiltshire, Northumberland). Here, the principle of being relational is evident and relevant: leaders and managers must role-model effective relationship-based working, not only with those they lead but also in their inter-agency and partnership working.

One of the common challenges facing those striving to develop Transitional Safeguarding was the question of how to define and measure success. We were provided with narratives about individual young people who had benefitted from the changes made locally to adopt a Transitional Safeguarding approach. These are helpful because they show how someone's life has improved and help people see what 'good looks like', what it is possible to achieve. However, it is too early to identify any measure of success (Cocker et al 2022a) at a system level. A further challenge is that, rather like early help (Bowyer 2022), the temptation is to narrowly define success, for example, a short-term reduction in demand on acute services, and so it becomes much easier to measure failure than success. One of the next tasks for all of us involved in this area of work is to continue building the evidence base for Transitional Safeguarding, including evaluating its impact on young people. In keeping with the participative principle, any success measure must include what young people say matters to them.

The importance of strengths-based and TIAs were common threads in all the examples included earlier. This chimes particularly with the relational principles of Transitional Safeguarding, which emphasises the importance of providing support that is person-centred, trauma-informed, and builds on young people's strengths. In terms of direct work with young people, taking the time to build strong relationships and valuing these was a key factor for success, as was enabling young people to have a sense of choice and agency over decision making. This foregrounding of choice reinforces the need to balance risk and rights, and to integrate participative approaches within protective interventions (as discussed in Chapter 2). This theme of TIAs also connects to the key principle of attending to equality, equity, diversity, and inclusion. Recognising the structural and/or collective trauma that some groups face is vital for enacting a trauma-informed response.

Experiences of racism, ableism, sexism, homophobia, classism, and other forms of discrimination are not only a direct source of harm to young people but can also make it hard for them to trust professionals who could help them navigate these risks. Local areas seeking to develop a Transitional Safeguarding approach must be courageous in identifying and redressing discrimination, exclusion, and inequality, and must see this as part and parcel of effective safeguarding activity.

Conclusion

Transitional Safeguarding is not a 'quick win'. The examples included in this chapter illustrate the significant commitment that people have shown to Transitional Safeguarding by making changes to improve the safety and well-being of young people. Leaders and practitioners know that the current systems are not working and want to change them, even though this is challenging to do. The tenacity and commitment of local agencies, partnerships, leaders, and practitioners shines through in these examples and shows that innovation can be led best by those who are closest to the communities they serve. There are many interesting and different ways of responding to what young people tell us needs to change. Key messages are to treat young people's expertise as a source of evidence, look around and learn from what others are doing while also being focused on your local context, and to ensure the change process is as collaborative, inclusive, and imaginative as possible. The next chapter explores system change in more detail.

10

Transitional Safeguarding as whole systems change

Introduction

This chapter explores what is meant by whole systems change and argues that this is an important paradigm for the development and implementation of a Transitional Safeguarding approach. As such, Transitional Safeguarding requires systems leadership which explicitly attends to complexity. Consideration is given to how change can be embedded, drawing on theoretical frameworks of innovation and implementation, and an example of a whole system change approach to reducing violence. Understanding Transitional Safeguarding as a whole system change brings some challenges for implementation and impact measurement; the key principles offer a way to think about these difficulties and so take small steps in the right direction. A discussion follows about how to frame Transitional Safeguarding in ways that enable helpful policy solutions. Finally, in an effort to model reflexivity and congruence, the endeavour of whole systems change is explored using the key principles of Transitional Safeguarding as a framework. Each key principle is considered in terms of what embodying the principles means for those seeking to develop Transitional Safeguarding at a local or national level.

Why Transitional Safeguarding is a 'systems' issue

A system can be broadly defined as a number of elements connected or linked together by dynamics which in turn influence or affect other elements or systems; some systems are complex because they involve unpredictability and emergence (OECD 2017). The concept of Transitional Safeguarding could be construed as a simple change proposition: young people who need support to be safe should receive this irrespective of their eighteenth birthday. However, the underlying problems and the required actions to address these are not simple at all; they are deeply complex issues that engage multiple aspects of the personal and professional system/s and wider society as a whole.

There are two key systems that are relevant to Transitional Safeguarding. The first, as noted in Chapter 2, relates to understanding individual young people's lives as complex ecosystems (Bronfenbrenner 1977). Young people are not simply elements *within* a system; their lives can be understood *as* a complex system, with each level of the system influencing the others. This ecological perspective is one of the key principles of Transitional Safeguarding and this is reflected in the whole systems model used to analyse safeguarding reviews covered within Chapter 8. Figure 10.1, adapted from Bronfenbrenner (1977), illustrates how we might think about a young person's ecosystem in the context of Transitional Safeguarding. Of course, all young people are different; the diagram is a high-level summary of a person's ecosystem.

The second systems lens that is significant to Transitional Safeguarding relates to the professional layer in Figure 10.1. This layer, encompassing professional services and structures and conceptualisations of need, risk, and of youth or adulthood, is in fact its own highly complex system. As the examples in Chapter 9 highlight, the professional system is complex and presents some challenges for local areas trying to redesign a more fluid safeguarding offer for young people. Figure 10.2 illustrates the different interacting layers of a local professional system, though again examples given are not exhaustive and will vary between different professional systems.

Transitional Safeguarding seeks to change the professional system, to better respond to young people, who are their own ecosystem; both of which are situated in wider social, political, and economic systems. Therefore, Transitional Safeguarding can

Figure 10.1: Individual ecosystem in relation to Transitional Safeguarding

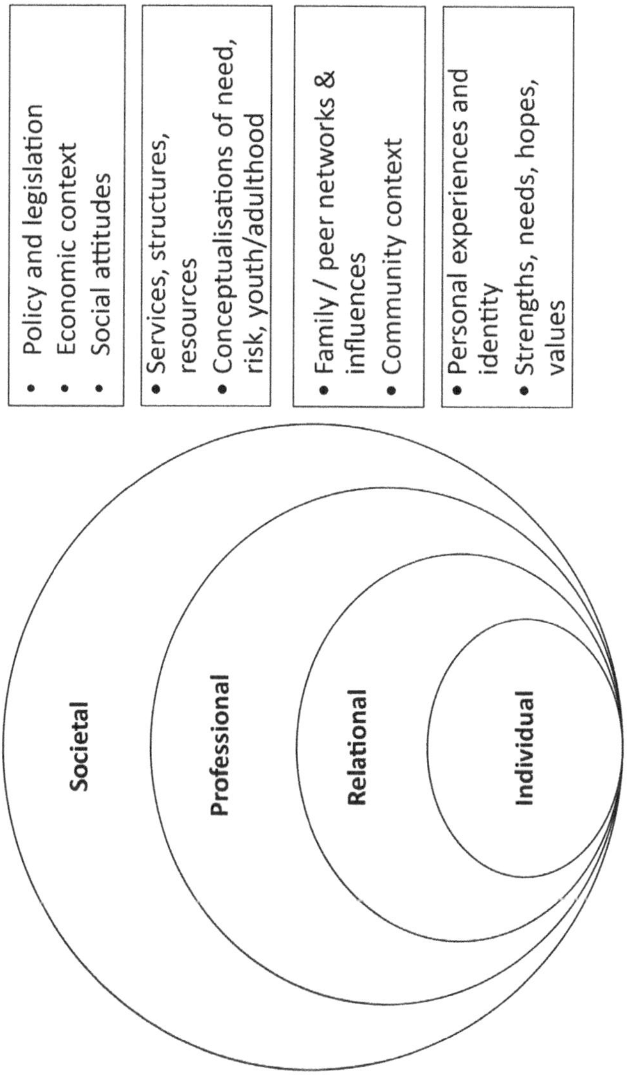

Figure 10.2: Professional system(s) relevant to Transitional Safeguarding

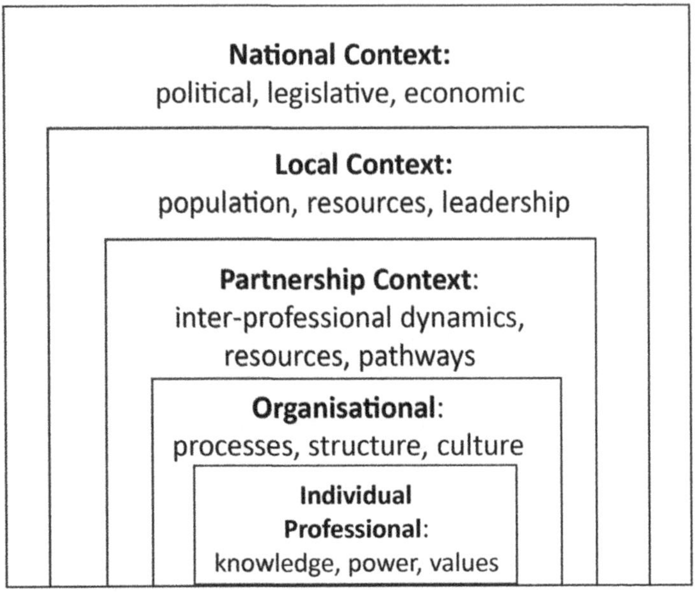

be understood as change being sought within a 'system of systems' (Arnold and Wade 2015). These include the policy and legislative systems governing safeguarding; the professional systems of local agencies and their various perspectives, standards, and regulatory frameworks; and the macro-level political and economic contexts that influence the legislative, professional, and interpersonal systems. Developing new interventions or services is certainly an important part of reforming the system – and some promising examples are offered in Chapter 9. However, Transitional Safeguarding should be understood not as a specific intervention or practice model, but as an issue of whole system change. This is not simple work by any means, but – as local areas are starting to demonstrate – it is possible.

The complexity of Transitional Safeguarding arises not only from these multiple systems interacting with each other, but from the inherent unpredictability of human beings and our 'messy' lives. The issue of how to adopt and embed Transitional Safeguarding – and the problems it seeks to address – can therefore be termed a 'wicked issue'. Wicked issues are described as having several key characteristics; they:

- involve multiple stakeholders, often with different ideas or explanations;
- are not definitively understandable and so there are no perfect solutions that will work in all contexts;
- involve 'liminality' existing 'between the original positions arrayed by law, custom, convention and ceremony' (Turner 1977, p 95);
- involve unpredictability and solutions can create unexpected consequences;
- are not comprised of elements connected by linear relationships, but instead are emergent as different elements compound, contradict or in some other way connect with each other. (Rittel and Webber 1973; Camillus 2008; OECD 2017)

Wicked issues are sometimes called VUCA issues, a term originating from post-Cold War military theory meaning issues characterised by volatility, uncertainty, complexity, and ambiguity (Bennis and Nanus 1985). Transitional Safeguarding can be understood as presenting all these features in various ways: mid-late adolescence and early adulthood are life stages that are by their very nature ambiguous, both in terms of individual young people's identity and in the contradictory nature of legislative frameworks (Holmes 2022a). Safeguarding practice is inherently complex and often involves managing uncertainty because of the unpredictable and multifaceted nature of people's lives. Further complexity arises from the multi-agency nature of safeguarding partnerships, with each agency working to its own duties and professional norms, and each staffed by a workforce of multifaceted people with their own perspectives and experiences. The balance of protecting people while upholding their participatory rights also presents complexity and ambiguity in practice. Volatility is a feature of some young people's safeguarding needs, particularly as risks can rapidly escalate. Uncertainty and volatility are features of professional systems too, with resources, policy, and regulatory activity subject to frequent change.

Complex system issues cannot be addressed through traditional top-down reform, command, and control management, or linear solutions. These kinds of approaches are ineffective when dealing with wicked issues (Camillus 2008) and can potentially worsen the situation, as layering discrete interventions within a complex system can mean that consequences shift from one part of the system to another (OECD 2017). An example of such a solution within the Transitional Safeguarding agenda might be to create a standalone Transitional Safeguarding service. A dedicated team might be *part* of the solution in a particular local context, and having specialist expertise and dedicated resources could be very helpful. However, this service would likely require its own eligibility criteria or threshold for access, very possibly resulting in a new silo or border to cross within an already fragmented system. These unintended consequences and risks require careful mitigation. So, while this kind of initiative can be a useful and important step towards system change, and could test or model a different approach, it is not in and of itself the system-wide change needed. To make progress towards whole systems change, it is necessary to engage in 'systems thinking'.

Systems thinking and systems leadership

Systems thinking has become increasingly popular within public services, notably public health (Chughtai and Blanchett 2017) and is defined in a variety of ways. Common elements of definitions seem to be about 'interconnections, the understanding of dynamic behaviour, systems structure as a cause of that behaviour, and the idea of seeing systems as whole rather than parts' (Arnold and Wade 2015, p 674). According to research focused on public sector innovation (OECD 2017), systems thinking involves a range of overlapping characteristics, as illustrated in Figure 10.3. Paying attention to the relationship between part of a system and striving for holistic solutions both require diverse perspectives to be valued (OECD 2017); this in turn suggests that the processes involved in systems thinking and systems change are not only technical and operational but also relational. Such an approach requires attention to be paid to the overall intended outcome

Figure 10.3: Characteristics of systems thinking

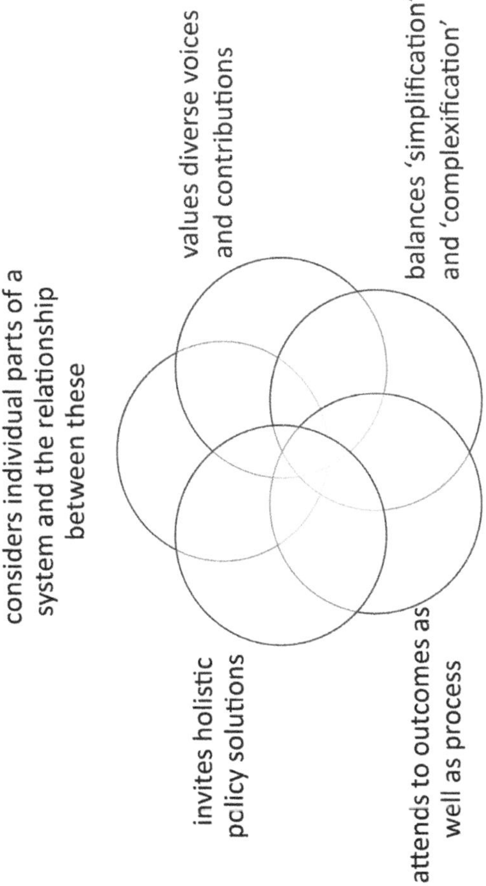
considers individual parts of a system and the relationship between these
values diverse voices and contributions
balances 'simplification' and 'complexification'
attends to outcomes as well as process
invites holistic policy solutions

('simplification') while also addressing multiple system factors simultaneously ('complexification') (OECD 2017).

Systems thinking has been critiqued by those who argue that technical approaches arising from systems engineering or computing are not helpful within complex public services (Senge 1987; Checkland 1999), and can invite reductionist approaches (Arnold and Wade 2015). There have been calls for a blended approach in which the problem and product focus found within systems engineering and design thinking is grounded in an understanding of social, economic, political, and community contexts (see Grohs et al 2018 for a discussion on this). Part of this social context is the beliefs and perceptions and values of stakeholders (Schön and Rein 1994), and so interrogating our own and other people's perspectives is key to systems thinking. Others note that some systems thinking literature fails to delineate between systematic (sequential and linear) thinking and systemic (relational and joined-up) thinking, and so misses the opportunity to position systems thinking as reflexive praxis (Ison and Blackmore 2014).

This offers two important prompts for Transitional Safeguarding. Firstly, recognising the belief systems at play is key to effective whole system change. Individual beliefs and perspectives influence (and are influenced by) the collective beliefs and perspectives created through interpersonal interactions, including within professional systems. Wider societal beliefs and attitudes are shaped by and shape these interpersonal and individual belief systems. Therefore, collaborative, inclusive debate about both the problems and solutions regarding Transitional Safeguarding is necessary to surface beliefs and values. Secondly, reflexivity and systemic thinking are important to the development of Transitional Safeguarding. This is because the interactions between system elements are not only procedural but also psychosocial, as they relate to human behaviour and emotion (Huegler and Ruch 2021). This suggests that any local agency or partnership wanting to develop Transitional Safeguarding must consider not only the 'hard' elements of their local system/s (such as service structures, procedures, resource allocation) but also 'soft' system elements (such as emotion, ethos, ego, and ethics). It is easy to overlook these soft elements when managing change. However, as the saying goes, 'the soft stuff is always harder than the hard stuff' and so must be attended to.[1] Many of the contributors to Chapter 9 have alluded to this, emphasising that good partnership working is key to success.

This brings us to the notion of systems leadership, which is necessary when tackling wicked issues (Ghate et al 2013; Camillus 2008). There is no universally agreed definition of 'systems leadership' (Bigland et al 2020), though it is generally understood to include a number of features which offer a useful lens when considering how to design and embed Transitional Safeguarding.

The first of these is that systems leadership is a *collective* form of leadership involving 'the concerted effort of many people working together at different places in the system and at different levels' (Ghate et al 2013, p 6). This speaks to the wide range of stakeholders involved in local safeguarding partnerships and the multi-agency collaboration required to help young people be and feel safe. The Solihull example in Chapter 9 is a good illustration of the way in which collective learning and cross-sector collaboration have been key to developing solutions that meet local need.

Secondly, systems leadership is 'leadership as participation', in which the highly relational, empathic, and reflexive nature of this kind of leadership are emphasised (Ghate et al 2013). This directly mirrors the relational principle of Transitional Safeguarding. In the introduction, we note that safeguarding is a verb not a noun; the same is true for systems leadership – it is a 'thing we do', not a state of being. The examples in Chapter 9 illustrate how vital active leadership is to the development of Transitional Safeguarding. The approach taken in Haringey is a helpful example of 'leadership by doing': proactive inquiry to learn about what needs to change, colleagues coalescing around a shared goal, joined-up strategic leadership, developing not only protocols but pledges and action plans, and centring relationships within the solution. All of these exemplify participative leadership.

Thirdly, systems leadership is explicitly concerned with leading beyond organisational and professional boundaries (Bolden et al 2019). This kind of leadership 'crosses boundaries, existing simultaneously in multiple dimensions' (Ghate et al 2013, p 6). Boundary-spanning can be understood as the consciously collaborative practice of reaching across dividing lines, whether institutional, geographical, or conceptual, to create connections and relationships in order to address complex problems (Williams 2002). This is particularly important in the context of Transitional Safeguarding, as 'siloed working' between agencies hampers effective safeguarding of children and adults (Brandon et al 2020; Preston-Shoot et al 2020) and is even more pronounced *between* these two safeguarding systems (as discussed in Chapter 8). In order to redress the unhelpful, and often unsafe, binaries of current safeguarding approaches, a boundary-spanning and system-wide approach to change is vital. This can be seen in the Northumberland example in Chapter 9; bringing together governance groups, promoting multi-agency knowledge exchange, and attending to practical issues alongside wider cultural barriers to change are all examples of boundary-spanning.

Systems leadership is not only the responsibility of those individuals or agencies with formal power and authority. People can and do exhibit these kinds of leadership behaviours at all levels and in a variety of ways. Non-statutory partners, practitioners working directly with young people, and young people themselves can and do all exercise systems leadership in different ways. The Oasis (Hope) example in Chapter 9 is an excellent example of how young people can lead change by informing service redesign, and how a voluntary sector organisation can lead and influence change across a locality.

Innovation, implementation, and impact: implications for Transitional Safeguarding

As discussed, Transitional Safeguarding is a complex issue and so it is important to avoid simplistic understandings of innovation as a linear process. Lefevre et al (2022) draw on the work of Albury et al (2018) in noting 'the majority of [innovation frameworks] were presented rather like a formula or manual, providing a comforting, but rather misleading, illusion of a pipeline whereby ideas, resources and the full range of prescribed activities could be fed in at one end so that aspired outcomes would flow out at the other' (Lefevre et al 2022, p 10).

Within adult social care, innovation has been defined as 'the practices adopted by providers, service users, local authorities or government to implement new models to solve a problem' (Department of Health and Social Care 2021, p 45). Within children's social care, innovation is described as 'a new practice, model or service that transforms mainstream ways of doing things' (Sebba et al 2017, p 6). Neither definition is an ideal fit for Transitional Safeguarding, which is not a prescribed model, practice, or service but a whole system approach. It is therefore more useful to consider Transitional Safeguarding as a 'social innovation', which 'aims to improve both the lives of individuals and the structures of society in ways that lead to better outcomes for all' (Lefevre et al 2022, p 4). The attention to both individuals *and* social structures highlights the whole system nature of such innovation and is a better fit with Transitional Safeguarding. Rather than locating innovation within services or practice, social innovation describes:

> Innovations that are social both in their ends and in their means. They are social in their ends because they are motivated by the goal of meeting a social need. They are social in their means because they leave behind a stronger social capital to act, and are usually … spread through organisations whose primary purposes are social. (Mulgan 2019, p 10)

This definition offers more space to consider the role of communities and social learning in driving change, and so aligns with the participative emphasis of Transitional Safeguarding. Seeing it as a social innovation also connects with the collective and participatory nature of systems leadership discussed previously and could help to avoid reductive and ineffective solutions. Innovation is not a straight path, but rather a winding journey involving 'multiple spirals' with 'feedback loops between every stage' (Mulgan 2019, p 25). The key message here for local areas keen to develop a Transitional Safeguarding approach is to resist those linear constructs of change management that can be 'comforting but misleading' and instead approach the issue as one of collaborative inquiry and experimentation. Emerging understandings, detours and delays, surprising insights, and unexpected challenges are all part of the process of social innovation. This understanding provides a helpful context for those aiming to improve safeguarding for young people and reassures innovators struggling to address the blocks and barriers in their Transitional Safeguarding journey.

Much of what is known about implementing new approaches relies on implementation science and evidence-based practice; both of which can assume what is being implemented is a bounded intervention, underpinned by empirical evidence of its effectiveness. But Transitional Safeguarding is not an intervention with clear edges and a defined target population. Indeed, the conscious 'smudging' of boundaries, whether age-related or service-oriented, is at the heart of Transitional Safeguarding. The Transitional Safeguarding work will necessarily look different in different places, according to local context. Therefore, it is not simply a case of 'rolling out' an evidence-based intervention in accordance with the manual and achieving the promised results.

It is useful that more recent research regarding implementation emphasises the importance of trusting relationships (Metz et al 2022). By developing trust between stakeholders, and attending to relational strategies as well as technical strategies, implementation efforts are more likely to achieve successful results (Metz et al 2022). Normalisation Process Theory (NPT) also offers useful insight here. Originating in healthcare and developed over a number of years, NPT attends to the complex relational processes involved in implementation and provides 'a set of sociological tools to understand and explain the social processes through which new or modified practices of thinking, enacting, and organising work are operationalised' (May et al 2009, p 2). NPT posits that the enacting and embedding of a new approach is enabled or impeded through four mechanisms: coherence, cognitive participation, collective action, reflexive monitoring (May and Finch 2009). Coherence here refers to a shared understanding of the meaning and use of what is being implemented; cognitive participation involves the engagement and 'buy-in' of those involved in implementation. Collective action refers to the shared investment of effort in what is being implemented; reflexive monitoring encompasses the formal and informal evaluation of the implementation process so that meaning, and coherence, are continually appraised (May and Finch 2009). This chimes with the tenets of systems leadership and is a useful framework for those developing their Transitional Safeguarding approach.

Applying traditional notions of 'best evidence' to a complex system innovation like Transitional Safeguarding can be difficult. In reviewing another whole system approach, Think Family authors note the 'lack of "acceptable" evidence on the effectiveness of messy, flexible, joined-up, relationship-based, whole systems practice' and highlight that individualised person-centred approaches make it 'problematic to construct an evaluation using a medical-style Randomised Controlled Trial (RCT) methodology' (Tew et al 2016, p 4).[2] In relation to early help, policy makers' desire to understand 'what works' has resulted in a narrow construct of evidence that privileges those interventions most amenable to RCT-style evaluations (Bowyer 2022). Specific targeted interventions are just one part of a whole system response, and yet – perhaps because their efficacy can more easily be measured quantitatively – they come to be seen *as the response*. Accordingly, 'what matters' will be defined not through collaborative engagement with intended beneficiaries and practitioners, but by 'what can be measured'.

RCTs are an important part of the evidence landscape but they are not the only source of evidence. Compared to medicine, social care has few trials to draw on – in part due to the disparity in research investment between health and social care (Bywaters 2008), and because such methods require significant funds and staff resources (Sebba et al 2017). Some argue that RCTs are not an effective approach within complex systems characterised by emergence, non-linearity, and localisation, because 'what "works" in a complex system at one place and time won't necessarily "work" in another system in a different place, or in the same system at a different time' (Lowe et al 2022, p 7). In addition, notions of 'rolling out' evidence-based models can arguably reinforce 'the fallacy of the pipeline' (meaning one-way dissemination of knowledge) and thus positions the practitioner as an 'empty vessel' (Green 2008).

All of the challenges noted previously could make Transitional Safeguarding seem too difficult to achieve; returning to the six key principles can help to steer a path through. Adopting an evidence-informed approach means drawing on knowledge from best available research and from professional wisdom and expertise from lived experience. We may not have definitive answers as to 'what works' for all young people, but we do not have to wait for a plethora of RCTs to be funded before we can act. Qualitative methods and theory align well with the idea of social innovation as a learning endeavour, and safeguarding reviews, such as those explored in Chapter 8, tell us plenty about how the current approach does *not* work. As shown in Chapter 9, local areas can undertake case file audits, service mapping, and consultation with professionals and communities to start to understand need and design more fluid pathways. Approaching system transformation in this way chimes with the principle of attending to equalities, equity, diversity, and inclusion too, as it prizes community-based knowledge, values seldom-heard voices, and can support the democratisation of knowledge and power. Rather than assuming evidence of 'what works' is externally defined and something practitioners must 'follow', the participative principle of Transitional Safeguarding invites a dialogical 'bottom-up' approach. Which young people are being turned away from services at 18? What happens to them and at what cost? What can we do to unlock creativity and capacity in the system? What small steps towards change feel possible now? These are all questions local areas and communities can answer, together.

To avoid one-way knowledge transfer, local areas developing Transitional Safeguarding can create opportunities for knowledge exchange and mobilisation, between professional groups and between professionals and people being supported. This can play an important role in spanning professional and epistemological (knowledge) boundaries. Two other Transitional Safeguarding principles are relevant here: harnessing professional expertise across disciplines can enable a more contextual or ecological perspective about young people's lives and can build a shared understanding of what a developmentally-attuned approach across the life course could look like. Guiding questions for local areas might include: How can we mobilise the vast knowledge and expertise across our locality to inform system-change efforts? Is our approach to training reinforcing unhelpful siloes? What can senior leaders learn from practice about what good looks like? What would success look like from young people's perspectives? How could we measure that in ways that are participative?

Seeing implementation as a social and relational act, rather than a linear project management approach, is also helpful. The emphasis on the social processes of putting ideas into action chimes with the relational principle of Transitional Safeguarding, as does the focus on developing trust and attending to relational strategies as well as technical strategies (Metz et al 2022). All of this is in line with the collective nature of systems leadership and reminds us again to pay attention to the 'soft stuff'. This is about exercising curiosity: What are we noticing about our professional cultures as we try to create change? Have we created enough space for imagination? Do we trust each other enough to experiment? Do we feel safe enough to try something and fail?

Whole systems change is not simple. Nonetheless, local areas have the necessary expertise and motivation to do it, and some have started the journey in relation to Transitional Safeguarding.

Learning from other whole system approaches

One fairly well-known example of a whole-system approach to a complex social issue is that of violence reduction, in which the term 'whole system approach' is increasingly used to describe what has previously been termed a 'public health approach' (for example, Craston et al 2020). Both terms emphasise the importance of taking an ecological perspective; understanding issues (and potential solutions) at the individual, relational, community, and societal level; and seeing these levels as interconnected and dynamic (Fraser and Irwin-Rogers 2021). A public health perspective is helpful to the framing of Transitional Safeguarding as it places prevention at the heart of a system-wide approach to improving outcomes. In the previously mentioned analysis of Think Family, the authors call for 'a coherent … understanding of primary, secondary and tertiary prevention across the life-course' (Tew et al 2016, p 6). This call to action could equally be applied to Transitional Safeguarding, in which the economic and moral arguments promote the need for prevention to be prioritised over rigid eligibility (Holmes 2022a).

While the World Health Organisation emphasises the role of targeted and evaluated interventions in its articulation of a public health approach (World Health Organization 2021), learning from Scotland offers a different picture. Specific interventions to address violence were applied 'against a backdrop of decreasing punitivism, investment in early years and education, and a large number of small-scale initiatives at local and public sector level ... alongside a dedicated media and communications strategy [designed] to change the conversation on violence [and] a shift in Scottish political rhetoric towards a more compassionate era of justice' (Fraser and Irwin-Rogers 2021, p 9). It is this multifaceted, multi-component, multi-level approach that warrants the Scottish approach to reducing violence as truly representing whole system, cultural, and social change (Youth Violence Commission 2018). Key to Scotland's success was adapting approaches applied in Cincinnati and Boston and tailoring these to the Scottish context (Fraser and Irwin-Rogers 2021). This chimes with Transitional Safeguarding being organised around a set of key principles that are adaptable to local circumstances (Holmes 2022a).

This recognition of local context is echoed in Public Health England's 2019 guidance for sector leaders, in which six core features are identified as characterising an effective, place-based, multi-agency approach to violence. These are:

- the focus on a population;
- the work is with and for communities;
- the approach is not constrained by organisational or professional boundaries;
- the focus on generating long-term as well as short-term solutions;
- data and intelligence are used to identify burdens on the population, including any inequalities';
- the approach is rooted in evidence of effectiveness to tackle the problem. (Public Health England 2019b, p 14)

A connection can be made between these ingredients of a whole system approach and the tenets of Transitional Safeguarding, in particular the emphasis on participatory engagement, (in)equalities, and taking an evidence-informed approach to determining what might work in a given context.

This same guidance outlines five principles for operationalising such an approach, known as the '5 Cs': collaboration; co-production; cooperation; counter-narrative; and community consensus (Public Health England 2019b). Again, alignment with the key principles of Transitional Safeguarding is evident. Collaboration across multi-agency partners, and between practice and policy, is a fundamental aspect of Transitional Safeguarding. Co-production of solutions, and problem definitions, is integral to local efforts to embed Transitional Safeguarding; meaningful participation with young people and those who care about them is particularly key here. Cooperation, in terms of Transitional Safeguarding, requires effective partnership working and collective imagining of a different approach for young people. This in turn promotes a counter-narrative to the binary paradigm that pervades existing safeguarding activity. Through meaningful inclusive engagement, community consensus can be developed as to what Transitional Safeguarding means in that particular locality. Examples in Chapter 9 illustrate some of these characteristics and principles in how local partners are developing their Transitional Safeguarding approach.

Framing of Transitional Safeguarding in terms of policy solutions

The framing of Transitional Safeguarding as a discrete solution or intervention must be resisted. Policy solutions can sometimes fail to distinguish between uncertainty (a lack of information or knowledge) and ambiguity (wherein a problem and solution/s can be interpreted in a variety of ways) (Cairney 2019a). Transitional Safeguarding policy solutions, if not careful, could seek to address uncertainty by pursuing evidence of 'what works' (Cairney 2019b) and thus contribute to the problems associated with evidence-based practice described earlier. Like innovation frameworks, the tendency to think of policy making as a straightforward linear process from setting priorities, implementing solutions, and evaluating impact (Benoit 2013) is a poor fit for Transitional Safeguarding. Rather than seeking to eliminate the ambiguity of Transitional Safeguarding it is arguably more helpful to acknowledge that multiple interpretations of both problems and solutions are inevitable and can in fact be highly beneficial to any social innovation.

Engaging with these multiple perspectives, as is necessary for the emergent and participatory nature of Transitional Safeguarding, helps to situate policy development as a social process of inquiry. This can help to avoid the linear approaches that are symptomatic of New Public Management,[3] instead reconceptualising the endeavour as one of collective and iterative learning. Human Learning Systems presents an alternative to the dominant paradigm of public service through management, markets, and metrics, instead arguing that creating positive outcomes relies on professionals understanding the complexity of people's lives and learning through exploration and experimentation alongside each other (Lowe et al 2022). Inherent to Human Learning Systems approaches is an acknowledgement of the power structures at play in people's personal and professional lives, and the importance of interrogating inclusion (or exclusion) within system analysis. This perspective connects with the focus on equity, equality, diversity, and inclusion within Transitional Safeguarding, and prompts a different approach to how the agenda for change might be usefully framed.

Earlier in this chapter, a simplistic change proposition was offered – that young people who need support to feel safe should receive this irrespective of their eighteenth birthday. From this, a problem definition of Transitional Safeguarding could be articulated as vulnerable young people being left without safeguarding support upon reaching 18, meaning their risks and difficulties often escalate in later adulthood.

However, this framing could lend itself to the kind of linear or simplistic solution that yields unintended consequences, actively undermines whole system change, or at best fails to achieve the intended outcome. A useful approach can be found in Bacchi's (2009) 'What's the problem represented to be?' (WPR) analytical framework for interrogating policy. Bacchi suggests applying six lines of enquiry to a policy dilemma, in order to disrupt the idea that complex problems are fixed and universally agreed upon, and so avoid the privileging of a technical process to policy solutions. Applying Bacchi's questions to the above problem definition highlighted the potential for unintended consequences, and 'solutions' that could be both counter to the notion of whole systems change but also to the core tenets of Transitional Safeguarding. If the problem is articulated as 'Vulnerable young people are being left without safeguarding support upon reaching 18, meaning that their risks and difficulties often escalate in later adulthood', it is easy to imagine a policy solution that seeks to identify 'vulnerable' young people, thus contributing to labelling and stigma, and potentially leading to punitive policy and public attitudes (Schneider et al 2014). Or perhaps this framing could locate the problem with adult safeguarding thresholds, inviting a solution such as a slightly different set of eligibility criteria but without addressing the problematic construct of vulnerability as static and individualistic. Expanding the problem definition to include the economic effects of a binary system might help to de-individualise the problem but could lend itself to the kind of policy solution that pursues narrowly defined evidence of 'what works' in order to generate savings to the public purse.

Bacchi's WPR questions were applied to a variety of alternative problem definitions, each bearing the risk of 'solutions' that could actively contradict the principles of Transitional Safeguarding and could create new problems by failing to engage with the system complexities. Subsequently, a new problem definition is tentatively offered here:

> The current systems (meaning the social, legal, policy, and professional systems that influence young people's safeguarding) are not connected, coherent nor relational enough to respond effectively, ethically, and cost-effectively to young people facing risk and harm as they make their individual journey into adulthood.

This problem definition, albeit imperfect and requiring much more consultation and reflection, can enable a useful positioning of Transitional Safeguarding. It frames Transitional Safeguarding not as a discrete solution to be applied, but instead as the connective tissue in a complex ecosystem. This is important, given the resource and time pressures facing professionals and policy makers. If Transitional Safeguarding can be understood as a way of joining up and enabling a variety of other developments and approaches, it might contribute to establishing the coherence and cognitive participation required to embed new ideas (May and Finch 2009). It is worthwhile, therefore, to emphasise the connection between this agenda and other sector activity and imperatives. These points of connection include the complementary relationship between Transitional Safeguarding, Contextual Safeguarding and Complex Safeguarding (Firmin et al 2019) and the alignment of Transitional Safeguarding with Making Safeguarding Personal (MSP) (Cocker et al 2021). The emphasis of Transitional Safeguarding on strengths-based and rights-based approaches also provides a strong connection with social work values and regulatory standards (Office of the Chief Social Worker for Adults 2021). There are clear connections between Transitional Safeguarding and Child First youth justice policy and the focus on improving transitions between youth and adult justice services (Holmes and Smith 2022). Transitional Safeguarding also aligns with key developments within health, including the NHS long-term plan and the embedding of integrated care systems, while the attention to exploitation and harm outside the home within Transitional Safeguarding chimes with children's services policy reform (Department for Education 2023b).

Framing Transitional Safeguarding as 'connective tissue', something that operates in the spaces between existing siloes, better reflects the complex relationships and behaviours comprising whole system change.

Applying the key principles of Transitional Safeguarding to the endeavour of whole systems change

The issues explored in this chapter suggest it is important to maintain congruence between the intended change and the way that change is pursued. In line with NPT's emphasis on reflexive monitoring and coherence (May and Finch 2009), and in order to critically reflect on the role we (the authors) play in enabling systems change, consideration is now given to how each of the six key principles of Transitional Safeguarding might inform ongoing activity to develop the approach and embed the concept.

Being evidence-informed means drawing on and valuing evidence in *all* its forms, creating opportunities for participatory research (Green 2008), building capacity for inclusive social research (Government Social Research Profession 2022), and ensuring that systems thinking or whole system change are seen not as abstract theories but as 'reflexive, transdisciplinary praxis' (Ison and Blackmore 2014, p 133).

Taking a contextual and/or ecological perspective means engaging with the complex ecosystem(s) of intertwined personal, professional, policy, and political spheres (Salmon et al 2020). Those of us advocating for Transitional Safeguarding must ensure our own interests do not inadvertently position Transitional Safeguarding as a new intervention within our specific professional field. Engaging interdisciplinary knowledge and diverse perspectives will help to retain a focus on the wider ecosystem as the concept develops.

Just like young people, the concept of Transitional Safeguarding must grow and evolve over time. This means demonstrating a maturation within the discourse, making the transition from arguing *why* Transitional Safeguarding is important to *how* it might be progressed. We must eschew familiar understandings of innovation as a discrete solution and instead need to 'think like a system and act like an entrepreneur' (Conway et al 2017). In terms of Transitional Safeguarding, this invites us to ask what kind of system would we create if we started with evidence rather than established norms? How would we use our collective resource if the explicit shared goal was to ensure best use of public money within a life-course approach?

In order to model the relational principle of Transitional Safeguarding, those of us aiming to promote systems change must be relational and inclusive in the continued development of the concept. This means reaching across boundaries in terms of knowledge disciplines (Williams 2002), building trusting relationships (Metz et al 2022), and seeing the practice of whole systems change practice as *being* not only *doing*.

Attending to issues of equity, equality, diversity, and inclusion is an important aspect of whole system change activity. This requires advocates of Transitional Safeguarding to relentlessly argue for greater diversity and inclusivity within evidence generation (including research funding), and links to the principle of evidence-informed practice in that it requires the explicit valuing of knowledge held by marginalised groups who are too often excluded from traditional constructs of evidence-based practice (Abimbola 2023). As white able-bodied authors, we want to challenge ourselves on this issue and hope to engage a diverse network of Transitional Safeguarding advocates and champions.

Lastly, of course, the development of the Transitional Safeguarding agenda – just like developing a local Transitional Safeguarding offer – must be participative. We have been privileged to work with organisations such as the National Leaving Care Benchmarking Forum and the Care Leavers National Movement, to ensure the voices of young people are shaping how we understand and describe the system-change endeavour. We are determined to engage more young people, particularly those whose voices are too often excluded, to keep informing and improving our work.

Conclusion

Transitional Safeguarding is a whole system approach, not an intervention within a system, and its development is an issue of whole system change. Developing and embedding the concept is an exercise in collective learning, it is not neat or linear. This can present a number of complexities, but there is much we can learn from other whole system approaches, from systems leadership and systems thinking, and from research regarding innovation and implementation.

The task ahead may be complex and difficult, but local areas and agencies are showing that it can be done. Their learning shows that by taking small steps, exercising curiosity, and collaboration, change is possible. The key principles of Transitional Safeguarding can act as an anchor to help navigate the complexity and challenges of whole system change.

The work feels hard because it *is* hard; and it is hard because it matters. On the days we feel daunted by the scale of the task, young people's ambition for change can be a motivating force. As one young person put it when crafting Chapter 1:

> I think it's about time that young people got to actually change the system to the way that it should be. Change it for everyone that comes after you. It's time to … see what we can do for other young people in the future, right?

Right.

Conclusion: Moving forward

This book captures what we have learned about Transitional Safeguarding over the past six years. We began with the voices of young people – it is their experiences that lie at the heart of this book. All young people need support moving into adulthood and this can include support to be safe. There remain significant gaps in safeguarding services for too many young people; this is something we have known about for some time, and so many of the ideas behind Transitional Safeguarding are not new. Over the past 25 years efforts have been made to address some of the issues that young people face. However helpful these changes have been in addressing specific issues, the evidence shows that making fragmented changes to various parts of the system does not achieve what is needed. Young people tell us this; colleagues tell us this. What is new is our argument that nothing short of whole systems change will do.

We cannot wait for the revolution – and evolution is slower still. We need to think about the ways in which change is possible *now* and in-so-doing, build on small steps as well as tackle some of the big issues. However, there is no silver bullet here. Whole systems change can mean a great many things. The key to this is clarity about how the small steps contribute to the systems change and understanding how efforts across different services or disciplines fit together to achieve the broader vision of a Transitional Safeguarding approach.

Various systems and structures govern and influence this work; at a macro level we have explored in the book some of the differences and similarities in existing legal and policy drivers in children's and adults' safeguarding that contribute to (but are not solely responsible for) gaps in safeguarding practices with young people. We have taken time in the book to explore the legal and social policy contexts in which we work in England in Chapters 3, 5, and 6. While challenging to navigate, the legal frameworks do not prohibit Transitional Safeguarding. It is possible for professionals working at all levels in local services to be creative within policy and practice frameworks to work around blocks and barriers created by the wholly separate systems for those aged under and over 18. Some examples include making use of the enabling aspects of law (powers in the Care Act 2014 and Children Act 2004) as well enacting the duties covered in legislation (see Chapters 5 and 7).

At a micro level, the experiences of young people are key. As we said in the introduction, unless young people are placed at the centre of this work then their needs will not be fully understood or addressed, and any system transformation will not achieve its goal. The perspectives from young people, shared in Chapter 1, enable us to understand what is wrong with existing systems, structures, and services as well as what is positive and valuable. Hearing young people express their views, needs, and aspirations is critically important; too much of the current service 'offer' to young people is experienced as 'doing to' rather than 'working with' them. Practitioners working with young people also need knowledge, skills, and legal literacy, including a comprehensive understanding of mental capacity and the relationship between it and executive functioning. This matters as too often young people in unsafe situations are described as having chosen to do 'x' or having made an unwise decision, and now that they are 16 or 18 there is nothing that can be done to prevent it. This is not a correct interpretation of the relevant legislation; they may have been manipulated, coerced, or forced into situations. We want to encourage practitioners to think beyond the simplistic binaries to be curious about young people's lives, and expect these to be complex and multifaceted, because all our lives are.

It is worth restating that Transitional Safeguarding is not a model. There is no manual that provides a step-by-step guide to enacting Transitional Safeguarding as a discrete intervention. The six overarching key principles that are described and discussed in Chapters 2, 8, and 10 in this book are designed to enable people in local areas to work flexibly within these principles according to their diverse contexts and circumstances. The six key principles of Transitional Safeguarding are:

- evidence-informed
- ecological and contextual
- developmental and transitional by design
- relational
- equalities-oriented
- participative

We are at the beginning of a journey to improve services for young people who are at risk of or experiencing abuse, neglect, or exploitation. This is not only about safeguarding services per se, nor is it about transitions between services, although both are part of the overall equation. We have explored some of the challenges, opportunities, and learning gleaned from local areas and agencies who have embarked on their own journey to develop a Transitional Safeguarding approach. These experiences from practice are highlighted in Chapters 4, 7, and 9.

Moving away from the safeguarding binary

One of the powerful drivers that create issues for safeguarding young people which we discuss in the book, specifically in Chapter 2, is the paradigm of binaries. These binaries include binaries in children's and adults' safeguarding legislation and practices; binaries in the life course, particularly between childhood and adulthood; and binaries in how professionals view a young person's situation pre and post-18 years. Further examples of these binary constructs can be seen in how professionals consider victim/perpetrator; vulnerability/culpability; and protection/autonomy. Understanding the dynamics and implications of these binaries is critical to improving practice with young people.

Holding young people responsible for their own adversity is unethical and unsafe, just as treating young people at risk as passive is developmentally inappropriate and ineffective. Inequality and poverty have particularly pernicious effects on young people's safety, and so understanding the socio-economic context is essential to taking Transitional Safeguarding forward. At its most damaging, young people face discrimination, homelessness, unemployment, poor mental health, criminalisation, and can experience other factors related to multiple exclusion, such as drug addiction and exploitation. Professional systems struggle to hold the 'both/and' constructs in mind when it comes to understanding binaries and this influences how young people are safeguarded. We know that public services face enormous cost pressures from long-term under-resourcing, which also impacts on the services that can be provided, even where there is a statutory duty to provide them. This is a challenging environment in which to consider or try to attempt transformational change, and yet we have found many people and partnerships who are prepared to think and do differently.

Leading change

To date, the amount of public money spent on developing and delivering a Transitional Safeguarding approach has been minimal. And yet this has not stopped innovation in this space. Similarly, there were very limited resources available to support the culture and practice shift in safeguarding adults – Making Safeguarding Personal (MSP). This did not stop MSP's development and eventual inclusion within the Care Act 2014 as *the* approach underpinning adult safeguarding in England. We think there are some parallels between the development of Transitional Safeguarding and MSP as they share core principles that underpin both approaches. They both entail involving people to achieve safety in their lives, and a change in practice across all parties involved in safeguarding. The difference between the two is that MSP was part of a wider shift towards personalisation in adult social care services and was aimed specifically at culture change. Transitional Safeguarding requires systems change and so is even more challenging. Both involve leadership at all levels to advocate for, drive, and deliver change.

To realise and publicise the benefits of and further develop Transitional Safeguarding, there are some essential requirements to consider:

- Start with young people. Build support offers wherein they participate as partners. Acknowledge the complexity of their lives and be driven by their individual needs and context, not the services that are available. Unless we acknowledge the importance of this, any change to systems and structures will not be effective.

- Communication and relationships are essential at every stage. This is a central tenet of innovation and system change, including Transitional Safeguarding. This includes between a young person and practitioners they are working with (who know the young person and are their advocate), between practitioners from different services, the horizontal and vertical relationships between operational and strategic managers and leaders within and between organisations, and the strategic planning groups that determine priorities and associated resources for their areas.
- Understand the nature of risks and harms that affect young people today and ensure that responses to these are not bound by age but are developmental and transitional by design.
- Be prepared to experiment, recognising not everything will succeed. System change is iterative, sometimes slow, and can be frustrating as well as rewarding. Maintaining a clear sense of purpose – holding onto your north star – is important to maintaining morale and momentum.

Regardless of organisation or role, anyone can promote Transitional Safeguarding – not only senior leaders. Of course, good leadership is essential, but practitioners can also lead change. Most often they have more power than those young people who are falling through the gaps in the current safeguarding systems. We hope that this book provides insight and inspiration to take forward Transitional Safeguarding and in so doing, makes a difference to young people's lives.

Notes

Introduction

[1] See www.padlet.com/transitionalsafeguarding

[2] The Special Issue on Transitional Safeguarding was published in January 2022. See: www.tandfonline.com/toc/cpra20/34/1

[3] See www.theinnovateproject.co.uk/

[4] Adultification is a concept that highlights how biased assumptions can mean certain children (Black children, for example) are more likely to be ascribed adult-like characteristics, thereby diminishing their perceived vulnerability. See Davis and Marsh (2022) for a fuller discussion.

Chapter 1

[1] Rosie is a participation and development worker at the National House Project.

[2] The National House Project provides support and expertise to local authorities around the country to set up and manage Local House Projects so that young people leave care in a planned and supported way, enabling young people to live connected and fulfilling lives.

[3] The Children and Families Act 2014 introduced a new duty on local authorities in England to advise, assist, and support fostered young people to stay with their foster families when they reach 18 up to age 21, if both parties agree. This is called 'staying put'.

[4] Child and Adolescent Mental Health Services.

[5] Deprivation of Liberty Safeguards – the procedure prescribed in law when it is necessary to deprive of their liberty a resident or patient who lacks capacity to consent to their care and treatment in order to keep them safe from harm (an amendment to the Mental Capacity Act 2005).

Chapter 2

[1] Home invasion, by those seeking an outpost to enable the distribution of drugs.

Chapter 3

[1] See the NSPCC website for an overview of child protection practices across the UK: https://learning.nspcc.org.uk/child-protection-system/history-of-child-protection-in-the-uk

[2] https://www.local.gov.uk/topics/social-care-health-and-integration/adult-social-care/resources-safeguarding-adults-boards/practitioners

[3] https://www.gov.scot/publications/adult-support-protection-scotland-act-2007-short-introduction-part-1-act/
[4] https://law.gov.wales/safeguarding

Chapter 4

[1] County Lines is where illegal drugs are transported from one area to another, often across police and local authority boundaries (although not exclusively), usually by children or vulnerable people who are coerced into it by gangs. The 'County Line' is the mobile phone line used to take the orders for drugs. Importing areas (areas where the drugs are taken to) are reporting increased levels of violence and weapons-related crimes as a result of this trend. (www.nationalcrimeagency.gov.uk/what-we-do/crime-threats/drug-trafficking/county-lines).
[2] Care leaver covenant: www.mycovenant.org.uk.

Chapter 5

[1] The Children Act 1989 included the duty to ascertain children's wishes and feelings during care proceedings. This was amended by the Children Act 2004, which extended this duty to earlier stages of social work intervention before court involvement.
[2] Social Work England: www.socialworkengland.org.uk/standards/professional-standards/
[3] International Federation of Social Workers: Global Definition of Social Work – International Federation of Social Workers (ifsw.org).
[4] It should be noted that the author of this chapter is the Chair of the Contextual Safeguarding UK Advisory Group.
[5] A £200m programme of investment in innovation and accompanying evaluation. See www.gov.uk/guidance/childrens-social-care-innovation-programme-insights-and-evaluation
[6] These are 1) to act in the best interests, and promote the physical and mental health and well-being, of those children and young people, 2) to encourage those children and young people to express their views, wishes, and feelings, 3) to take into account the views, wishes, and feelings of those children and young people, 4) to help those children and young people gain access to, and make the best use of, services provided by the local authority and its relevant partners, 5) to promote high aspirations and seek to secure the best outcomes for those children and young people, 6) for those children and young people to be safe, and for stability in their home lives, relationships, and education or work, and 7) to prepare those children and young people for adulthood and independent living (DfE 2018c).

Chapter 6

[1] Chapter 14 of the statutory guidance describes in detail the range of safeguarding duties and responsibilities that should be undertaken by different organisations and agencies (DHSC 2023).

2 **Empowerment** – People being supported and encouraged to make their own decisions and informed consent. 'I am asked what I want as the outcomes from the safeguarding process and these directly inform what happens.'
Prevention – It is better to take action before harm occurs. 'I receive clear and simple information about what abuse is, how to recognise the signs, and what I can do to seek help.'
Proportionality – The least intrusive response appropriate to the risk presented. 'I am sure that the professionals will work in my interest, as I see them and they will only get involved as much as needed.'
Protection – Support and representation for those in greatest need. 'I get help and support to report abuse and neglect. I get help so that I am able to take part in the safeguarding process to the extent to which I want.'
Partnership – Local solutions through services working with their communities that have a part to play in preventing, detecting, and reporting neglect and abuse. 'I know that staff treat any personal and sensitive information in confidence, only sharing what is helpful and necessary. I am confident that professionals will work together and with me to get the best result for me.'
Accountability – Accountability and transparency in delivering safeguarding. 'I understand the role of everyone involved in my life and so do they.'

3 This website provides a range of tools about MSP: https://www.local.gov.uk/our-support/partners-care-and-health/care-and-health-improvement/safeguarding-resources/making-safeguarding-personal [Accessed 13 November 2023].

Chapter 7

1 With huge thanks to Sarah Williams and Michael Preston-Shoot for some of the legal information contained in this chapter.

2 https://www.gov.uk/government/collections/case-management-guidance

3 Annex A, The Youth to Adult Transitions Framework Process Map 2021: https://assets.publishing.service.gov.uk/government/uploads/system/uploads/attachment_data/file/1001348/Annex_A_Youth_to_Adult_Transitions_Framework_Process_Map_2021.pdf

4 Eligible young people are aged 16 or 17, have been looked after for a period or periods totalling at least 13 weeks starting after their fourteenth birthday and ending at least one day after their sixteenth birthday, and are still in care. There is a duty to support these young people up to the age of 18, wherever they are living. (CLCA explanatory notes – www.legislation.gov.uk).

5 Relevant young people are those aged 16 and 17 who meet the criteria for eligible children but who leave care. Regulations may exclude certain groups, such as children who return home permanently and children who receive respite care. Local authorities may, for example, take highly dependent children for short periods to give their carers a break. This group would remain the responsibility of their families and would not be eligible for the new arrangements even if their periods of respite care added up to the prescribed period for eligibility. (CLCA explanatory notes – www.legislation.gov.uk).

[6] Former relevant young people are those who, before reaching the age of 18, were either eligible or relevant children. (CLCA explanatory notes – www.legislation.gov.uk).
[7] *Shah v London Borough of Barnet* [1983] 1 All ER 226 (HL).
[8] Baker J, GW v A Local Authority [2014] EWCOP20, para. 45.
[9] This links to a special issue about Transitional Safeguarding published in January 2022: www.tandfonline.com/toc/cpra20/34/1 [Accessed 13 November 2023].

Chapter 8

[1] The study received ethical approval from the School of Social Work Ethics Committee at the University of East Anglia. Fifty-nine reviews that were undertaken between 2014 and 2021 were identified and analysed. The full results of the study will be presented in a forthcoming work by Cocker et al.
[2] This links to Government advice on financial support young people aged between 16 and 19 may be able to access to help them participate in education and training: www.gov.uk/topic/schools-colleges-childrens-services/support-for-children-young-people [Accessed 13 November 2023].
[3] This is defined as 'the co-existence of two or more chronic conditions in the same individual and includes both physical and mental health conditions (Smith et al 2013, p 10).

Chapter 9

[1] See: www.padlet.com/transitionalsafeguarding [Accessed 13 November 2023].
[2] See https://vimeo.com/770791854/5b80707cc5 [Accessed 13 November 2023].
[3] For West Midlands information please see: www.westmidlands-vrp.org/tackling-exploitation-abuse/); for Southend, Essex, and Thurrock, see: https://www.escb.co.uk/media/2152/set-expoitation-strategy-2019-24-final.pdf [Accessed 13 November 2023].
[4] See: www.padlet.com/transitionalsafeguarding [Accessed 13 November 2023].

Chapter 10

[1] A quote often attributed to ex-CEO of PepsiCo, Roger Enrico, though variations are widely used in business management literature.
[2] A whole family approach involving multiple stakeholders and practices, discussed in Chapter 5.
[3] New Public Management emerged in the 1980s and was an attempt to make the public sector more 'business-like' and to improve the efficiency of government by applying management models from the private sector.

References

Abimbola, S. (2023) 'The art of medicine: when dignity meets evidence', *The Lancet*, 401(10374): 340–341.

Adams, G., Dobles, I., Gómez, L., Kurtiş, T., and Molina, L. (2015) 'Decolonizing psychological science: introduction to the special thematic', *Journal of Social and Political Psychology*, 3(1): 213–238.

Albury, D., Beresford, T., Dew, S., Horton, T., Illingworth, J., and Langford, K. (2018) Against the odds: successfully scaling innovation in the NHS, Innovation Unit/Health Foundation. https://www.health.org.uk/publications/against-the-odds-successfully-scaling-innovation-in-the-nhs [Accessed 30 October 2023].

American Psychiatric Association (2013) *Diagnostic and Statistical Manual of Mental Disorders –DSM-5*, Arlington, VA: APA Publishing.

American Psychological Association (2016) Clinical practice guideline for treatment of posttraumatic stress disorder (PTSD) in adults. https://www.apa.org/ptsd-guideline/ptsd.pdf [Accessed 30 October 2023].

Anonymous Safeguarding Adult Board (undated) *Safeguarding Adults Review Briefing: 'Colin'*. https://www.kirklees.gov.uk/beta/adult-social-care-providers/pdf/sar-colin-national-briefing.pdf [Accessed 30 October 2023].

APPG (2017) APPG for ending homelessness: Homelessness prevention for care leavers, prison leavers and survivors of domestic violence (July). https://www.crisis.org.uk/media/237534/appg_for_ending_homelessness_report_2017_pdf.pdf [Accessed 30 October 2023]

Arnett, J. (2000) 'Emerging adulthood: a theory of development from the late teens through the twenties', *American Psychologist*, 55(5): 469–480.

Arnett, J.J. (2004) *Emerging Adulthood: The Winding Road from the Late Teens through the Twenties*, New York: Oxford University Press.

Arnett, J.J. (2007) 'Emerging adulthood: what is it, and what is it good for?', *Child Development Perspectives*, 1: 68–73.

Arnold, R. and Wade, J. (2015) 'A definition of systems thinking: a systems approach', *Procedia Computer Science*, 44: 669–678.

Arnstein, S. (1969) 'Eight rungs on the ladder of citizen participation', *Journal of the American Institute of Planners*, 35(4): 216–224.

Asmussen, K., Masterman, T., McBride, T., and Molloy, D. (2022) Trauma-informed care: understanding the use of trauma-informed approaches within children's social care. https://www.eif.org.uk/report/trauma-informed-care-understanding-the-use-of-trauma-informed-approaches-within-childrens-social-care [Accessed 30 October 2023].

Association of Directors of Adult Social Services (ADASS) (2019) *A Framework for Making Decisions on the Duty to Carry Out Safeguarding Adults Enquiries*, London: ADASS/ LGA. https://www.adass.org.uk/media/7326/adass-advice-note.pdf [Accessed 30 October 2023].

Association of Directors of Adult Social Services (ADASS) (2022) *ADASS Spring Budget Survey 2022*, London: ADASS. Available at: https://www.adass.org.uk/adass-spring-budget-survey-2022 [Accessed 30 October 2023].

Association of Directors of Children's Services (ADCS) (2013) *What Is Care For? Alternative Models of Care for Adolescents*. ADCS Position Statement, Manchester: ADCS.

Association of Directors of Children's Services (2021) *Safeguarding Pressures: Phase 7*, Manchester: ADCS.

Association of Directors of Children's Services (2022) *Safeguarding Pressures: Phase 8*, Manchester: ADCS.

Audit Commission (2008) *Are We There Yet? Improving Governance and Resource Management in Children's Trusts*, London: Audit Commission. https://lx.iriss.org.uk/sites/default/files/resources/AreWeThereYet29Oct08REP.pdf [Accessed 30 October 2023].

Bacchi, C. (2009) *Analysing Policy: What's the Problem Represented to Be?*, London: Pearson Education.

Bachmann, M.O., O'Brien, M., Husbands, C., Shreeve, A., Jones, N., Watson, J., Reading, R., Thoburn, J., and Mugford, M. (2009) 'Integrating children's services in England: national evaluation of children's trusts', *Child: Care, Health and Development*, 35: 257–265.

Baginsky, M., Hickman, B., Harris, J., Manthorpe, J., Sanders, M., O'Higgins, A., Schoenwald, E., and Clayton, V. (2020) *Evaluation of MTM's Signs of Safety Pilots Evaluation Report*, London: Department for Education.

Bandura, A. (1977) 'Self-efficacy: toward a unifying theory of behavioral change', *Psychological Review*, 84(2): 191–215.

Barlow, C., Kidd, A., Green, S.T., and Darby, B. (2022) 'Circles of analysis: a systemic model of child criminal exploitation', *Journal of Children's Services*, 17(3): 158–174.

Barnardo's (2019) Toolkit for supporting care leavers in custody 2019, HM Prison and Probation Service. https://www.nicco.org.uk/directory-of-resources/toolkit-for-supporting-care-leavers-in-custody [Accessed 30 October 2023].

Bateman, F. and Cocker, C. (2021) Safeguarding Adults Review: Madeleine, Croydon Safeguarding Adults Board. https://www.croydonsab.co.uk/wp-content/uploads/2022/03/PDF-Madeleine-SAR-Final-Report.pdf [Accessed 30 October 2023].

Bateman, T. (2017) The state of youth justice 2017: An overview of trends and developments. National Association of Youth Justice. https://thenayj.org.uk/cmsAdmin/uploads/state-of-youth-justice-2020-final-sep20.pdf [Accessed 30 October 2023].

Batty, D. (2003) 'Catalogue of cruelty', *The Guardian*, 27 January. https://www.theguardian.com/society/2003/jan/27/childrensservices.childprotection?CMP=share_btn_link [Accessed 1 January 2022].

Batty, D. (2005) 'Timeline: a history of child protection', *The Guardian* 18 May. https://www.theguardian.com/society/2005/may/18/childrensservices2 [Accessed 1 January 2022].

Beckett, H., Holmes, D. and Walker, J. (2017) *Child Sexual Exploitation Definition & Guide for Professionals*, Luton and Dartington: The International Centre: Researching Child Sexual Exploitation, Violence and Trafficking, and Research in Practice. https://bettercarenetwork.org/sites/default/files/Child%20Sexual%20Exploitation%20Extended%20Text.pdf [Accessed 30 October 2023].

Beckett, H. and Lloyd, J. (2022) 'Growing pains: developing safeguarding responses to adolescent harms', in D. Holmes (ed) *Safeguarding Young People: Rights, Risks, Resilience and Relationships*, London: Jessica Kingsley Publications.

Bennis, W. and Nanus, B. (1985) *Leaders: The Strategies for Taking Charge*, New York: Harper & Row.

Benoit, F. (2013) *Public Policy Models and Their Usefulness in Public Health: The Stages Model.* Montréal, Québec: National Collaborating Centre for Healthy Public Policy.

Bigland, C., Evans, D., Bolden, R., and Rae, M. (2020) 'Systems leadership in practice: thematic insights from three public health case studies', *BMC Public Health*, 20: 1735.

Bion, W.R. (1962) *Learning from Experience*, London: Heinemann.

Blankenstein, N.E., Crone, E.A., van den Bos, W., and van Duijvenvoorde, A.C.K. (2016) 'Dealing with uncertainty: testing risk- and ambiguity-attitude across adolescence', *Developmental Neuropsychology*, 41(1–2): 77–92.

Bolden, R., Gulati, A., and Edwards, G. (2019) 'Mobilizing change in public services: insights from a systems leadership development intervention', *International Journal of Public Administration*, 43: 26–36.

Bostock, L., Munro, E., Khan, M., Lynch, A., Baker, C., Newlands, F., and Antonpoulou V. (2020) *Havering: Face to Face Pathways: Final Evaluation Report*. London: Department for Education/Tilda Goldberg for Social Work and Social Care, University of Bedfordshire.

Bowyer, S. (2022) What is early help? Concepts, policy directions and multi-agency perspectives. Ofsted and Research in Practice. https://www.gov.uk/government/publications/early-help-concepts-policy-directions-and-multi-agency-perspectives [Accessed 30 October 2023].

Brammer, A. (2020) *Social Work Law*, Harlow: Pearson Education.

Brandon, M., Bailey, S., and Belderson, P. (2010) Building on the learning from SCRs: a two-year analysis of child protection data base notifications 2007–2009. https://assets.publishing.service.gov.uk/media/5a7ab80bed915d71db8b2048/DFE-RR040.pdf [Accessed 30 October 2023].

Brandon, M., Belderson, P., Warren, C., Howe, D., Gardner, R., Dodsworth, J., and Black, J. (2008) Analysing child deaths and serious injury through abuse and neglect: What we can learn? A biennial analysis of SCRs 2003–2005. https://dera.ioe.ac.uk/7190/1/dcsf-rr023.pdf [Accessed 30 October 2023].

Brandon, M,. Bailey, S., Belderson, P., Gardner, R., Sidebotham, P., Dodsworth, J., and Black, J. (2009) Understanding SCRs and their impact: A biennial analysis of SCRs 2005–07. https://dera.ioe.ac.uk/11151/1/DCSF-RR129(R).pdf [Accessed 30 October 2023].

Brandon, M., Sidebotham, P., Bailey, S., and Belderson, P. (2011) *A Study of Recommendations Arising from Serious Case Reviews 2009–2010*, London: Department for Education.

Brandon, M., Sidebotham, P., Bailey, S., Belderson, P., Hawley, C., Ellis, C., and Megson, M. (2012) *New Learning from SCRs: A Two-Year Analysis of SCRs 2009–2011 (Vol. RR226)*. https://assets.publishing.service.gov.uk/media/5a7a0893ed915d6d99f5cab0/DFE-RR226_Report.pdf [Accessed 30 October 2023].

Brandon, M., Sidebotham, P., Belderson, P., Cleaver, H., Dickens, J., Garstang, J., Harris, J., Sorensen, P., and Wate, R. (2020) *Complexity and Challenge: A Triennial Analysis of SCRs 2014–2017 Final Report March 2020*, London: Department for Education. https://assets.publishing.service.gov.uk/government/uploads/system/uploads/attachment_data/file/869586/TRIENNIAL_SCR_REPORT_2014_to_2017.pdf [Accessed 30 October 2023].

Braye, S. and Preston-Shoot, M. (2017a) 'Self-neglect and hoarding', in A. Cooper and E. White (eds) *Safeguarding Adults Under the Care Act: Understanding Good Practice*, London: Jessica Kingsley Publications, pp 40–56.

Braye, S. and Preston-Shoot, M. (2017b) *Learning from Safeguarding Adults Reviews: A Report for the London Safeguarding Adults Board*, London: London ADASS. https://londonadass.org.uk/wp-content/uploads/2014/12/London-SARs-Report-Final-Version.pdf [Accessed 30 October 2023].

Braye, S. and Preston-Shoot, M. (2020a) 'Adult safeguarding', in S. Braye and M. Preston-Shoot (eds) *The Care Act 2014, Wellbeing in Practice*, London: SAGE.

Braye, S. and Preston-Shoot, M. (2020b) 'Overview of the Care Act', in S. Braye and M. Preston-Shoot (eds) *The Care Act 2014, Wellbeing in Practice*, London: SAGE.

Braye, S., Orr, D., and Preston Shoot, M. (2015) 'Serious case review findings on the challenges of self-neglect: indicators for good practice', *The Journal of Adult Protection*, 17(2): 75–87.

Broadhurst, K., Wastell, D., White, S., Hall, C., Peckover, S., Thompson, K., Pithouse, A., and Davey, D. (2010) 'Performing "initial assessment": identifying the latent conditions for error at the front-door of local authority children's services', *The British Journal of Social Work*, 40(2): 352–370.

Bronfenbrenner, U. (1974) 'Developmental research, public policy, and the ecology of childhood', *Child Development*, 45(1): 1–5.

Bronfenbrenner, U. (1977) 'Toward an experimental ecology of human development', *American Psychologist*, 32(7): 513.

Bronfenbrenner, U. (2005) *Making Human Beings Human: Bioecological Perspectives on Human Development*, Thousand Oaks, CA, Sage Publications.

Butler-Sloss, E. (1988) *Report of the Inquiry into Child Abuse in Cleveland 1987 Cm 412*, London: Her Majesty's Stationery Office.

Butterworth, S., Singh, S.P., Birchwood, M., Islam, Z., Munro, E.R., Vostanis, P., Paul, M., Khan, A., and Simkiss, D. (2017) 'Transitioning care-leavers with mental health needs: "they set you up to fail!"', *Child and Adolescent Mental Health*, 22: 138–147.

Bynner, J. (2005) 'Rethinking the youth phase of the life course: the case for emerging adulthood?', *Journal of Youth Studies*, 8: 367–384.

Bywaters, P. (2008) 'Learning from experience: developing a research strategy for social work in the UK', *British Journal of Social Work*. 38(5): 936–952.

Bywaters, P. and Skinner, G. (2022) *The Relationship between Poverty and Child Abuse and Neglect: New Evidence*. Nuffield Foundation.

Cabinet Office (2008) *Think Family: Improving the Life Chances of Families at Risk*, London: Cabinet Office Social Exclusion Task Force.

Cairney, P. (2019a) *Fostering Evidence-Informed Policymaking: Uncertainty versus Ambiguity*, Montreal, Quebec: National Collaborating Centre for Healthy Public Policy.

Cairney, P. (2019b) 'Evidence and policy making', in A. Boaz, H. Davies, A. Fraser, and S. Nutley (eds) *What Works Now?*, Bristol: Policy Press.

Camillus, J. (2008) 'Strategy as a wicked problem', *Harvard Business Review*, May. https://hbr.org/2008/05/strategy-as-a-wicked-problem [Accessed 30 October 2023].

Campbell, F., Biggs, K., Aldiss, S.K., O'Neill, P.M., Clowes, M., McDonagh, J., While, A., and Gibson, F. (2016) 'Transition of care for adolescents from paediatric services to adult health services', *Cochrane Database Systematic Reviews*, 29(4): CD009794.

Care Council for Wales (2017) Social Services and Wellbeing (Wales) Act 2014: Getting in on the Act. https://socialcare.wales/cms-assets/documents/hub-downloads/Principles-Resource-Guide_March-17.pdf [Accessed 30 October 2023].

Care Quality Commission (2014) *From the Pond into the Sea: Children's Transitions to Adult Health Services*, Gallowgate: CQC.

Carr, H. and Goosey, D. (2017) *Law for Social Workers* (14th edn), Oxford: Oxford University Press.

Centre for Mental Health (2010) *The Economic and Social Costs of Mental Health Problems in 2009/10*. Centre for Mental Health.

Charlton, J. (2000) *Nothing about Us without Us: Disability, Oppression and Empowerment*, Oakland, CA: University of California Press.

Checkland, P. (1999) 'Systems thinking. Rethinking management information systems', in W.L. Currie and B. Galliers (eds) *Rethinking Management Information Systems*, Oxford: Oxford University Press, pp 45–56.

Children's Commissioner (2023) Children's Mental Health Services 2021–22 (March 2023), London: Children's Commissioner. https://www.childrenscommissioner.gov.uk/wp-content/uploads/2023/03/Childrens-Mental-Health-Services-2021-2022-1.pdf [Accessed 30 October 2023].

Children's Commissioner for England (2019) *The Characteristics of Gang-Associated Children and Young People. Technical Report*, London: Office of the Children's Commissioner.

Children's Society (2017) Criminal exploitation and county lines: a toolkit for working with children and young people. https://www.childrenssociety.org.uk/information/professionals/resources/county-lines-toolkit [Accessed 30 October 2023].

Child Safeguarding Practice Review Panel (2020) *It Was Hard to Escape: Safeguarding Children at Risk from Criminal Exploitation*, London: Crown Copyright. https://assets.publishing.service.gov.uk/government/uploads/system/uploads/attachment_data/file/870035/Safeguarding_children_at_risk_from_criminal_exploitation_review.pdf [Accessed 30 October 2023].

Child Safeguarding Practice Review Panel (2022) Child protection in England: national review into the murders of Arthur Labinjo-Hughes and Star Hobson, HM Government. https://assets.publishing.service.gov.uk/government/uploads/system/uploads/attachment_data/file/1078488/ALH_SH_National_Review_26-5-22.pdf [Accessed 30 October 2023].

Chowdry, H. and Fitzsimons, P. (2016) *The Cost of Late Intervention: Analysis*, London: Early Intervention Foundation.

Chughtai, S. and Blanchet K. (2017) 'Systems thinking in public health: a bibliographic contribution to a meta-narrative review', *Health Policy Plan*, 32: 585–594.

Clarke, A., Burgess, G., Morris, S., and Udagawa, C. (2015) 'Estimating the scale of youth homelessness in the UK: final report', Cambridge Centre for Housing and Planning Research. https://www.cchpr.landecon.cam.ac.uk/Research/Start-Year/2014/Estimating-the-scale-of-youth-homelessness-in-the-UK/Report [Accessed 30 October 2023].

Cockbain, E. (2013) 'Grooming and the "Asian sex gang predator": the construction of a racial crime threat', *Race & Class*, 54(4): 22–32.

Cocker, C. and Hafford-Letchfield, P. (eds) (2014) *Rethinking Anti-Discriminatory and Anti-Oppressive Theories for Social Work Practice*, Basingstoke: Palgrave.

Cocker, C. and Allain, L. (2019) *Social Work with Looked After Children* (3rd edn), London: Sage/Learning Matters.

Cocker, C., Minnis, H., and Sweeting, H. (2018) 'Potential value of the current mental health monitoring of children in state care in England', *BJPsych Open*, 4(6): 486–491.

Cocker, C., Cooper, A., and Holmes, D. (2022a) 'Transitional Safeguarding: transforming how adolescents and young adults are safeguarded', *British Journal of Social Work*, 52(3): 1287–1306.

Cocker, C., Cooper, A., and Holmes, D. (2022b) 'Transitional Safeguarding: bridging the gap between children's and adults' safeguarding responses', in D. Holmes (ed) *Safeguarding Young People: Risk, Rights, Resilience and Relationships*. London: Jessica Kingsley Publishing, pp 203–222.

Cocker, C., Cooper, A., Holmes, D., and Bateman, F. (2021) 'Transitional Safeguarding: presenting the case for developing Making Safeguarding Personal for young people in England', *The Journal of Adult Protection*, 23(3): 144–157.

Coleman, J. and Hagell, A. (2022) 'Understanding the age of adolescence', in D. Holmes (ed) *Safeguarding Young People: Risk, Rights, Resilience and Relationships*, London: Jessica Kingsley Publications.

Commission on Young Lives (2022) Hidden in plain sight: a national plan of action to support vulnerable teenagers to succeed and to protect them from adversity, exploitation and harm. https://thecommissiononyounglives.co.uk/wp-content/uploads/2022/11/COYL-FINAL-REPORT-FINAL-VERSION.pdf [Accessed 30 October 2023].

Conway, R., Masters, J., and Thorold, J. (2017) *From Design Thinking to Systems Change: How to Invest in Innovation for Social Impact*, London: RSA Action and Research Centre.

Cooper, A. (2019) *Making Safeguarding Personal Outcomes Framework: Project Summary Report 2018/19*, London: LGA/ADASS. https://www.local.gov.uk/sites/default/files/documents/25.155%20Making%20Safeguarding%20Personal%20Outcomes%20Framework_03.pdf [Accessed 30 October 2023].

Cooper, A. and Bruin, C. (2017) 'Adult safeguarding and the Care Act (2014)—the impacts on partnerships and practice', *Journal of Adult Protection*, 19(4): 209–219.

Cooper, A. and White, E. (eds) (2017), *Safeguarding Adults under the Care Act: Understanding Good Practice*, London, Jessica Kingsley Publications.

Cooper, A., Cocker, C., and Briggs, M. (2018) 'Making Safeguarding Personal and social work practice with older adults: findings from local authority survey data in England', *British Journal of Social Work*, 48: 1014–1032.

Cooper, A., Lawson, J., Lewis, S., and Williams, C. (2015) 'Making Safeguarding Personal: Learning and messages from the 2013/14 programme', *Journal of Adult Protection*, 17(3): 153–165.

Cooper, A., Briggs, M., Lawson, J., Hodson, B., and Wilson, M. (2016) *MSP Temperature Check*, London: Association of Directors of Adult Social Services.

Corby, B., Shemmings, D., and Wilkins, D. (2012) *Child Abuse: An Evidence Base for Confident Practice* (4th edn), Maidenhead: Open University Press.

Cossar, J., Brandon, M., and Jordan, P. (2011) *Don't Make Assumptions: Children's and Young People's Views of the Child Protection System and the Messages for Change*, London: Office of the Children's Commissioner.

Cossar, J., Brandon, M. and Jordan, P. (2016) '"You've got to trust her and she's got to trust you": children's views on participation in the child protection system', *Child & Family Social Work*, 21: 103–112.

Côté, J. (2014) 'The dangerous myth of emerging adulthood: an evidence-based critique of a flawed developmental theory', *Applied Developmental Science*, 18(4): 177–188.

Craston, M., Balfour, R., Henley, M., Baxendale, J., and Fullick, S. (2020) *Process Evaluation of the Violence Reduction Units, Research Report 116*, London: Home Office.

Crenshaw, K. (1991) 'Mapping the margins: intersectionality, identity politics, and violence against women of color', *Stanford Law Review*, 43: 1241–1299.

Criado Perez, C. (2019) *Invisible Women: Exposing Data Bias in a World Designed for Men*, London: Chatto and Windus.

Cullen, N. (2020) *Burnt Bridges? A Thematic Review of the Deaths of Five Men on the Streets of Halifax During Winter 2018/19.* Calderdale Safeguarding Adult Board. https://safeguarding.calderdale.gov.uk/wp-content/uploads/2021/06/burnt-bridges.pdf [Accessed 30 October 2023].

Davis, J. and Marsh, N. (2020) 'Boys to men: the cost of "adultification" in safeguarding responses to Black boys', *Critical and Radical Social Work*, 8(2): 255–259.

Davis, J. and Marsh, N. (2022) 'The myth of the universal child', in D. Holmes (ed) *Safeguarding Young People: Risk, Rights, Relationships and Resilience*. London: Jessica Kingsley Publishers.

Dearden, L. (2018) 'Grooming gangs abused more than 700 women and girls around Newcastle after police appeared to punish victims', *The Independent*, 23 February. https://www.independent.co.uk/news/uk/crime/grooming-gangs-uk-britain-newcastle-serious-case-review-operation-sanctuary-shelter-muslim-asian-a8225106.html [Accessed 30 October 2023].

Dent, R.J. and Cocker, C. (2005) 'Serious case reviews – lessons for practice in cases of child neglect', in B. Daniel and J. Taylor (eds) *Neglect: Issues for Health and Social Care*, London: Jessica Kingsley Publications.

Department for Education (2010) The Children Act 1989 guidance and regulations volume 3: planning transition to adulthood for care leavers. https://www.gov.uk/government/publications/children-act-1989-transition-to-adulthood-for-care-leavers [Accessed 30 October 2023].

Department for Education (2014a) *Rethinking Support for Adolescents in or on the Edge of Care: Children's Social Care Innovation Programme*, London: Department for Education.

Department for Education (2014b) *Statutory Guidance on Children Who Run Away or Go Missing from Home or Care*, London: Department for Education.

Department for Education (2018) *Extending Personal Adviser Support to all Care Leavers to Age 25. Statutory Guidance for Local Authorities*, London: Department for Education.

Department for Education (2021) *Reforms to Unregulated Provision for Children in Care and Care Leavers. Government Consultation Response*, London Department for Education.

Department for Education (2023a) Regulating supported accommodation for looked after children and care leavers aged 16 and 17: Government consultation response March 2023. https://assets.publishing.service.gov.uk/government/uploads/system/uploads/attachment_data/file/1145589/Supported_accommodation_-_government_response.pdf [Accessed 30 October 2023].

Department for Education (2023b) *Stable Homes, Built on Love: Implementation Strategy and Consultation. Children's Social Care Reform 2023*, London: Department for Education.

Department for Education and Department of Health (2015) Special educational needs and disability code of practice: 0 to 25 years. Statutory guidance for organisations which work with and support children and young people who have special educational needs or disabilities. https://assets.publishing.service.gov.uk/government/uploads/system/uploads/attachment_data/file/398815/SEND_Code_of_Practice_January_2015.pdf [Accessed 30 October 2023].

Department of Health (2007) *Putting People First: A Shared visions and Commitment to the Transformation of Adult Social Care*, London: HMSO.

Department of Health (2012) *Caring for Our Future: Reforming Care and Support*, London: Crown Copyright.

Department of Health (2017a) *Statutory Guidance to Support Local Authorities Implement the Care Act 2014*, London: HMSO.

Department of Health (2017b) *Strengths-based social work practice with adults: Roundtable report*, London: Department of Health https://assets.publishing.service.gov.uk/government/uploads/system/uploads/attachment_data/file/652773/Strengths-based_social_work_practice_with_adults.pdf [Accessed 30 October 2023].

Department of Health and Home Office (2000) *No Secrets: Guidance on Developing and Implementing Multi-Agency Policies and Procedures to Protect Vulnerable Adults from Abuse*, London: HMSO.

Department of Health and Social Care (2019) *Strengths-Based Approach: Practice Framework and Practice Handbook*, London: Department of Health https://assets.publishing.service.gov.uk/government/uploads/system/uploads/attachment_data/file/778134/stengths-based-approach-practice-framework-and-handbook.pdf [Accessed 30 October 2023].

Department of Health and Social Care (2021) People at the heart of care: Adult social care reform white paper. https://assets.publishing.service.gov.uk/media/6234b0a6e90e0779a18d3f46/people-at-the-heart-of-care-asc-reform-accessible-with-correction-slip.pdf [Accessed 30 October 2023].

Department of Health and Social Care (2022) Revisiting safeguarding practice. https://www.gov.uk/government/publications/revisiting-safeguarding-practice [Accessed 30 October 2023].

Department of Health and Social Care (2023) Care and support statutory guidance, updated 19 January. https://www.gov.uk/government/publications/care-act-statutory-guidance/care-and-support-statutory-guidance [Accessed 30 October 2023].

Dickens, J., Taylor, J., Cook, L., Garstang, J., Hallett, N., Okpokiri, C., and Rimmer, J. (2022) *Annual Review of Local Child Safeguarding Practice Reviews*, London: The Child Safeguarding Practice Review Panel. https://assets.publishing.service.gov.uk/government/uploads/system/uploads/attachment_data/file/1123918/Annual_review_of_local_child_safeguarding_practice_reviews.pdf [Accessed 30 October 2023].

Dooley, T. (2019) Transitions panel: life in motion – does age matter? Unpublished report to the Havering Safeguarding Adults Board, 20 May.

Downey, C. and Crummy A. (2022) 'The impact of childhood trauma on children's well-being and adult behavior', *European Journal of Trauma and Dissociation*. https://doi.org/10.1016/j.ejtd.2021.100237 [Accessed 30 October 2023].

Droy, R. and Lawson, J. (2017) *Making Safeguarding Personal Supporting Increased Involvement of Service Users*, London: Local Government Association and ADASS.

Elder, G.H., Jr. (1974) *Children of the Great Depression: Social Change in Life Experience*, Chicago: University of Chicago Press.

Elder, G. Jr. (1994) 'Time, human agency, and social change: perspectives on the life course', *Social Psychology Quarterly*, 57(1): 4–15.

Elder, G., Jr. (1998) 'The life course as development theory', *Child Development*, 69(1): 1–12.

Eshalomi, F. (2020) *Gang-Associated Girls: Supporting Young Women at Risk*, London: Greater London Assembly.

Farmer, L. (2017) The importance of strengthening prisoners' family ties to prevent reoffending and reduce intergenerational crime, Ministry of Justice. https://assets.publishing.service.gov.uk/government/uploads/system/uploads/attachment_data/file/642244/farmer-review-report.pdf [Accessed 30 October 2023].

Faulkner, A. (2012) The right to take risks: service users' views of risk in adult social care, Joseph Rowntree Foundation. https://www.jrf.org.uk/sites/default/files/jrf/migrated/files/right-to-take-risks-faulkner.pdf [Accessed 30 October 2023].

Featherstone, B., White, S., and Morris, K. (2014) *Reimagining Child Protection*, Bristol: Policy Press.

Featherstone, B., Gupta, A., Morris, K., and White, S. (2018) *Protecting Children: A Social Model*, Bristol: Policy Press.

Firmin, C. (2020) *Contextual Safeguarding and Child Protection: Rewriting the Rules*, Abingdon: Routledge.

Firmin, C. and Lloyd, J. (2020) *Contextual Safeguarding. A 2020 Update on the Operational, Strategic and Conceptual Framework*, Luton: University of Bedfordshire.

Firmin, C. and Knowles, R. (2022) 'Has the purpose outgrown the design?', in D. Holmes (ed) *Safeguarding Young People: Risk, Rights, Resilience and Relationships*, London: Jessica Kingsley Publications.

Firmin, C., Wroe, L., and Skidmore, P. (2020) *A Sigh of Relief. A Summary of the Phase One Results from the Securing Safety Study*, Luton: University of Bedfordshire.

Firmin, C., Horan J., Holmes, D., and Hopper, G. (2019) *Safeguarding during Adolescence – The Relationship between Contextual Safeguarding, Complex Safeguarding and Transitional Safeguarding*, Dartington: Research in Practice, University of Bedfordshire, Rochdale Borough Council, and Contextual Safeguarding Network.

Flynn, M. (2007) 'The murder of Steven Hoskin: a serious case review', Cornwall Adult Protection Committee. https://www.hampshiresab.org.uk/wp-content/uploads/2007-December-Serious-Case-Review-regarding-Steven-Hoskin-Cornwall.pdf [Accessed 29 October 2023].

Flynn, M. (2021) Safeguarding adults review: Joanna, Jon and Ben. Norfolk Safeguarding Adults Board. https://www.norfolksafeguardingadultsboard.info/assets/SARs/SAR-Joanna-Jon-and-Ben/SAR-Rpt-Joanna-JonBen_EXEC-SUMMARY02-June2021.pdf [Accessed 30 October 2023].

Forrester, D., Goodman, K., Cocker, C., Binnie, C., and Jensch, G. (2009) 'What is the impact of public care on children's welfare? A review of research findings from England and Wales and their policy implications', *Journal of Social Policy*, 38: 439–456.

Forrester, D., Lynch, A., Bostock, L., Newlands, F., Preston, B., and Cary, A. (2017) *Family Safeguarding Hertfordshire: Evaluation Report*, London: Department for Education.

Fraser, A. and Irwin-Rogers, K. (2021) *A Public Health Approach to Violence Reduction: Strategic Briefing*, Dartington: Research in Practice.

Gamble, J. and McCallum, R. (2022) Local Child Safeguarding Practice Review: Child Q. City and Hackney Safeguarding Children Partnership. https://chscp.org.uk/wp-content/uploads/2022/03/Child-Q-PUBLISHED-14-March-22.pdf [Accessed 30 October 2023].

Geronimus, A.T., Hicken, M., Keene, D., and Bound, J. (2006) '"Weathering" and age patterns of allostatic load scores among blacks and whites in the United States', *American Journal of Public Health*, 96(5): 826–833.

Ghate, D., Lewis, J., and Welbrown, D. (2013) Systems Leadership for Exceptional Times. Synthesis Paper. Virtual Staff College. https://thestaffcollege.uk/wp-content/uploads/2022/04/Systems-Leadership-Full-Report-Staff-College.pdf [Accessed 30 October 2023].

Giddens, A. and Sutton, P. (2021) *Sociology* (9th edn), Cambridge: Polity Press.

Glover Williams, A. and Finlay, F. (2019) 'County lines: how gang crime is affecting our young people', *Archive of Diseases in Childhood*, 104: 730–732.

Goff, P.A., Jackson, M., Di Leone, B., Culotta, C., and Ditomasso, N. (2014) 'The essence of innocence: consequences of dehumanizing black children', *Journal of Personality and Social Psychology*, 106(4): 526–545.

Gorin, S. and Jobe, A. (2013) 'Young people who have been maltreated: different needs – different responses?', *British Journal of Social Work*, 43(7): 1330–1346.

Government Social Research Profession (2022) A guide to inclusive social research practices produced as part of the Government Social Research Strategy 2021–2025. https://www.gov.uk/government/publications/a-guide-to-inclusive-social-research-practices/a-guide-to-inclusive-social-research-practices [Accessed 30 October 2023].

Gradus, J.L. and Galea, S. (2022) 'Reconsidering the definition of trauma', *The Lancet Psychiatry*, 9(8): 608–609.

Green, L.W. (2008) 'Making research relevant: if it is an evidence-based practice, where's the practice-based evidence?', *Family Practice*, 25(1): 20–24.

Griffiths R. (2022) 'Transitional Safeguarding in London Borough of Hackney: a case study', *Practice: Social Work in Action*, 34(1): 41–50.

Grohs, J., Kirk, G., Soledad, M., and Knight, D. (2018) 'Assessing systems thinking: A tool to measure complex reasoning through ill-structured problems', *Thinking Skills and Creativity*, 28: 110–130.

Gunner, J. (2017) 'Working towards recovery and resolution, including mediation and restorative justice', in A. Cooper and E. White (eds) *Safeguarding Adults Under the Care Act: Understanding Good Practice*, London: Jessica Kingsley Publications, pp 74–90.

Gupta, A. and Blumhardt, H. (2016) 'Giving poverty a voice: families' experiences of social work practice in a risk-averse child protection system', *Families, Relationships and Societies*, 5(1): 163–172. https://bristoluniversitypressdigital.com/view/journals/frs/5/1/article-p163.xml [Accessed 30 October 2023].

Hafford-Letchfield, P., Lambley, S., Spolander, G., and Cocker, C. (2014) *Inclusive Leadership: Managing to Make A Difference in Social Work and Social Care*, Bristol: Policy Press.

Hall, B. (2012) 'Reflective social work practice with older people: the professional and the Organisation', in B. Hall and T. Scragg (eds) *Social Work with Older People: Approaches to Person-Centred Practice*, Maidenhead: Open University Press.

Hallet, S. (2016) 'An uncomfortable comfortableness: "care", child protection and child sexual exploitation', *British Journal of Social Work*, 46(7): 2137–2152.

Hanson, E. and Holmes, D. (2014) *That Difficult Age: Developing a More Effective Response to Risks in Adolescence*, Dartington, Research in Practice/Association of Directors of Children's Services.

Harris, J., Tinarwo, M., and Ramanathan, R. (2020) *Leeds Partners in Practice: Reimagining Child Welfare Services for the 21st Century. Final Evaluation Report*, London: Department for Education.

Harris, M. and Fallot, R.D. (2001) 'Envisioning a trauma-informed service system: a vital paradigm shift', *New Directions for Mental Health Services*, 89: 3–22.

Harris, M. and Edwards, M. (2023) *Young People in Transition in the Criminal Justice System: Evidence Review*. Alliance for Youth Justice. https://barrowcadbury.org.uk/wp-content/uploads/2023/06/FINAL-AYJ-Young-people-in-transition-in-the-criminal-justice-system-Evidence-review-April-2023.pdf [Accessed 30 October 2023].

Hart, R. (1992) *Children's Participation from Tokenism to Citizenship*, Florence: UNICEF Innocenti Research Centre.

Health and Social Care Committee (2021) *Has the Provision of Mental Health Services for Children and Young People Improved?* https://ukparliament.shorthandstories.com/children-young-people-mental-health/index.html [Accessed 30 October 2023].

Health Foundation (2021) *Social Care Funding Gap*, London: The Health Foundation.

Helyar-Cardwell, V. and Moran, K. (2020) *Timely Justice: Turning 18: A Briefing on the Impact of Turning 18 in the Criminal Justice System*, London: Just for Kids Law.

Hendrick, H. (2003) *Child Welfare: Historical Dimensions, Contemporary Debates*, Bristol: Policy Press.

Hendry, L.B. and Kloep, M. (2007), 'Conceptualizing emerging adulthood: inspecting the emperor's new clothes?', *Child Development Perspectives*, 1: 74–79.

Hertfordshire. Evaluation Report. Department for Education. Reference: DFE-RR574

Hickle, K. (2020) 'Introducing a trauma-informed capability approach in youth services', *Child Soc*, 34(6): 537–551.

Hickle, K. and Lefevre, M. (2022) 'Learning to love and trust again: a relational approach to developmental trauma', in D. Holmes (ed) *Safeguarding Young People: Risk, Rights, resilience and Relationships*, London: Jessica Kingsley, pp 159–176.

Hill, N. and Warrington, C. (2022) 'Nothing about me without me', in D. Holmes (ed) *Safeguarding Young People: Risk, Rights, Relationships and Resilience*, London: Jessica Kingsley Publishers.

HM Government (2013) *Care Leaver Strategy: A Cross-Departmental Strategy for Young People Leaving Care*, London: Crown Copyright. https://assets.publishing.service.gov.uk/government/uploads/system/uploads/attachment_data/file/266484/Care_Leaver_Strategy.pdf [Accessed 30 October 2023].

HM Government (2020) *Working Together to Safeguard Children*, London: HMSO. https://www.gov.uk/government/publications/working-together-to-safeguard-children--2 [Accessed 30 October 2023].

HM Government (2021) Joint national protocol for transitions in England: joint protocol for managing the cases of children moving from Youth Offending Teams to the National Probation Service. Youth Justice Board, National Probation Service. https://www.gov.uk/government/publications/joint-national-protocol-for-transitions-in-england [Accessed 30 October 2023].

HM Government (2022) *SEND Review: Right Support, Right Place, Right Time*, London: HMSO.

HM Government (2023) Multi-agency practice principles for responding to child exploitation and extra-familial harm. Research in Practice. https://tce.researchinpractice.org.uk/wp-content/uploads/2023/03/FINAL-Multi-agency-Practice-Principles-for-responding-to-child-exploitation-and-extrafamilial-harm-Designed-.pdf [Accessed 30 October 2023].

HMI Probation (2016) Transitions arrangements: a follow-up inspection. HM Inspectorate of Probation. https://www.justiceinspectorates.gov.uk/hmiprobation/inspections/transitions-followup/ [Accessed 30 October 2023].

Holland, S., Tannock, S., and Collicut, H. (2011) 'Everybody's business? A research review of the informal safeguarding of other people's children in the UK', *Children & Society*, 25(5): 406–416.

Holmes, D. (2022a) 'Transitional Safeguarding: the case for change', *Practice: Social Work in Action*, 34(1): 7–23.

Holmes, D. (ed) (2022b) *Safeguarding Young People: Risk, Rights, Resilience and Relationships*, London: Jessica Kingsley.

Holmes, D. and Smale, E. (2018) *Mind the Gap: Transitional Safeguarding – Adolescence to Adulthood*, Dartington: Research in Practice.

Holmes, D. and Smith, L. (2022) Transitional Safeguarding. HM Inspectorate of Probation. https://www.justiceinspectorates.gov.uk/hmiprobation/wp-content/uploads/sites/5/2022/03/Academic-Insights-Holmes-and-Smith-RM.pdf [Accessed 30 October 2023].

Holmström, C. (2020) 'Transitions to adult social care', in S. Braye and M. Preston-Shoot (eds) *The Care Act 2014: Wellbeing in Practice*, London: Sage/Learning Matters, pp 159–172.

Home Office (2018) *Criminal Exploitation of Children and Vulnerable Adults: County Lines Guidance*, London: HMSO.

House of Commons Health and Social Care Committee (2020) *Social care: funding and workforce*. Third Report of Session 2019–21. https://committees.parliament.uk/publications/3120/documents/29193/default/ [Accessed 30 October 2023].

House of Commons Home Affairs Committee (2013) *Child sexual exploitation and the response to localised grooming*. Second Report of Session 2013–14. https://publications.parliament.uk/pa/cm201314/cmselect/cmhaff/68/68i.pdf [Accessed 30 October 2023].

House of Commons Housing, Communities and Local Government Committee (2019) *Funding of local authorities' children's services*. Fourteenth Report of Session 2017–19. https://publications.parliament.uk/pa/cm201719/cmselect/cmcomloc/1638/1638.pdf [Accessed 30 October 2023].

House of Commons Justice Committee (2016) *The treatment of young adults in the criminal justice system*. Seventh Report of Session 2016–17. https://publications.parliament.uk/pa/cm201617/cmselect/cmjust/169/169.pdf [Accessed 30 October 2023].

House of Commons Levelling Up, Housing and Communities Committee (2022) *Long-term funding of adult social care Second Report of Session 2022–23*. https://publications.parliament.uk/pa/cm5803/cmselect/cmcomloc/19/report.html#heading-3 [Accessed 30 October 2023].

Howe, D. (2005) *Child Abuse and Neglect: Attachment, Development and Intervention*, London: Palgrave.

Huegler, N. and Ruch, G. (2021) 'Risk, vulnerability and complexity: transitional Safeguarding as a reframing of binary perspectives', *Practice: Social Work in Action*, 34(1): 25–39.

Human Trafficking Foundation (2022) *Child Criminal Exploitation and The Need for Consistency*, London: Human Trafficking Foundation: Human Trafficking Foundation.

Hutchison E. (2014) 'Life course theory', in J. Roger and R. Levesque (eds) *Encyclopedia of Adolescence*, New York: Springer, pp 1586–1594.

Idzelis Roth, M., Nelson-Dusek, S. and Skrypek, M. (2013) *Innovations in Child Protection Services in Minnesota*, Chicago: Casey Family Programs.

Independent Review of Children's Social Care (2022) The independent review of children's social care – final report. https://assets.publishing.service.gov.uk/government/uploads/system/uploads/attachment_data/file/1141532/Independent_review_of_children_s_social_care_-_Final_report.pdf [Accessed 30 October 2023].

Institute of Public Care (2013) *Evidence Review - Adult Safeguarding*, London: Skills for Care. Available at: https://ipc.brookes.ac.uk/files/publications/Evidence_Review_-_Adult_Safeguarding.pdf [Accessed 30 October 2023].

Irwin-Rogers, K., Muthoo, A. and Billingham, L. (2020) *Youth Violence Commission Final Report*. Youth Violence Commission.

Ison, R. and Blackmore, C. (2014) 'Designing and developing a reflexive learning system for managing systemic change', *Systems*, 2: 119–136.

Jago, S., Arocha, L., Brodie, I., Melrose, M., Pearce, J., and Warrington, C. (2011) *What's Going On to Safeguard Children and Young People from Sexual Exploitation?*, Luton: University of Bedfordshire.

Jay, A. (2014) *Independent Inquiry into Child Sexual Exploitation in Rotherham 1997–2013*. https://www.rotherham.gov.uk/downloads/file/279/independent-inquiry-into-child-sexual-exploitation-in-rotherham [Accessed 1 January 2022].

Jobe, A. and Gorin, S. (2013) '"If kids don't feel safe they don't do anything": young people's views on seeking and receiving help from Children's Social Care Services in England', *Child & Family Social Work*, 18(4): 429–438.

Johansson, T. (2021) 'Becoming and belonging: modern passages and transitions from childhood to adulthood', *British Journal of Sociology of Education*, 42(3): 440–446.

Johnson, A. and Avery, C. (2022) 'Preparing for adult life: safety planning in transition', *Practice: Social Work in Action*, 34(1): 51–59.

Johnson, S.B., Blum, R.W., and Giedd, J. M. (2009) 'Adolescent maturity and the brain: the promise and pitfalls of neuroscience research in adolescent health policy', *Journal of Adolescent Health*, 45(3): 216–221.

Joint Targeted Area inspection (2016) *'Time to listen'– A Joined Up Response to Child Sexual Exploitation and Missing Children*, Manchester: OFSTED. https://assets.publishing.service.gov.uk/media/5a81dd5c40f0b62305b91382/Time_to_listen___a_joined_up_response_to_child_sexual_exploitation_and_missing_children.pdf. Accessed on 30.10.23

Joint Targeted Area inspection (2018) *Protecting Children from Criminal Exploitation, Human Trafficking and Modern Slavery: An Addendum*, Manchester: OFSTED. https://assets.publishing.service.gov.uk/government/uploads/system/uploads/attachment_data/file/756031/Protecting_children_from_criminal_exploitation_human_trafficking_modern_slavery_addendum_141118.pdf [Accessed 30 October 2023].

Jones, P. (2013) 'Adult mental health disorders and their age at onset', *The British Journal of Psychiatry*, 202(S54): S5–S10.

Kenward, H. (2002) *Ainlee Labonte: Chapter Eight Integrated Review*. Newham Area Child Protection Committee.

Kellett, M. (2009) 'Children and young people's participation', in H. Montgomery and M. Kellett (eds) *Children and Young People's Worlds: Developing Frameworks for Integrated Practice*, Bristol: Policy Press, pp 43–60.

Kerr, H., Widger, K., Cullen-Dean, G., Price, J., and O'Halloran, P. (2020) 'Transition from children's to adult services for adolescents/young adults with life-limiting conditions: developing realist programme theory through an international comparison', *BMC Palliative Care*, 19(1): 1–11.

Kessler, R., Bergland, P., Demler, O., Jin, R., Merikangas, K., and Walters, E. (2005) 'Lifetime prevalence and age-of-onset distributions of DSM-IV disorders in the National Comorbidity Survey Replication', *Arch Gen Psychiatry*, 62: 593–602.

Kezelman, C., Hossack, N., Stavropoulos, P., and Burley, P. (2015) *The Cost of Unresolved Childhood Trauma and Abuse in Adults in Australia*, Sydney: Adults Surviving Child Abuse and Pegasus Economics.

Klee, D. and Williams, C. (2014) *Making Safeguarding Personal*, London: Local Government Association. https://www.local.gov.uk/sites/default/files/documents/Making%20Safeguarding%20Personal%202012-13%20full%20report.pdf [Accessed 30 October 2023].

Kneale, D., Henley, J., Thomas, J., and French, R. (2021) 'Inequalities in older LGBT people's health and care needs in the United Kingdom: a systematic scoping review', *Ageing and Society*, 41: 493–515.

Krieger, N. (2020) 'Measures of racism, sexism, heterosexism, and gender binarism for health equity research: from structural injustice to embodied harm – an ecosocial analysis', *Annual Review of Public Health*, 41(1): 37–62.

Lalor, K. and McElvaney, R. (2010) 'Child sexual abuse, links to later sexual exploitation/high-risk sexual behavior, and prevention/treatment programs', *Trauma, Violence, & Abuse*, 11(4): 159–177.

Laming Report (2003) *The Victoria Climbie Inquiry: Report of an Inquiry by Lord Laming*, London: Stationery Office.

La Valle, I. and Graham, B. (2016) Child sexual exploitation: support in children's residential homes. Department for Education. https://assets.publishing.service.gov.uk/government/uploads/system/uploads/attachment_data/file/582354/Child-sexual-exploitation-support-in-childrens-homes.pdf [Accessed 30 October 2023].

Lawson, J. (2017) 'The Making Safeguarding Personal approach to practice', in A. Cooper and E. White (eds) *Safeguarding Adults Under the Care Act: Understanding Good Practice*, London: Jessica Kingsley, pp 20–39.

Lawson, J., Lewis, S., and Williams, C. (2014) *Making Safeguarding Personal: Guide*. Association of Directors of Adult Social Services and Local Government Association.

Leeds City Council (no date) One minute guide: restorative practice. https://www.leeds.gov.uk/one-minute-guides/restorative-practice [Accessed 30 October 2023].

Lefevre, M., Hickle, K., and Luckock, B. (2018) '"Both/and" not "either/or": reconciling rights to protection and participation in working with child sexual exploitation', *British Journal of Social Work*, 49(7): 1837–1855.

Lefevre, M., Hampson, M., and Goldsmith, C. (2022) 'Towards a synthesised directional map of the stages of innovation in children's social care', *The British Journal of Social Work*, 183: 1–21.

Lefevre, M., Hickle, K., Luckock, B., and Ruch, G. (2017) 'Building trust with children and young people at risk of child sexual exploitation: the professional challenge', *The British Journal of Social Work*, 47(8): 2456–2473.

Lennox, C. (2014) 'The health needs of young people in prison', *British Medical Bulletin*, 112(1): 17–25.

Levine, J. (2016) 'Mental health issues in survivors of sex trafficking', *Cogent Medicine*, 4(1): doi.org/10.1080/2331205X.2017.1278841.

Levy, A. and Kahan, B.J. (1991) *The Pindown Experience and the Protection of Children: The Report of the Staffordshire Child Care Inquiry 1990*, Stafford: Staffordshire County Council.

LGiU (2013) *Whole-Place Community Budgets. An LGiU Essential Guide*, London: LGiU.

Liebel, M. (2021) *Decolonizing Childhoods: From Exclusion to Dignity*, Bristol: Policy Press.

Lister, R. (2021) *Poverty* (2nd edn), Cambridge: Polity Press.

Local Government Association (2012) *Sector-Led Improvement in Local Government*. London: Local Government Association. https://www.local.gov.uk/sites/default/files/documents/sli-local-government-pdf--f4c.pdf [Accessed 30 October 2023].

Local Government Association/Association of Directors of Adult Social Services (LGA/ADASS) (2014), *Making Safeguarding Personal Case Studies 2013/14*, London: Local Government Association. https://www.local.gov.uk/sites/default/files/documents/Making%20Safeguarding%20Personal%202013-2014%20-%20Case%20Studies.pdf [Accessed 30 October 2023].

Local Government Association/Association of Directors of Adult Social Services (LGA/ADASS) (2018a) *Making Safeguarding Personal Toolkit*, London: Local Government Association. https://www.local.gov.uk/msp-toolkit [Accessed 30 October 2023].

Local Government Association/Association of Directors of Adult Social Services (LGA/ADASS) (2018b) *Making Safeguarding Personal Toolkit, Case Study 15 Transitional Safeguarding – Adolescence to Adulthood*, London: Local Government Association. https://www.local.gov.uk/sites/default/files/documents/case-example_15_Transitional_safeguarding_adolescence_to_adulthood%20WEB.pdf [Accessed 30 October 2023].

Local Government Association/Association of Directors of Adult Social Services (LGA/ADASS) (2019a) *Making Decisions on the Duty to Carry Out Safeguarding Adults Enquiries*, London: Local Government Association.

Local Government Association/Association of Directors of Adult Social Services (LGA/ADASS) (2019b) *Myths and Realities about MSP*, London: Local Government Association. https://www.local.gov.uk/sites/default/files/documents/25.144%20MSP%20Myths_04%20WEB.pdf [Accessed 30 October 2023].

Local Government Association/Association of Directors of Adult Social Services (LGA/ADASS) (2019c) *Making Safeguarding Personal Case Studies 2018/19*, London: Local Government Association. https://www.local.gov.uk/sites/default/files/documents/25.143%20Making%20Safeguarding%20Personal_04%20WEB_0.pdf [Accessed 30 October 2023].

Local Government Association/Association of Directors of Adult Social Services (LGA/ADASS) (2019d) *Briefing for Practitioners, Analysis of Safeguarding Adults Reviews*, London: Local Government Association and Directors of Adult Social Services. https://www.local.gov.uk/topics/social-care-health-and-integration/adult-social-care/resources-safeguarding-adults-boards/practitioners [Accessed 30 October 2023].

Local Government Association/Association of Directors of Adult Social Services (LGA/ADASS) (2020) *Understanding What Constitutes a Safeguarding Concern and How to Support Effective Outcomes*, London: Local Government Association. https://www.local.gov.uk/sites/default/files/documents/25.168_Understanding_what_constitutes_a_safeguarding_07.1.pdf [Accessed 30 October 2023].

Lowe, T., Padmanabhan, C., McCart, D., McNeill, K., Brogan, A., and Smith, M. (2022) *Human Learning Systems: A Practical Guide for the Curious*. Centre for Public Impact. https://www.humanlearning.systems/ [Accessed 30 October 2023].

Luke, N., Sinclair, I., Woolgar, I., and Sebba, J. (2014) *What Works in Preventing and Treating Poor Mental Health in Looked After Children?*, London: NSPCC, Rees Centre Oxford University.

Lymbery, M. (2014) 'Austerity, personalisation and older people: the prospects for creative social work practice in England', *European Journal of Social Work*, 17(3): 367–382.

Mahon, D. (2022) 'Implementing trauma informed care in human services: an ecological scoping review', *Behavioral Sciences* (2076–328X), 12(11): 431.

Manchester Safeguarding Partnership (2020) *Manchester's Complex Safeguarding Strategy 2020–2023*. https://www.manchestersafeguardingpartnership.co.uk/resources/complex-safeguarding/ [Accessed 30 October 2023].

Manthorpe, J. and Martineau, S. (2011), 'Serious case reviews in adult safeguarding in England: an analysis of a sample of reports', *British Journal of Social Work*, 41(2): 224–241.

Manthorpe, J. and Martineau, S. (2015) 'What can and cannot be learned from serious case reviews of the care and treatment of adults with learning disabilities in England? Messages for social workers', *British Journal of Social Work*, 45(1): 331–348.

Manthorpe, J. and Martineau, S. (2016) 'Serious case reviews into dementia care: an analysis of context and content', *British Journal of Social Work*, 46(2): 514–531.

Manthorpe, J. and Martineau, S. (2017) 'Engaging with the new system of safeguarding adults reviews concerning care homes for older people', *British Journal of Social Work*, 47(7): 2086–2099.

Manthorpe, J., Klee, D., Williams, C., and Cooper, A. (2014) 'Making Safeguarding Personal: developing responses and enhancing skills', *Journal of Adult Protection*, 16(2): 96–103.

Manthorpe, J., Stevens, M., Samsi, K., Aspinal, F., Woolham, J., Hussein, S., Ismail, M., and Baxter, K. (2015) 'Did anyone notice the transformation of adult social care? An analysis of Safeguarding Adult Board Annual Reports', *Journal of Adult Protection*, 17(1): 19–30.

Markauskaite, L. and Goodyear, P. (2017) *Epistemic Fluency and Professional Education: Innovation, Knowledgeable Action and Actionable Knowledge*, Dordrecht: Springer.

Marmot, M. (2020) 'Health equity in England: the Marmot review 10 years on', *BMJ*, 24;368: m693.

Martineau, S. and Manthorpe, J. (2020) 'Safeguarding adults reviews and homelessness: making the connections', *Journal of Adult Protection*, 22(4): 181–197.

Mason, K., Cornes, M., Dobson, R., Meakin, A., Ornelas, B., and Whiteford, M. (2017/18) 'Multiple exclusion homelessness and adult social care in England: exploring the challenges through a researcher-practitioner partnership', *Research, Policy and Planning*, 33(1): 3–14.

Mason, K., Biswas Sasidharan, A., Cooper, A., Shorten, K., and Sutton, J. (2022) 'Discriminatory abuse: time to revive a forgotten form of abuse?' *Journal of Adult Protection*, 24(2): 115–125.

May, C. and Finch, T. (2009) 'Implementation, embedding, and integration: an outline of Normalization Process Theory', *Sociology*, 43(3): 535–554.

May, C.R., Mair, F., Finch, T., MacFarlane, A., Dowrick, C., Treweek, S., Rapley, T., Ballini, L., Ong, B.N., Rogers, A., Murray, E., Elwyn, G., Légaré, F., Gunn, J., and Montori, V.M. (2009) 'Development of a theory of implementation and integration: Normalization Process Theory', *Implementation Science*, 4(29): doi.org/10.1186/1748-5908-4-29.

McNamara, R. and Morgan, S. (2016) *Risk Enablement: A Frontline Briefing*, Dartington: Research into Practice for Adults. https://www.local.gov.uk/sites/default/files/documents/Practice_Tool_10%20risk%20enablement%20chart%20WEB.pdf [Accessed 30 October 2023].

Meltzer, H., Gohuard, R., Corbin, T., Goodman, R., and Ford, T. (2003) The mental health of young people looked after by local authorities in England: the report of a survey carried out in 2002 by Social Survey Division of the Office for National Statistics on behalf of the Department of Health, London: Office for National Statistics/Stationery Office.

Meyer, I.H. (2003) 'Prejudice, social stress, and mental health in lesbian, gay, and bisexual populations: conceptual issues and research evidence', *Psychological Bulletin*, 129(5): 674–697.

Metz, A., Jensen, T., Farley, A., Boaz, A., Bartley, L., and Villodas, M, (2022) 'Building trusting relationships to support implementation: a proposed theoretical model', *Frontiers in Health Services* 2: doi.org/10.3389/frhs.2022.894599.

Ministry of Justice (2022) Transition of Young People from the Children and Young People Secure Estate to Adult Custody Policy Framework. https://www.gov.uk/government/publications/transition-of-young-people-from-the-children-and-young-people-secure-estate-to-adult-custody-policy-framework [Accessed 30 October 2023].

Mistry, D. and Chauhan, S. (2003) 'Don't leave race on the side', Community Care, 31 July. https://www.communitycare.co.uk/2003/07/31/dont-leave-race-on-the-side/ [Accessed 30 October 2023].

Molina, J. and Levell, J. (2020) *Children's Experience of Domestic Abuse and Criminality: A Literature Review*, London: Victims Commissioner for England and Wales.

Morgan, D. (2019) *Safeguarding Adults Review: Mr D.* Portsmouth Safeguarding Adults Board. http://www.portsmouthsab.uk/wp-content/uploads/2019/05/PSAB-Mr-D-2019-Executive-Summary-vFINAL.pdf [Accessed 30 October 2023].

Mulgan, G. (2019) *Social Innovation: How Societies Find the Power to Change*, Bristol: Policy Press.

Munro, E. (2004) 'The impact of child abuse inquiries since 1990', in N. Stanley and J. Manthorpe (eds) *The Age of the Inquiry*, London: Routledge.

Munro, E. (2011) The Munro Review of Child Protection: Final Report – A Child-Centred System, Norwich: The Stationery Office. https://assets.publishing.service.gov.uk/government/uploads/system/uploads/attachment_data/file/175391/Munro-Review.pdf [Accessed 30 October 2023].

Munro, E. (2019) 'Decision-making under uncertainty in child protection: creating a just and learning culture', *Child & Family Social Work*, 24(1): 123–130.

Munro, E. and Simkiss, D. (2020) 'Transitions from care to adulthood: messages to inform practice', *Paediatrics and Child Health*, 30(5): 175–179.

Munro, E. and Turnell, A. (2020) *You Can't Grow Roses in Concrete Part 2. Action Research Final Report, Signs of Safety England Innovation Programme*, Australia: Elia International.

Munro, E., Turnell, A., and Murphy, T. (2016) *'You Can't Grow Roses in Concrete' Organisational Reform to Support High Quality Signs of Safety Practice*, Munro, Turnell & Murphy Child Protection Consultancy

Narendorf, C. (2017) 'Intersection of homelessness and mental health: a mixed methods study of young adults who accessed psychiatric emergency services', *Children and Youth Services Review*, 81: 54–62.

National Institute for Clinical Excellence (2018) *Decision Making and Mental Capacity*, London: NICE. https://www.nice.org.uk/guidance/ng108 [Accessed 30 October 2023].

National Institute for Health and Care Excellence (2016a) *Transition from Children's to Adults' Services – Quality Standard*, London: National Institute for Health and Care Excellence. https://www.nice.org.uk/guidance/qs140/resources/transition-from-childrens-to-adults-services-pdf-75545472790213 [Accessed 30 October 2023].

National Institute for Health and Care Excellence (2016b) *Transition from Children's Services to Adults' Services for Young People Using Health or Social Care Services – NICE Guidance*, London: National Institute for Health and Care Excellence. https://www.nice.org.uk/guidance/ng43/resources/transition-from-childrens-to-adults-services-for-young-people-using-health-or-social-care-services-pdf-1837451149765 [Accessed 30 October 2023].

Neinstein, L.S. (2013) 'The new adolescents: an analysis of conditions, behaviors, risks, and access to services among emerging young adults'. Volume 208 Suppl. Los Angeles: University of Southern California

Neinstein, L. and Irwin, C. (2013) 'Young adults remain worse off than adolescents', *Journal of Adolescent Health*, 53(5): 559–561.

NHS Digital (2014) Safeguarding Adults Return, Annual Report, England 2013–14, Experimental Statistics, NHS Digital. https://digital.nhs.uk/data-and-information/publications/statistical/safeguarding-adults/2013-14 [Accessed 30 October 2023].

NHS Digital (2022a) *Safeguarding Adults, England, 2021–22*, NHS Digital. https://digital.nhs.uk/data-and-information/publications/statistical/safeguarding-adults [Accessed 30 October 2023].

NHS Digital (2022b) *Mental Health of Children and Young People in England 2022 – Wave 3 Follow Up to the 2017 Survey*. https://digital.nhs.uk/data-and-information/publications/statistical/mental-health-of-children-and-young-people-in-england/2022-follow-up-to-the-2017-survey#Chapter-index [Accessed 30 October 2023].

NHSE (2022) Monitoring the quality of care and safety for people with a learning disability and/or people who are autistic in inpatient care. https://www.england.nhs.uk/learning-disabilities/care/monitoring-the-quality-of-care-and-safety-for-people-with-a-learning-disability-and-or-people-who-are-autistic-in-inpatient-care/Norfolk [Accessed 27 November 2022].

NHSE, LGA, and ADASS (2015) Building the right support. https://www.england.nhs.uk/wp-content/uploads/2015/10/ld-nat-imp-plan-oct15.pdf [Accessed 27 November 2022].

Norfolk Safeguarding Adults Board (2021) Seven Minute Briefing on Transitional Safeguarding. https://www.norfolksafeguardingadultsboard.info/document/618/7-Minute-Briefing-Form-Transitional-Safeguarding-28.7.21-V2.pdf?t=0188652650ae6bce6dfb6f7d59265a0d6e22d26 [Accessed 30 October 2023].

Norrie, C., Stevens, M., Graham, K., Manthorpe, J., Moriarty, J., and Hussein, S. (2014) 'Investigating models of adult safeguarding in England – a mixed methods approach', *Journal of Adult Protection*, 16(6): 377–388.

NSPCC (2021) History of child protection in the UK. https://learning.nspcc.org.uk/child-protection-system/history-of-child-protection-in-the-uk [Accessed 1 January 2022].

OECD (2017) *Systems Approaches to Public Sector Challenges: Working with Change*, Paris: OECD Publishing.

Office for Health Improvement and Disparities (2023) *Young people's substance misuse treatment statistics 2021 to 2022: report*. OHID.

Office of the Chief Social Worker for Adults and Research in Practice (2021) Bridging the gap: transitional safeguarding and the role of social work with adults – knowledge briefing. Department of Health and Social Care. https://assets.publishing.service.gov.uk/government/uploads/system/uploads/attachment_data/file/990426/dhsc_transitional_safeguarding_report_bridging_the_gap_web.pdf [Accessed 30 October 2023].

Ofsted (2018) Protecting children from criminal exploitation, human trafficking and modern slavery: an addendum. Ofsted, CQC, HMIP & HMICFRS. https://www.gov.uk/government/publications/joint-inspections-of-child-sexual-exploitation-and-missing-children [Accessed 30 October 2023].

Ofsted (2022) *'Ready or Not': Care Leavers' Views of Preparing to Leave Care*, London: HMSO. https://www.gov.uk/government/publications/ready-or-not-care-leavers-views-of-preparing-to-leave-care [Accessed 30 October 2023].

Oliver, M. (2013) 'The social model of disability: thirty years on', *Disability & Society*, 28(7): 1024–1026.

Owens, R., Ruch, G., Firmin, C., Millar, H., and Remes, E. (2020) *Relationship-Based Practice and Contextual Safeguarding*, Luton: University of Bedfordshire.

Parole Board (2021) Guidance for Parole Board Members on Young Adult Prisoners. https://www.gov.uk/government/publications/guidance-for-parole-board-members-on-young-adult-prisoners [Accessed 30 October 2023].

Partners in Care and Health (2022) Health and social care, integrated care and safeguarding adults. Local Government Association (LGA) and Association of Directors of Adult Social Services (ADASS).

Parton, N. (2003) 'From Maria Colwell to Victoria Climbie: Reflections on a generation of public inquiries into child abuse'. Plenary paper for the BASPCAN conference, July. http://www.gptsw.net/wp-content/uploads/Parton1.pdf [Accessed 1 January 2021].

Parton, N. (2004) 'From Maria Colwell to Victoria Climbié: reflections on a generation of public inquiries into child abuse', *Child Abuse Review*, 13(2): 80–94.

Parton, N. (2009) 'Challenges to practice and knowledge in child welfare social work: from the "social" to the "informational"?', *Children and Youth Services Review*, 31(7): 715–721.

Phoenix, J. (2012) 'Out of place: the policing and criminalisation of sexually exploited girls and young women'. London: Howard League for Penal reform. https://howardleague.org/wp-content/uploads/2016/04/Out-of-place.pdf [Accessed 30 October 2023].

Pike, L. and Walsh, J. (2015) *Making Safeguarding Personal 2014/15 Evaluation Report*, London: Local Government Association.

Preston-Shoot, M. (2017) *Safeguarding Adult Review: Ms A (Date of Birth: 20th March 1995)*, London: Havering Safeguarding Adults Board.

Preston-Shoot, M. (2019) 'Self-neglect and safeguarding adult reviews: towards a model of understanding facilitators and barriers to best practice', *Journal of Adult Protection*, 21(4), 219–234.

Preston-Shoot, M. (2020), *Adult Safeguarding and Homelessness, a Briefing on Positive Practice*, London: ADASS & LGA. www.local.gov.uk/adult-safeguarding-and-homelessness-briefing-positive-practice [Accessed 30 October 2023].

Preston-Shoot, M. (2021) 'On (not) learning from self-neglect safeguarding adult reviews', *The Journal of Adult Protection*, 23(4): 206–224.

Preston-Shoot, M., Cocker, C. and Cooper A. (2022) 'Learning from safeguarding adult reviews about Transitional Safeguarding: Building an evidence base', *Journal of Adult Protection*, 24(2): 90–101.

Preston-Shoot, M., Braye, S., Preston, O., Allen, K., and Spreadbury, K. (2020) *Analysis of Safeguarding Adult Reviews April 2017 – March 2019 Findings for Sector-Led Improvement*, London: Local Government Association and Directors of Adult Social Services. https://www.local.gov.uk/publications/analysis-safeguarding-adult-reviews-april-2017-march-2019 [Accessed 30 October 2023].

Prior, D., Farrow, K., Hughes, N., Kelly, G., Manders, G., White, S., and Wilkinson, B. (2011) *Maturity, Young Adults and Criminal Justice: A Literature Review*. Commissioned by the Barrow Cadbury Trust for the Transition to Adulthood Alliance.

Pritchard, J. (2013) 'How recovery and healing should fit into the adult safeguarding process', in J. Pritchard (ed) *Good Practice in Promoting Recovery and Healing for Abused Adults*, London: Jessica Kingsley Publications, pp 17–37.

Public Health England (2019a) *A framework for supporting teenage mothers and young fathers*. Public Health England and Local Government Association.

Public Health England (2019b) *A Whole-System Multi-Agency Approach to Serious Violence Prevention. A Resource for Local System Leaders in England*, London: HM Government.

Rees, G. and Stein, M. (1999) *The Abuse of Adolescents within the Family* (NSPCC Policy Practice Research Series), London: NSPCC.

Reeve, K. and Batty, E. (2011) *The Hidden Truth About Homelessness: Experiences of Single Homelessness in England*, London: Crisis.

Research in Practice (2020) *2019 Triennial Analysis of Serious Case Reviews: Local Safeguarding Partnerships*, Dartington: Research in Practice.

Richmond and Wandsworth Safeguarding Adults Board (2020) Minding the Gap: Mental Health Transitions Framework 2020–2023. https://sabrichmondandwandsworth.org.uk/media/1449/mental_health_transitions_protocol.pdf [Accessed 30 October 2023].

Riosa, P.B., McArthur, B.A., and Preyde, M. (2011) 'Effectiveness of psychosocial intervention for children and adolescents with comorbid problems: a systematic review', *Child and Adolescent Mental Health*, 16: 177–185.

Rittel, H.W.J. and Webber, M. (1973) 'Dilemmas in a general theory of planning', *Policy Sciences*, 4(2): 155–169.

Rodger, J., Allen, T. and Elliott, S. (2020) *Family Safeguarding Evaluation Report*, London: Department for Education.

Rosenfeld, R.G. and Nicodemus, B.C. (2003) 'The transition from adolescence to adult life: physiology of the 'transition' phase and its evolutionary basis', *Hormone Research in Adolescence*, 60 (Suppl 1): 74–77.

Ruch, G. and Julkenen, I. (2016) *Relationship-Based Research in Social Work*, London: Hachette.

Ruch, G., Turney, D., and Ward, A. (2018) *Relationship-Based Social Work, Getting to the Heart of Practice* (2nd edn), Philadelphia: Jessica Kingsley Publishers.

Rutter, M. (1996) 'Transitions and turning points in developmental psychopathology: as applied to the age span between childhood and mid-adulthood', *International Journal of Behavioral Development*, 19(3): 603–626.

Saleeby, D. (1996) 'The strengths perspective in social work practice: extensions and cautions', *Social Work*, 41(3): 296–305.

Salmon, J., Hesketh, K., Arundell, L., Downing, K., and Biddle, S. (2020) 'Changing behavior using ecological models', in M. Hagger, L. Cameron, K. Hamilton, N. Hankonen, and T. Lintunen (eds) *The Handbook of Behavior Change*, Cambridge: Cambridge University Press, pp 237–250.

Samsonsen, V. and Turney, D. (2017) 'The role of professional judgement in social work assessment: a comparison between Norway and England', *European Journal of Social Work*, 20(1): 112–124.

Sawyer, S., Azzopardi, P., Wickremarathne, D., and Patton, G. (2018) 'The age of adolescence', *The Lancet Child and Adolescent Health*, 2(3): 223–228.

Schneider, A., Ingram, H., and deLeon, P. (2014) 'Democratic policy design: social construction of target populations', in P. Sabatier and C. Weible (eds) *Theories of the Policy Process*. Avalon Publishing.

Schön, D.A. and Rein, M. (1994) *Frame Reflection: Toward the Resolution of Intractable Policy Controversies*, New York: Basic Books.

Schwartz, S.J., Tanner, J.L., and Syed, M. (2015) 'Emerging adulthood', in S.K. Whitbourne (ed) *The Encyclopedia of Adulthood and Aging*. https://doi.org/10.1002/9781118521373.wbeaa263 [Accessed 30 October 2023].

Sebba, J., Luke, N., McNeish, D., and Rees, A. (2017) *Children's Social Care Innovation Programme: Final Evaluation Report*, London: Department for Education.

Sebba, J., Berridge, D., Luke, N., Fletcher, J., Bell, K., Strand, S., Thomas, S., Sinclair, I., and O'Higgins, A. (2015) *The Educational Progress of Looked After Children in England: Linking Care and Educational Data*, Oxford/Bristol: Rees Centre/University of Bristol.

Senge, P. (1987) 'Catalyzing systems thinking within organizations', System Dynamics Group, Massachusetts Institute of Technology, pp 855–887.

Sheehan, L., O'Donnell, C., Brand, S.L., Forrester, D., Addiss, S., El-Banna, A., Kemp, A., and Nurmatov, U. (2018) *Signs of Safety: A Mixed Methods Systematic Review*, Cardiff: Cardiff University and What Works Centre for Children's Social Care.

Shemmings, D. (2000) 'Professionals' attitudes to children's participation in decision-making: dichotomous accounts and doctrinal contests', *Child & Family Social Work*, 5(3): 235–243.

Sidebotham, P., Brandon, M., Bailey, S., Belderson, P., Dodsworth, J., Garstang, J., Harrison, E., Retzer, A., and Sorensen, P. (2016) *Pathways to Harm, Pathways to Protection: A Triennial Analysis of SCRs 2011–2014*, London: Department for Education.

Signs of Safety (no date) *What Is Signs of Safety?*. https://www.signsofsafety.net/what-is-sofs/ [Accessed 30 October 2023].

Sinclair, R. and Bullock, R. (2002) *Learning from Past Experience: A Review of Serious Case Reviews*, London: Department of Health.

Smith, S.M., Bayliss, E.A., Mercer, S.W. Gunn, J., Vestergaard, M., Wyke, S., Salisbury, C., and Fortin M.(2013) 'How to design and evaluate interventions to improve outcomes for patients with multimorbidity', *Journal of Comorbidity*, 3(1): 10–17.

Social Care Institute for Excellence (2022) Safeguarding Adults Review on Whorlton Hall: Executive Summary. http://www.safeguardingdurhamadults.info/media/41326/Whorlton-Hall-Safeguarding-Adults-Review-Executive-Summary-December-2022-pdf/pdf/WhorltonHallSafeguardingAdultsReviewExecutiveSummaryDecember2022.pdf?m=638058557112270000 [Accessed 30 October 2023].

Spicer, J., Moyle, L., and Coomber, R. (2020) 'The variable and evolving nature of "cuckooing" as a form of criminal exploitation in street level drug markets', *Trends in Organized Crime*, 23: 301–323.

Spreadbury, K. and Hubbard, R. (2020) *The Adult Safeguarding Practice Handbook*, Bristol: Policy Press.

Staines, J. (2016) *Risk, Adverse Influence and Criminalisation Understanding the Over-Representation of Looked After Children in the Youth Justice System*, London: Prison Reform Trust.

Stephens, T. and Webber, S. (2022) *Child Practice Review Report CTMSB 04/2021: Extended Child Practice Review - Child T.* Cwm Taf Morgannwg Safeguarding Board. https://www.cwmtafmorgannwgsafeguardingboard.co.uk/En/NewsEvents/pdfs/ChildPracticeReviewCTMSB042021ChildTFinalReportEMBARGOED.pdf [Accessed 30 October 2023].

Staempfli, A. (2020) Enabling evidence-informed practice: knowledge briefing. Practice Supervisors Development Programme. https://practice-supervisors.rip.org.uk/ [Accessed 19 December 2022].

Stein, M. (2004) *What Works for Young People Leaving Care?*, London: Jessica Kingsley Publishers.

Stein, M. (2006a) 'Research review: young people leaving care', *Child and Family Social Work*, 11(3): 273–279.

Stein, M. (2006b) 'Wrong turn. The consensus that children in care are failing, and that the system is to blame is plain wrong', *The Guardian*, 6 December. http://www.theguardian.com/society/2006/dec/06/childrensservices.guardiansocietysupplement1 [Accessed 30 October 2023].

Stein, M. and Morris, M. (2010) Increasing the Number of Care Leavers in 'Settled, Safe Accommodation'. Research Report. Knowledge Review, 3. London: C4EO.

Suris, J.C. and Akre, C. (2015) 'Key elements for, and indicators of, a successful transition: an international Delphi study', *Journal of Adolescent Health*, 56(6): 612–618.

Taggart, D. (2018) Trauma-informed approaches with young people: Frontline Briefing. Dartington, Research in Practice

Taylor, M. and Tapper, L. (2017) 'Participative practice and family group conferencing', in A. Cooper and E. White (eds) *Safeguarding Adults Under the Care Act: Understanding Good Practice*, London: Jessica Kingsley Publications, pp 57–73.

Tew, J., Morris, K., White, S., Featherstone, B., and Fenton, S.J. (2016) 'What has happened to "Think Family"– challenges and achievements in implementing family inclusive practice', *Pavilion Annual Parental Mental Health and Child Welfare Work*, 1. https://www.birmingham.ac.uk/Documents/college-social-sciences/social-policy/family-potential/what-happened-to-think-family-pavillion-yearbook.pdf [Accessed 30 October 2023].

Treisman, K. (2016) *Working with Relational and Developmental Trauma in Children and Adolescents*, Abingdon: Taylor & Francis Group.

Treseder, P. (1997) *Empowering Children and Young People*, London: Save the Children.

Turner, V. (1977) *The Ritual Process*, Ithaca, NY: Cornell University Press.

Tymula, A., Rosenberg Belmaker, L.A., Roy, A.K., Ruderman, L., Manson, K., Glimcher, P.W., and Levy, I. (2012) 'Adolescents' risk-taking behavior is driven by tolerance to ambiguity', *Proceedings of the National Academy of Sciences*, 109(42): 17135–17140.

Tyrell, F.A. and Yates, T.M. (2018) 'Emancipated foster youth's experiences and perceptions of the transition to adulthood', *Journal of Youth Studies* 21(8): 1011–1028.

UK Research & Innovation (2022) 'What is social science?' https://www.ukri.org/about-us/esrc/what-is-social-science/quantitative-research/ [Accessed 19 December 2022].

United Nations (2020) *Youth*. https://www.un.org/en/global-issues/youth [Accessed 30 October 2023].

University of Birmingham, Barrow Cadbury Trust and Transition to Adulthood Alliance (2013) Taking Account of Maturity: A Guide for Probation Practitioners. https://t2a.org.uk/wp-content/uploads/2013/07/T2A-Maturity-Guide_online.pdf [Accessed 30 October 2023].

Valentine, G. (2003) 'Boundary crossings: transitions from childhood to adulthood', *Children's Geographies*, 1(1): 37–52.

Van den Steene, H., van West, D., and Glazemakers, I. (2019) 'Towards a definition of multiple and complex needs in children and youth: Delphi study in Flanders and international survey', *Scandinavian Journal of Child and Adolescent Psychiatry and Psychology*, 7: 60–67.

Vinall, I. (2020) An Adult Safeguarding Review and a Children's Safeguarding Practice Case Review regarding Michelle. Royal Borough of Windsor & Maidenhead's multi agency adults and children safeguarding arrangements and West of Berkshire Adults Safeguarding Board. https://nationalnetwork.org.uk/2020/michelle-final-report.pdf [Accessed 30 October 2023].

Vinter, R. (2022) 'Sebastian Kalinowski: couple jailed for murdering teenage son', *The Guardian*, 3 November. https://www.theguardian.com/uk-news/2022/nov/03/sebastian-kalinowski-couple-jailed-murder-teenage-son [Accessed 30 October 2023].

Wallace, M. and Cocker, C. (2022) 'Following the death of Ms A: a local authority response to Transitional Safeguarding', *Practice: Social Work in Action*, 34(1): 61–69.

Wall, E. and Olofsson, A. (2008) 'Young people making sense of risk: how meanings of risk are materialized within the social context of every-day life', *Young*, 16(4): 431–448.

Walker-McAllister S. and Cooper A. (2022) 'Transitional Safeguarding: a strategic response', *Practice: Social Work in Action*, 34(1): 71–82.

Warrington, C. (2016) *Young Person-Centred Approaches in Child Sexual Exploitation (CSE) – Promoting Participation and Building Self-Efficacy*, Dartington: Research in Practice.

Warwickshire Safeguarding Adults Board (2011) *Serious Case Review: The murder of Gemma Hayter 9th August 2010 – Public Summary*. https://www.safeguardingwarwickshire.co.uk/images/downloads/SCR-of-Gemma-Hayter.pdf [Accessed 30 October 2023].

Wachtel, T. (2003) 'Restorative practice in everyday life: beyond the formal ritual', *Reclaiming Children and Youth: The Journal of Strength-Based Interventions*, 12(2): 83–87.

Wachtel, T. (2013) Defining restorative. International Institute for Restorative Practices. https://www.iirp.edu/images/pdf/Defining-Restorative_Nov-2016.pdf [Accessed 17 February 2023].

Waterhouse, R. (2000) *Lost in Care: The Waterhouse Report: Summary: Report of the Tribunal of Inquiry into the Abuse of Children in the Former County Council Areas of Gwynedd and Clwyd since 1974 (Children in Wales)*, London: HMSO.

Werner, E. (2001) 'Protective factors and individual resilience', in J. Shonkoff and S. Meisels (eds) *Handbook of Early Childhood Intervention* (2nd edn), Cambridge: Cambridge University Press.

White, E. (2017) 'Assessing and responding to risk', in A. Cooper and E. White, (eds) *Safeguarding Adults under the Care Act: Understanding Good Practice*, London, Jessica Kingsley Publications, pp 110–127.

Whittaker, A., Densley, J., Cheston, L., Tyrell, T., Higgins, M., Felix-Baptiste, C., and Havard, T. (2019) 'Reluctant gangsters revisited: the evolution of gangs from postcodes to profits', *European Journal on Criminal Policy and Research*, 26(1): 1–23.

Widom, C., Czaja, S. and Dutton, M (2008) 'Childhood victimization and lifetime revictimization', *Child Abuse & Neglect*, 32(8): 785–796.

Wilkinson, J. (2018) *Developing and Leading Trauma-Informed Practice: Leaders' Briefing*, Dartington, Research in Practice.

Williams, C. (2013) *Safeguarding Adults Learning from Peer Challenges*, London: Local Government Association.

Williams, P. (2002) 'The competent boundary spanner', *Public Administration*, 80(1): 103–124.

Williams, P. and Clarke, B. (2016) *Dangerous Associations: Joint Enterprise, Gangs and Racism: An Analysis of the Process of Criminalisation of Black, Asian and Minority Ethnic Individuals*, London: Centre for Crime and Justice Studies.

Williams, S. (2020) *Safeguarding Adult Review – Jasmine. Richmond and Wandsworth Safeguarding Adults Board.* https://nationalnetwork.org.uk/2020/safeguarding-_adults_review_jasmine.pdf [Accessed 30 October 2023].

Willis, E.R. and McDonagh, J.E. (2018) 'Transition from children's to adults' services for young people using health or social care services', (NICE Guideline NG43), *Archives of Disease in Childhood – Education and Practice* 103: 253–256.

Wood, A. (2021) *Wood Report: Sector Expert Review of New Multi-Agency Safeguarding Arrangements*, London: Department for Education. https://assets.publishing.service.gov.uk/government/uploads/system/uploads/attachment_data/file/987928/Wood_Review_of_multi-agency_safeguarding_arrangements_2021.pdf [Accessed 30 October 2023].

World Health Organization (2021) The violence prevention alliance (VPA) approach. https://www.who.int/groups/violence-prevention-alliance/approach [Accessed 30 October 2023].

Worrall, D.A., Kiernan, K., Anderton, N. and Cottrell, D. (2004) 'Working with young people with complex needs: Practitioners' views', *Child & Adolescent Mental Health*, 9(4): 180–186.

Wright, M. (2021) 'London's teenage homicides hit record high as social media blamed for fuelling violence', *The Telegraph*, 31 January. https://www.telegraph.co.uk/news/2021/12/31/londons-teenage-homicides-hit-record-high-two-teens-killed-single/ [Accessed 30 October 2023].

Wroe, L.E. (2021) Tackling extra-familial harm – relationships of care and trust, or relationships or surveillance and control?. https://www.contextualsafeguarding.org.uk/blog/tackling-extra-familial-harm-relationships-of-care-and-trust-or-relationships-or-surveillance-and-control/ [Accessed 30 October 2023].

Wroe, L.E. (2022) 'When helping hurts: a zemiological analysis of a child protection intervention in adolescence — implications for a critical child protection studies', *Social Sciences*, 11(6): 263.

Wroe, L.E. and Lloyd, J. (2020) 'Watching over or working with? Understanding social work innovation in response to extra-familial harm', *Social Sciences*, 9(4): 37.

Wroe, L.E. and Pearce, J. (2022) 'Young people negotiating intra and extra-familial harm and safety: social and holistic approaches', in D. Holmes (ed) *Safeguarding Young People: Risk, Rights, Resilience and Relationships*, London: Jessica Kingsley Publications.

Youth Justice Board (2021) Strategic Plan 2021–2024. Youth Justice Board for England and Wales. https://assets.publishing.service.gov.uk/media/603f6d268fa8f577c44d65a8/YJB_Strategic_Plan_2021_-_2024.pdf [Accessed 30 October 2023].

Youth Violence Commission (2018) *Interim Report*. https://www.yvcommission.com/ [Accessed 30 October 2023].

Index

Note: References to figures appear in *italic* type; those in **bold** type refer to tables.

Printed and bound by CPI Group (UK) Ltd, Croydon, CR0 4YY

28/10/2024

14582427-0003